Authorized Lives

Studies in Indian and Tibetan Buddhism

THIS SERIES WAS CONCEIVED to provide a forum for publishing outstanding new contributions to scholarship on Indian and Tibetan Buddhism and also to make accessible seminal research not widely known outside a narrow specialist audience, including translations of appropriate monographs and collections of articles from other languages. The series strives to shed light on the Indic Buddhist traditions by exposing them to historical-critical inquiry, illuminating through contextualization and analysis these traditions' unique heritage and the significance of their contribution to the world's religious and philosophical achievements.

STUDIES IN INDIAN AND TIBETAN BUDDHISM

Authorized Lives

Biography and the Early Formation of Geluk Identity

Elijah S. Ary

Wisdom

Wisdom Publications, Inc.
199 Elm Street
Somerville MA 02144 USA
wisdompubs.org

Library of Congress Cataloging-in-Publication Data

Ary, Elijah S., 1972– author.
Authorized lives : biography and the early formation of Geluk identity / Elijah S. Ary.
pages cm
Includes bibliographical references and index.
ISBN 978-1-61429-164-0 (pbk. : alk. paper) — ISBN 1-61429-164-0 (pbk. : alk. paper) — ISBN 978-1-61429-180-0 (Ebook)
1. Dge-lugs-pa (Sect)—History. 2. Buddhist hagiography—Tibet Region—History. 3. Tson-kha-pa Blo-bzan-grags-pa, 1357–1419. 4. Mkhas-grub Dge-legs-dpal-bzan-po, 1385–1438. I. Title.
BQ7586.A78 2015
294.3'9230922—dc23

2014020594

ISBN 978-1-61429-164-0 ebook ISBN 978-1-61429-180-0

19 18 17 16 15
5 4 3 2 1

Author photo on page 179 is by Kris Snibbe. Cover and interior design by Gopa&Ted2. Typeset by LC. Set in Diacritical Garamond Pro 10.5/13.

Wisdom Publications' books are printed on acid-free paper and meet the guidelines for permanence and durability of the Production Guidelines for Book Longevity of the Council on Library Resources.

This book was produced with environmental mindfulness. We have elected to print this title on 30% PCW recycled paper. As a result, we have saved the following resources: 3 trees, 2 million BTUs of energy, 319 lbs. of greenhouse gases, 1,735 gallons of water, and 116 lbs. of solid waste. For more information, please visit our website, www.wisdompubs.org.

Printed in the United States of America.

MIX
Paper from responsible sources
FSC® C011935

Please visit www.fscus.org.

Contents

Publisher's Acknowledgment

THE PUBLISHER gratefully acknowledges the generous contribution of the Hershey Family Foundation toward the publication of this book.

Preface

DURING THE COURSE of my research for my master's thesis—on a polemical work by the eminent scholar Jetsun Chökyi Gyaltsen (1469–1544, hereafter Jetsunpa)—I came across a passage in one of Jetsunpa's biographies that suggested he had rewritten the monastic "textbooks," or *yig cha*, of Sera Jé, a Geluk monastic community he guided for nearly thirty years. This would have been around the turn of the sixteenth century, a century after the Geluk lineage was founded. Having closely studied and debated Jetsunpa's philosophical works during my own six-year monastic education at Sera, I found this passage intriguing, for it suggested that there had been an earlier *yig cha* before Jetsunpa's works achieved the central position they hold today. I decided to press the issue further and soon discovered that among the older texts Jetsunpa was said to have replaced were the writings of Sera Jé's founder, Lodrö Rinchen Sengé (fourteenth–fifteenth centuries), also known as Kunkhyenpa. According to the aforementioned biography, Jetsunpa's logic for replacing these works was that he felt they did not correspond adequately to the teachings of the founder of the Geluk lineage, Tsongkhapa Losang Drakpa (1357–1419).

As I began to consider the significance of this revelation, I realized its implications for some larger questions concerning orthodoxy and the early history of the Geluk school. For one, the proposition that Jetsunpa was able to displace a *yig cha* challenges the common assumption that criticism of the views expressed in the *yig cha* of one's college is a serious offense punishable by public humiliation and even exclusion from the monastic community. Clearly in this case such disapprobation did not occur. Given the usual loyalty to the *yig cha* of a college, what might have convinced the denizens of Sera to allow their central textbooks to be completely reconstituted? I also wondered what Lodrö Rinchen Sengé's misinterpretations might have been and what about them was so egregious that his works needed to be removed from the Sera Jé canon altogether. And if Lodrö Rinchen Sengé's works were so inconsistent with Tsongkhapa's thought, why was this fact not recognized and amended earlier? Was there more to this *yig cha* displacement than was being stated? These questions became the fundamental questions behind my doctoral thesis at Harvard and, in turn, the germ of the present book.

My first impulse was to investigate the philosophical issues at play. To do this, or so I thought, one need only compare Lodrö Rinchen Sengé's works with Jetsunpa's against the backdrop of Tsongkhapa's teachings.

With hopes of locating Sera Jé's original *yig cha,* I undertook a series of trips to Tibet. I had received mixed information from a variety of Tibetan scholars concerning the whereabouts of Lodrö Rinchen Sengé's texts. Unfortunately, despite repeated journeys to Lhasa and much searching, I came up empty-handed.

I then considered whether I might look at the matter from another angle, and I began to follow a hunch that extraphilosophical matters may have been at least as much at stake as those strictly concerned with doctrine. To pursue this line of inquiry, I looked into the lives of the actors in question by turning my attention to another genre of writing that is very common in Tibet: the genre of life-story writing.

On one of my trips to Lhasa, I managed to secure a copy of a manuscript version of a "secret biography" (*gsang ba'i rnam thar*) composed by Jetsunpa himself of the figure Khedrup Gelek Palsang (1385–1438), widely considered today to be one of Tsongkhapa's two principal disciples. The manuscript is written entirely in cursive *dbu med* script, features red ink for important words and names, and employs extremely laudatory language. Although it is not unusual for such biographical literature to extol and even exaggerate the hero's spiritual exploits, I began to ponder the significance of this particular text's repeated insistence on its hero's special relationship to his master.

Having received my own early education in matters Gelukpa from within the Geluk tradition itself, I did not at first see the acclamations of Khedrup and his relationship to Tsongkhapa as anything out of the ordinary. Indeed, Khedrup's authority and place within the Geluk tradition as one of Tsongkhapa's two chief disciples has long been established. But as I began to look more closely at Khedrup's life according to other historical sources, I started to see the rhetoric in Jetsunpa's work as curious. It appeared to prefigure a shift in the portrayal of Khedrup's position vis-à-vis his master Tsongkhapa, a position that, as it turns out, had previously been rather ambiguous. Might this apparent elevation of Khedrup's status have had a bearing on Jetsunpa's own life and career? Were Jetsunpa's overt efforts to elevate Khedrup in fact directly related to Jetsunpa's displacement of the older *yig cha* of Sera Jé? These are the questions that animate the present work.

Only a few months after defending my thesis, I was notified that the Paltsek Center for Research on Old Tibetan-Language Texts in Lhasa had located and republished multiple Madhyamaka works by Lodrö Rinchen Sengé, Sera Jé's founder. I was overjoyed that the works had finally been discovered, and I at once ordered a copy. Insights gained from examining those works has informed my conclusions here. But as it turns out, the most fruitful analysis remains not of philosophy but of biography and biographical rhetoric—an investigation that traces shifts in representations a generation back beyond Khedrup, emcompassing also the earliest biographies of his master, Tsongkhapa. In reading through the biographies first of Tsongkhapa, then Khedrup, and finally Jetsunpa himself, I hope to provide a glimpse of the complex intersection of lives, the telling of lives, and the positioning of philosophy and doctrinal authority within those tellings. This work is therefore also an exercise in reading closely—reading rhetoric, and discerning the best ways to make use of the enormously rich resource that biography presents for deepening our understanding of Tibet's complex religious culture.

Acknowledgments

I would like to express my gratitude to my copyeditor, piiopah damiano, for his extensive revisions and to everyone at Wisdom Publications, particularly David Kittelstrom, whose keen eye, concise eloquence, and unwavering gentle, yet firm encouragement guided this work throughout the editorial process. I could not have hoped for a better editor. I also thank the chairs of the Studies in Indian and Tibetan Buddhism series, José Cabezón and Tom Tillemans, for including my work in the series, and to José and to Georges Dreyfus for their developmental suggestions.

I am deeply appreciative of my teachers, Geshé Tsultrim Chöpel, Janet Gyatso, Leonard van der Kuijp, and Charles Hallisey, whose knowledge and insight were invaluable for the dissertation that was the starting point of this book.

Thank you to my parents and family for all their support, and to my good friends Kris and Bonnie, and their lovely children Sophie and Sebastian, for putting up with me in their home, sometimes for months at a time, and for getting my mind off things by making me laugh when I needed it. Your friendship is truly of the most rare and precious kind.

Finally, words cannot express the depth of gratitude and indebtedness I feel toward my wife, Emmanuelle, whose love and indefatigable support have forever been a source of strength and encouragement. Thank you for believing in me in times when I no longer did, thank you for helping me back up when my strength faltered, thank you for rejoicing in my enthusiasm at small, seemingly insignificant discoveries, and for your encouragement at all times. And thank you for all the times you came to me with a cup of warm honeyed tea, smiled, and said, "Remember, the only good book is a done book!"

Introduction

> *And as they move we shall arrange them in all sorts of patterns of which they were ignorant, for they thought when they were alive that they could go where they liked; and as they speak we shall read into their sayings all kinds of meanings which never struck them, for they believed when they were alive that they said straight off whatever came into their heads. But once you are in a biography all is different.*
>
> —Virginia Woolf, *The Common Reader*

In Western contexts there is commonly a notion, however implicit, that biographical works convey truths—truths about the subject's life, education, and career; truths about the historical and social context in which he or she thrived; and even truths about his or her intimate personal and emotional life. There is an expectation that the biographer will present his or her subject factually and objectively. In Tibetan biographies, however, it is not unusual for authors to make use of highly exaggerated panegyric in discussing their heroes, especially if the biographical subject is a key figure for the biographer's tradition or lineage. Tibetan biography often contains such marvelous and seemingly exaggerated accounts that these works have historically been considered by Tibetologists to have nothing at all to do with human events,[1] to be "of no direct historical worth."[2]

As more recent studies of Tibetan biography have shown, these dismissive evaluations fail to take into consideration that, despite the adulatory language and fabulous stories, life-writing in Tibet nevertheless contains a plethora of historical information—information evident not only once the panegyrics are set aside but right amid the flowery language itself. Even the wondrous dreams and visions common to this genre are informative of not only who the author's audience might have been but also of the author's

1. Tucci 1949, 1:150–51.

2. Snellgrove 1957, 85.

intentions in composing the work. Such elements can even shed light on the historical and political climate at the time of composition.

Literally translated, the Tibetan term for biography, *rnam thar*, means "completely liberated." It implies that the lifestory being told is an account of the hero's journey to full liberation from the fetters of cyclic existence, which is, at least ideally speaking, the purpose of a Buddhist life.[3] This distinct genre of Tibetan literature is generally broken down into two main emic categories: outer (*phyi*) and inner (*nang*).[4] Outer biography most often gives an account of the more directly observable physical aspects of the hero's life, such as his[5] birth, family background, education, travels, teaching career, and death. Although the hero's personal dreams can be discussed briefly on occasion, this type of content is most often reserved for the inner biography. In accordance with its label, the inner biography is mostly an account of the hero's inner, or spiritual, life. Typically it discusses the less visible and more personal interior aspects of his life, such as the meditative cycles the hero practiced, empowerments he received, and teachings imparted to him. It is not unusual for an inner biography to leave out details concerning the hero's birth and upbringing, or even his travels, in order to focus primarily on his spiritual education.

One subtype of inner biography is the *secret* biography (*gsang rnam*). The title "secret" does not imply that such biographies are kept locked up and out of view to all; indeed, what good would a biography be if it could not be read by anyone? Rather, a secret biography is dubbed "secret" because its purpose is to recount the most intimate details of the hero's spiritual life: the aspects he would have kept secret (dreams, premonitions, meditative and visionary experiences, spiritual attainments, and so on) from all save his closest teachers and associates. And yet, by virtue of existing in written (and often published) form, biography always stands as a potentially public rendering of private events. The question then occurs: why did Tibetan authors write so overtly about features of a life that were ostensibly meant to be kept secret?

Jan Willis has posited that every Tibetan biography contains elements from all of the three classic subgenres of biography: outer, inner, and secret.[6] Each one of these "levels" of life-writing serves a specific function: the outer

3. Gyatso 1998, 6.

4. For Tibetan classificatory schemes, see Gyatso 1998, 102–6.

5. I use the male pronoun due to the fact that the large majority of Tibetan biographical literature is about men. Nevertheless there are a few examples of autobiographies by women, an excellent discussion of which is Schaeffer 2005. See also Schaeffer 2004.

6. See Willis 1995, 5–6; and Willis 1985, 312.

level acts as a historical record, providing the reader with dates and historical vitae; the inner level serves as an inspirational model whereby readers are moved to feel greater devotion for the biography's hero and a desire to emulate his model life; and the secret level serves as a practical or "instructional" guide for advanced practitioners desirous of achieving the same meditative effects and states as the hero.[7] Willis's scheme does not necessarily hold true for all Tibetan biographies. The examples in this book demonstrate the imperfect fit of such general assertions about intentions or content. But it remains valid to note that many Tibetan authors seem to have felt the need to compose separate biographies to address different dimensions of the lives of their heroes. For example, Khedrup composed not only a full-length "outer" biography of his teacher, Tsongkhapa, but felt the need to produce a "secret" biography as well. Significantly, the latter work differs from the outer biography in structure, content, and focus. Tsongkhapa's secret biography is the starting point of my study of biography and philosophical lineage in the first chapter.

According to Willis, secret biography served in part as an instructional model for advanced tantric practitioners.[8] But secret biography was also read by noninitiates and possibly even by lay patrons,[9] such as those who helped sponsor the creation of the work.[10] They may or may not have followed or even fathomed the texts' instructions. But what is important here is the possibility that secret biography, like Tibetan biography in general, may have served purposes beyond the historical, inspirational, and instructional models that Willis describes. Willis neglects the crucial political functions that biography and secret biography can also have in the Tibetan context.

Janet Gyatso has argued that one agenda of life-story writing in Tibet was "to assert the religious achievements of a master and his or her lineage

7. Willis 1995, 5–6.

8. A similar claim is recorded by Janet Gyatso, whose Tibetan informants assert that while anyone can read secret biography, only the initiate can decipher its true meaning (Gyatso 1998, 7).

9. Gyatso 1998, 124.

10. In Central Tibet, due to the arid climate, the creation and printing of literary works such as biography were highly meritorious acts, but they were painstaking tasks that required the support of patrons sympathetic to the biography's subject or author. Such patrons had to be wealthy enough to ship large amounts of wood with which to make printing blocks from the outer regions of Tibet to the center (see Ehrhard 2000). For a discussion of editorial practices and processes concerning a master's collected writings, see Schaeffer 1999.

in contrast to those of rival schools."[11] I would add that it has also served that function in rivalries within the same tradition. Biography can also be a tool for drumming up economic support and ensuring the continued aid of benefactors by providing them with the "proof," often in the form of accounts of near-incredible spiritual feats, that the hero is worthy of their support and veneration. Critically, this worthiness of support also extends by association to the hero's followers. In this way, a whole lineage can be positioned as worthy of the vital support of wealthy patrons, thereby making it possible for the lineage to survive. Indeed, through his work a biographer, who most frequently self-identifies as belonging to the hero's lineage, is also making a statement about himself, not to mention his own worthiness of veneration and economic support.

Few scholars have attempted to explore in depth the specific political or social dimensions or motivations of philosophical disputes. The majority of contemporary Tibetological scholarship on Buddhist philosophy has focused primarily, if not exclusively, on elucidating the intricate details of philosophical tenets and debates themselves.[12] Karma Phuntso's work on the philosophical positions of Mipham Namgyal Gyatso (1846–1912), for example, gives us a very useful and articulate account of the development of Madhyamaka scholarship in Tibet and of the rivalries it engendered. It also discusses the political climate prior to and during his subject's life.[13] Nevertheless, Phuntso's historical focus remains primarily on providing his readers with a backdrop to the philosophical positions and debates that developed throughout the different Buddhist traditions in Tibet and not at all on the influence politics may have had on the philosophical positions taken or argued.

One scholar to have recently broken from this tradition is Donald Lopez, who in his recent work on Gendun Chöphel (1903–51) offers a translation and analysis of the latter's Madhyamaka commentary. Lopez links the criticisms voiced by his subject to other key aspects of the figure's life, such as his strong political opinions and his views on religion, which had been largely

11. J Gyatso 1998, 102.

12. If we consider the works of scholars such as Wayman (1997; 1999), Hopkins (1999a; 1999b; 1987a), Thurman (1978; 1982; 1984), Cabezón (1988; 1992; 2001), Garfield (2002; and in Nāgārjuna 1995 and Tsongkhapa 2006), Thupten Jinpa (2002), Dreyfus (1997; 2003), and Karma Phuntso (2005), who have led the way in scholarly inquiry into this key dimension of Tibetan Buddhist culture, all—even the masterful doxographic historian David Seyfort Ruegg—have overlooked what other historical issues, such as lineage, institutional affiliation, and political loyalties, might be ingredients in the actual content of philosophical dispute as such.

13. See Phuntso 2005.

influenced by his travels.[14] What Lopez does, then, is show that Gendun Chöphel's philosophical opinions, which greatly displeased many contemporary Gelukpa scholars, are in fact informed by his other political and intellectual preoccupations.

Matthew Kapstein is also somewhat of an exception to the tendency mentioned above. In his discussion of Sumpa Khenpo Yeshé Paljor's (1704–88) work on canonicity, given under its short title *The Purificatory Gem*,[15] Kapstein remarks that doctrinal concerns (in this case canonicity) were influenced and restricted by political and sectarian convictions.[16] He also points out that lineage history and "particular currents in Buddhist philosophical thought" were connected, one being the subject matter for the other.[17] Kapstein therefore begins to get at the fact that doctrinal and philosophical issues not only influenced but were also influenced by nondoctrinal matters such as lineage construction, religious politics, and personal motives.

Aside from these works, the influence of extraphilosophical elements and issues on philosophical positioning and argument has yet to be seriously investigated. This work therefore breaks from the tradition of most modern Tibetological research by looking at the formative period of the Geluk school and attending to the often contentious processes through which the now-accepted philosophical and lineage orthodoxies emerged. In this it attempts to position philosophical matters within personal and institutional exigencies. More specifically, this work considers how biography is used as a tool in constructing authority and creating intellectual and textual community. Rather than focusing primarily on the content of the dispute between Lodrö Rinchen Sengé and Jetsunpa, we will look instead at the roles that lineage creation, loyalty, institutional structure, and consensus building played in philosophical dispute. An examination of the socioeconomic and political implications of Jetsunpa's *Secret Biography of the Omniscient Khedrup* not only allows us to discern how Jetsunpa's text actually serves to adjust the author's own position and status, it also helps us to see how attention to biographical rhetoric can serve to fill out, in critical ways, our understanding of Tibetan Buddhist intellectual history. In this way the present work moves forward the study of Tibetan religions by not only discussing important developments of early Geluk history but also by

14. See Lopez 2006.

15. *Gsung rab rnam dag chu'i dri ma sel byed nor bu ke ta ka*. See Kapstein 2000b, 121–37.

16. Kapstein 2000b, 130.

17. Kapstein 2000b, 108–9.

showing the importance of considering philosophical texts, positions, and disputes in terms of their human communities rather than as separate from them.

Philosophy, *Yig cha*, and Community

It is important to note that philosophy, in Indo-Tibetan Buddhism, has a primarily salutary function. It is seen as a means by which one deepens one's understanding of ultimate reality, which in turn allows one to be liberated from the throes of cyclic existence (*saṃsāra*). Indeed, as Karma Phuntso puts it,

> The pursuit of philosophy without a soteriological vision, from an Indo-Tibetan Buddhist perspective, is mere ratiocination with no worthy purpose or benefit. Philosophy is a beacon to guide you through the byways of religious practice to the higher goal of liberation and enlightenment, and not an independent end in itself. It becomes meaningful when it has a soteriological cause to stand for.[18]

Gelukpas maintain that a proper understanding of emptiness—an understanding that is "the *summum bonum* to be realized or attained as a soteriological goal"[19]—is achieved through meditative experience, but that meditation is of little or no use without prior discursive knowledge of the tenets propounded by the Prāsaṅgika-Madhyamaka system. As was the case with monks at each of the three major Geluk institutions surrounding Lhasa, contemporary Gelukpas are expected to engage in a rigorous curriculum of philosophical study.[20] The standard course of study in a Geluk monastery is comprised of about twelve different levels or classes, each lasting one or more years. The entire course of study can last upward of twenty years. As monks progress through each stage, they study and debate in great detail key elements found in specific texts.

18. Phuntso 2005, 11.

19. Phuntso 2005, 35.

20. Not all monks engage in such academic activities. Historically, only about 30 percent of the monastic population (depending on the monastery) are estimated to have participated in scholastic training at the advanced levels. The rest were engaged in various nonacademic activities such as commerce, trade, and management of arable lands for the monastery. There were even groups of "fighting monks," or *dobdob* (*ldob ldob*), that allegedly comprised up to 15 percent of monastic inhabitants (Goldstein 1989, 24–25).

Three layers of texts are studied in the Geluk education centers. These layers might be represented as concentric rings, each one slightly smaller than the next. The first layer, the outermost ring, is constituted by the classic works of Indian Buddhist philosophers—most frequently Nāgārjuna, Asaṅga, Candrakīrti, Dharmakīrti, Bhāvaviveka, Buddhapālita, Vasubhandu, Śantarākṣita, and Kamalaśīla. These texts, referred to as *rgya gzhung* ("Indian treatises"), are often in compact verse translated into Tibetan and are usually accepted as authoritative by all Tibetan Buddhist scholars regardless of their sectarian affiliations. The texts serve as a common scriptural basis for philosophical discussion between scholars of the different Tibetan Buddhist traditions and thereby carry authority for the largest community of readers.

The second layer, the middle ring, is made up of commentaries considered authoritative only by members of the Geluk tradition. It includes Tsongkhapa's treatises on both exoteric and esoteric matters and the commentarial interpretations thereof by his disciples Gyaltsap Darma Rinchen and Khedrup Gelek Palsang. The collected writings of these three figures, referred to collectively as the Jé Yabsé Sum (*rje yab sras gsum*),[21] or "lordly father and his two sons," serve as both the defining limits of what is and is not an acceptable view for the Geluk school and as the doctrinal framework through which the tradition defines itself. As mentioned in the preface, to disagree with them, deny their validity, or criticize them is one of the gravest offenses a Gelukpa can commit. Indeed, to deny the absolute authority of the writings of the Jé Yabsé Sum is to renege one's identity as a Gelukpa.[22] A Gelukpa is therefore defined today not merely by his or her adherence to the views and teachings of Tsongkhapa but also by his or her adherence to Tsongkhapa's views as interpreted and presented by Gyaltsap and Khedrup.

But even the works of Tsongkhapa and his chief interpreters can be difficult to comprehend at times and may require further explanation and commentary. This is provided by a third layer of textual authority, the innermost ring constituted by "textbooks," or *yig cha*. These are essentially commentaries

21. Implicitly expressed with this term is the notion that Tsongkhapa had only two chief disciples. Had there been three disciples, then the term sum (*gsum*, three) would be replaced by the term shi (*bzhi*, four), indicating that together with the "father" (i.e., Tsongkhapa), the total number of people being referred to is four. Interestingly, in Paṇchen Sönam Drakpa's history of the Geluk school there is one case where the expression *jé yapsé shi* (*rje yab sras bzhi*) is indeed used to refer to Tsongkhapa, Gyaltsap, Khedrup, and Dulzin Drakpa Gyaltsen (1374–1434/36). See Paṇchen Sönam Drakpa, *Mind's Ornament*, 164.

22. Such a refusal is an outright betrayal of Tsongkhapa's teachings as a whole (see Dreyfus 2003, 319–20).

on Tsongkhapa's works composed by monastic founders, abbots, and other influential figures from particular monasteries and monastic colleges. They serve as the basis for studying and understanding Tsongkhapa's teachings, though their authority is only accepted by those at the college in which they are studied.[23]

Yig cha hold a very important place within the schools of the Geluk tradition.[24] While the aforementioned Indian works are not necessarily used directly by teachers and students, *yig cha* are constantly taught, read, debated, and referred to during the entire course of study. Not only are they the basis for philosophical study within one's college, they also serve to define the community that takes them as authoritative. *Yig cha* thus also function to exclude from that community all those who do not recognize their authority. As Guy Newland remarks:

> From a dGe lugs religious perspective, debate manuals [*yig cha*] engender analytical skills and lay the foundations of right view, thus providing a solid conceptual basis from which yogic inquiry into the nature of reality can proceed. We may also observe that (1) minor differences among the manuals are focal points for the intellectual expression of collegial solidarity and intercollegiate tensions, while (2) their far broader commonalities in structure and content contribute to the socialization of the monastic elite within a shared worldview.[25]

Thus, a monk from Sera's Jé college is not merely one who lives there but, more importantly, one who accepts the college's *yig cha* to be authoritative and correct interpretations of Tsongkhapa's thought.[26] Furthermore, the subtle differences in how Tsongkhapa's views are understood and explained serve

23. Occasionally, however, an author may have had an impact on another college either directly or through a disciple. This was the case at Ganden's Jangtsé college, for example, where Jetsunpa's works are accepted as authoritative scripture due to the influence of his disciples, Gomdé Namkha Gyaltsen and Khyungtruk Jampa Tashi, the latter of whom was also Jetsunpa's younger brother.

24. The manuals of Drepung's Loseling and Ganden's Shartsé colleges were composed by Paṇchen Sönam Drakpa, while Gomang college relies on the works of the first Jamyang Shepa, Ngawang Tsondrü (1648–1722). Ganden Jangtsé's *yig cha* consists of works by Jetsun Chökyi Gyaltsen, Gomdé Namkha Gyaltsen (1532–92), and Khyungtruk Jampa Tashi (fifteenth–sixteenth cent.s). Sera Mé's were composed by Khedrup Gendun Tenpa Dargyé (1493–1568).

25. Newland 1996, 211.

26. Personal oral communication with Geshé Karma Sönam, circa. 1989.

as the basis for communal cohesion and distinction. A useful way of looking at this is through the lens of "textual community."

In his work on the effects of literacy on medieval European culture, historian Brian Stock describes textual communities as "groups of people whose social activities are centered around texts, or, more precisely, around a literate interpreter of them."[27]

Similarly, in her work on textual practices in eighteenth-century Lankan monastic culture, Anne Blackburn has defined a textual community as "a group of individuals who think of themselves to at least some degree as a collective, who understand the world and their appropriate place within it in terms significantly influenced by their encounter with a shared set of written texts or oral teachings based on written texts, and who grant special status to literate interpreters of authoritative written texts."[28] Put simply, then, a textual community is a group of individuals whose sense of identity as a community derives largely from the shared acceptance and performance—reading, chanting, and debating, for example—of a specific text or series of texts, either oral or written, composed by a specific interpreter or set of interpreters deemed by the community to be authoritative.

The performative aspect is important for heightening the group's sense of self-definition and cohesion. In the Tibetan monastic context, most activities—from morning prayers to evening debates—take place in groups and focus on a shared set of texts deemed authoritative by the monastic community itself. Even the teaching sessions, during which one studies the authoritative textbooks with a designated teacher, are most often conducted in groups.

The notion of textual community allows us to better comprehend just how *yig cha* dynamics can be at the very center of a college's identity and thus how criticism or repudiation of *yig cha* could lead to strong reactions, especially when the criticism comes from within the community itself. This is why the case of Jetsunpa caught my attention.

As mentioned in the preface, Jetsunpa allegedly felt that the works of his precursor, Lodrö Rinchen Sengé, contained slight misrepresentations of the views propounded by Tsongkhapa and his chief disciples and therefore warranted replacement. But how could Jetsunpa criticize or even refute his own college's *yig cha*, let alone replace them with his own, without provoking the community's wrath? One possibility is that criticism of one's own college's *yig cha* was not as grave an offense in the early stages of the Geluk school's

27. Stock 1983, 522.

28. Blackburn 2001, 12.

development as it later became. Many figures were composing commentarial works on Tsongkhapa's thought, and contrary to the situation nowadays, it may be that there was no standard Geluk textual authority. Another possibility, one pursued herein, is that Jetsunpa portrayed himself as a member of a seminal lineage in the transmission of Tsongkhapa's views. Part of this effort, I argue, was achieved by his composing a biography of one of the lineage's key figures.

I began my research with an in-depth reading and translation of a key and telling panegyrical account of Khedrup's spiritual life, his *Secret Biography* by Jetsun Chökyi Gyaltsen, in order to better comprehend its place within the larger tradition of Khedrup biographies. I looked at how Khedrup is portrayed in other biographical and historical sources, both earlier and later than Jetsunpa's. As I came to discover, Jetsunpa's own fortunes are also rooted in key shifts that occur in the biographical tradition of the seminal figure for the powerful Geluk school, the master Tsongkhapa himself. There is, therefore, a certain logic for this work to start with a study of Tsongkhapa's biography.

As we go through key moments in the development of Tsongkhapa's and Khedrup's life stories (chapters 1 and 2, respectively), we will glimpse important issues relating to institution, lineage, orthodoxy, community, and authority in Tibetan Buddhism. The final chapter concentrates on Jetsunpa himself, showing how all of these issues come together in his apparent suppression of Lodrö Rinchen Sengé's commentarial writings on the thought of Tsongkhapa. We will look at Jetsunpa's own life and historical context, at his preoccupations with doctrinal cohesion, and at his ostensible critiques of Lodrö Rinchen Sengé's views. We will see that biography can be used to do more than simply inspire, inform, and instruct. Crucially, biography can also be used to make important legitimation claims that bear directly upon the formulation of both sectarian and personal identity and the creation of community in the great philosophical colleges of the monasteries of Tibetan Buddhism.

1. Tsongkhapa

Source Material: Biographical Accounts of Tsongkhapa

TIBETAN-LANGUAGE BIOGRAPHIES OF the Geluk tradition's founding figure, Tsongkhapa Losang Drakpa, are many and vary in length as well as content. Some number several hundred folios, while others count as few as four. Some discuss Tsongkhapa's life in its entirety; others choose instead to focus on one or two particular aspects or events. The dates at which these works were composed span the centuries from his death right up to the present day.[29]

The vast majority of late works on Tsongkhapa's life, by both Tibetan and Western scholars, take as their starting point the biographical account by his disciple Khedrup entitled *Entryway of Faith: The Wondrous Biography of the Lord Teacher Tsongkhapa.*[30] This is the earliest-known biographical source for Tsongkhapa after his own brief autobiographical *Realization Narrative.*[31] Over the last five centuries or so, Khedrup's account has come to be the standard source for all other renditions of Tsongkhapa's life.

After Khedrup, several of Tsongkhapa's followers composed biographies in homage to their spiritual master and guide, some writing in prose and others in verse. While Akuching Sherap Gyatso (1803–75), in his record of

29. While I have chosen to focus primarily on the biographical and autobiographical literature available for Tsongkhapa, I have also consulted other works contained in Tsongkhapa's collected works. These include the account of how he gave a tooth to Khedrup (Tsongkhapa, *Meeting with Lhodrak Drupchen and The Gift of the Tooth to Khedrup Jé*) and Tsongkhapa's letter to his master Umapa, found in Tsongkhapa's *Miscellaneous Writings* (80a–82a). Additionally, for the analyses undertaken in this chapter, I have consulted Khedrup's *Eulogy to Tsongkhapa* (Khedrup Jé, *Miscellaneous Writings*, 4a–6b) and his *Prayer for Tsongkhapa's Rebirth* (Khedrup Jé, *Miscellaneous Writings*, 6b–8a).

30. *Rje btsun bla ma tsong kha pa chen po'i ngo mtshar rmad du byung ba'i rnam par thar pa dad pa'i 'jug ngogs.*

31. *Rtog brjod mdun legs ma.* For a translation of this work, see Thurman 1982, 40–46.

Tibetan biographical works, lists fourteen biographies of Tsongkhapa,[32] all composed either by Tsongkhapa's direct disciples or by later members of the Gelukpa community,[33] the influential Russian Tibetologist A. I. Vostrikov lists fifteen rare and six more popular such biographies.[34] Of the latter six, only three date back to the first one hundred years following Tsongkhapa's death. These are: Tsongkhapa's own *Realization Narrative*, the short autobiographical prayer by Tsongkhapa himself which discusses his spiritual education and attainments; the *Supplement*, composed by Jampal Gyatso, a disciple and contemporary of Tsongkhapa and teacher of Khedrup; and *Entryway of Faith* by Khedrup. Of the fourteen rare biographies mentioned by the Tibetan biographer and historian Kharnak Lotsāwa in his account of rare biographies of Tsongkhapa and his followers,[35] two—the *Golden Wick* (*Gser gyi mchod sdong*) and the *Jewel Treasury* (*Nor bu'i bang mdzod*),[36] both by Sangsang Neringpa Chimé Rapgyé (fifteenth cent.)—have since been found and published, thanks to the efforts of Rakra Rinpoché Thupten Chödar.

Today, the standard account of Tsongkhapa's life is a biography now called the *Great Biography* by Chahar Geshé Losang Tsultrim (1740–1810).[37] Chahar wrote extensively on a vast array of topics, and his biography of Tsongkhapa discusses a broad range of aspects of Tsongkhapa's life, including his

32. Chandra 1963, 503–14.

33. Sketches of Tsongkhapa's life of varying lengths are also found in even greater numbers embedded within other Tibetan historical works, such as Gö Lotsāwa Shonu Pal's (1392–1481) *Blue Annals*, composed circa 1478 (see translation in Gö Lotsāwa 1976, 1073–79); Lechen Kunga Gyaltsen's (1432–1506) *Lamp Illuminating the History of the Kadam Tradition* (*Bka' gdams chos 'byung gsal ba'i sgron me*, 340b–384a) composed in 1494; Paṇchen Sönam Drakpa's (1478–1554) *Mind's Ornament: The History of the Old and New Kadam Traditions* (*Bka' gdams gsar rnying gi chos 'byung yid kyi mdzes rgyan*, 45–60) composed in 1429; Desi Sangyé Gyatso's *Golden Vaiḍūrya* (*Dga' ldan chos 'byung bai ḍūrya ser po*, 5–70); and Kharnak Lotsāwa Paljor Gyatso's (sixteenth–seventeenth cent.) *History of Ganden* (1b–10a), to name but a few.

34. Vostrikov 1994, 191–94, notes 561 and 562.

35. Chandra 1963, 672.

36. Chimé Rapgyé's *Jewel Treasury* is an account of Tsongkhapa's disciples and does not deal in any real detail with Tsongkhapa's actual life. Instead it gives an account of who his disciples were and where they came from. It is probably one of the first classifications of Tsongkhapa's followers according to their specific characteristics and not just according to their places of origin. Because of this, and despite it being considered one of Tsongkhapa's biographies, I have left it out of the present section. I use it in the next chapter in my discussion of Khedrup's place among Tsongkhapa's disciples.

37. Chahar's works have now been republished in New Delhi. See Chahar Geshé, *Collected Works.*

previous incarnations prior to and during the time of the Buddha; his life in Tibet, complete with details of his birth, education, travels, teaching career, public activities (such as the institution of the *Mönlam* prayer festival and the founding of Ganden Monastery in 1409); and his meditative and visionary achievements. The text also gives a list of Tsongkhapa's disciples and the monasteries they went on to establish around Tibet.

Since 1959, a number of Western scholars have contributed significantly to making Tsongkhapa's extraordinary contribution accessible to Western students of Tibetan Buddhist history, religion, and philosophy (see, e.g., Tsongkhapa 2000). Though some present their readers with an account of Tsongkhapa's outstanding life, the vast majority focus instead on Tsongkhapa's philosophical views or on his explanation of the stages of the path to enlightenment (*lam rim*).[38] Surprisingly enough, though there are many

38. Robert Thurman has published two works in which he presents the life story of this remarkable figure for a larger audience of Western readers. In his introductory chapter of *Tsong Khapa's Speech of Gold in the Essence of True Eloquence* (Thurman 1984), Thurman gives a short biography based on multiple biographies of Tsongkhapa written by various Tibetan authors throughout history. Thurman's *Life and Teachings of Tsong Khapa* (Thurman 1982), a collection of works on Tsongkhapa by Tibetan and Western scholars, offers translations of several of those biographies including Tsongkhapa's autobiographical *Realization Narrative* (*rtogs brjod*) and the versified *Supplication* by Jamyang Chöjé. The main biography of Tsongkhapa given in Thurman's work, however, is taken from the teachings of the contemporary Gelukpa scholar Geshé Ngawang Dhargyey (1921–95), who is said to have based his account on the earliest Tibetan biography of Tsongkhapa written by Khedrup, entitled *Entryway of Faith: The Wondrous Biography of the Lord Teacher Tsongkhapa*. Upon analysis, however, it is clear that although Geshé Dhargyey's account does make use of information found within Khedrup's work, it also relates stories that are not found in this work and relies instead on other sources, such as the *Supplement* by Tokden Jampal Gyatso (1356–1428, hereafter simply Jampal Gyatso), which will be discussed in more detail later on. It is my impression that Dhargyey's account is actually based on the aforementioned biography by Chahar Geshé.

Rudolf Kaschewsky's monumental 1971 work *Das Leben des Lamaistischen Heiligen Tsongkhapa Blo-Bzaṅ-Grags-Pa (1357–1419)*, a somewhat dated work and available only in German, is essentially a translation of the no less monumental work on Tsongkhapa's life by Chahar Geshé.

Other Western-language biographies of Tsongkhapa include Françoise Wang's *Dje Tsongkhapa: Rencontre avec un Maître Remarquable* (Wang 2000). This work is based mainly on the teachings of Wang's Buddhist master, Gosok Rinpoché, and is more of a pious rendition of Tsongkhapa's life than a scholarly work. In fact, Wang does not rely directly on any Tibetan biographies of Tsongkhapa, and though she does mention the versified *Supplication* by Jamyang Chöjé as one of her sources, she is in fact referring to the translated version of the text given in Thurman's *Life and Teachings of Tsong Khapa* (Thurman 1982, 47–55).

Translations such as Thurman's are not the only places to find biographical sketches of Tsongkhapa in English. Alex Wayman, for example, devotes eleven pages of his work *Calming the Mind and Discerning the Real* to a discussion of Tsongkhapa's life, which he says is based

short biographies to be found in Western scholarship, a translation or close study of Khedrup's *Great Biography of Tsongkhapa*, which is clearly one of the most important sources for the figure's life, has yet to be published.[39]

For the sections that follow I have drawn upon Chimé Rapgyé's *Jewel Treasury* as well as other early biographies found in both the Kumbum (*Sku 'bum*) and Lhasa editions of Tsongkhapa's collected writings.[40] These works consist of Khedrup's *Entryway of Faith* and his *Secret Biography of Tsongkhapa*; the *Supplement* and the *Very Secret Biography of Tsongkhapa* (*Rnam thar shin tu gsang ba*), both by Jampal Gyatso; and the *Supplication*, a versified biography in praise of his master by Jamyang Chöjé, who founded Drepung Monastery in 1416 at Tsongkhapa's request. I discuss each of these works in turn below. I have also consulted some more recent biographies, namely those by the first Jamyang Shepa Ngawang Tsöndrü (1648–1721/22)[41] and Gyalwang Chöjé Losang Trinlé Namgyal (nineteenth cent.).[42]

Each of Tsongkhapa's biographies, whether composed early or later, in some way tells of how intellectually and spiritually gifted he was. Some, like Khedrup's *Entryway of Faith*, tell of the great master's travels and intellectual education, while others, such as Jamyang Chöjé's *Supplication*, focus more directly on his spiritual education and accomplishments. *Entryway of Faith*, for example, relates in great detail the stories of Tsongkhapa's conception, birth, early and advanced education, his career as a teacher, and eventually his death. In contrast, the *Secret Biography of Tsongkhapa* and the *Very Secret Biography of Tsongkhapa*, by Khedrup and Jampal Gyatso respectively, dis-

on two Tibetan biographies by Khedrup and by Akya Losang Tenpai Gyaltsen (1708–68). Alex Berzin, too, has a short version of Tsongkhapa's life on his website, the Berzin Archives (http://www.berzinarchives.com/bioghaphies/short_biography_lama_tsongkhapa.html). Like the biography given in Thurman's *The Life and Teachings of Tsong Khapa*, it too is based largely on the teachings of Geshé Dhargyey. In his work on guru devotion in Tibetan Buddhism, Gareth Sparham also gives a version of Tsongkhapa's life story based largely on Khedrup's account (Tsongkhapa 1999), and the recently published translation of Thuken Losang Chökyi Nyima's (1737–1802) monumental *Crystal Mirror of Philosophical Systems* (2009) also contains a version of Tsongkhapa's biography.

39. Thurman has stated that he has completed a translation of this work and that its publication is forthcoming (1982, 3), but more than thirty years later, it remains a desideratum.

40. Gene Smith and the Tibetan Buddhist Resource Center (TBRC) have reproduced in digital format both the Kumbum (W22272) and Lhasa (W635) editions of Tsongkhapa's collected works. I primarily cite the Kumbum edition in this book.

41. Jamyang Shepa I, *Cittamaṇi Garland.*

42. Gyalwang Chöjé, *Wondrous Jewel Garland.*

cuss other more spiritual matters, such as Tsongkhapa's relationship with various deities like Vajrabhairava and Mañjuśrī.

Throughout the various biographies, Tsongkhapa's relationship to Mañjuśrī occupies a central place. According to his biographers, it is largely thanks to this relationship that Tsongkhapa became the erudite scholar, the great practitioner, and the Buddhist master that he did. Moreover, Mañjuśrī is seen as playing an essential role in Tsongkhapa's enlightenment. In what follows, rather than produce yet another biographical sketch of Tsongkhapa, I will look more closely at the relationship between Tsongkhapa and Mañjuśrī, the bodhisattva of wisdom. For the particulars of the relationship between Tsongkhapa and the bodhisattva become a flashpoint for the complex interweaving of lives and biography that eventuates in Jetsunpa's own career and biography.

Tsongkhapa and Mañjuśrī

Gelukpa authors depict Tsongkhapa's connection to the bodhisattva of wisdom in two ways. On one hand, he is portrayed as an emanation (*sprul pa*)[43] of Mañjuśrī, who purposely took birth in Tibet at a critical moment in order to direct the country's inhabitants on the path to enlightenment.[44] In other contexts, however, Tsongkhapa is described not as an emanation but as a worshipper and disciple of Mañjuśrī. He is a follower who pays homage to the deity as his *yidam* (*yi dam*), or "tutelary deity," and who is blessed with visions and revelations from Mañjuśrī. It is thanks to these revelations that he

43. The Tibetan term most often given in the sources used here is *sprul pa* ("emanation" or "incarnation"). It carries a more intentional connotation than the term *'phrul pa* ("manifestation" or "appearance"), most often used to describe manifestations of deities in worldly realms. Though the term *'phrul pa* is used on occasion, the more usual use of *sprul pa* would seem to indicate that Tsongkhapa's biographers mean to imply that Mañjuśrī emanated in this world as Tsongkhapa intentionally and for specific reasons. Though the term is actually closer in sense to "incarnation," I have opted for "emanation" to avoid confusion with the terms *yang srid* and *sprul sku*.

44. Sermé Drakpa Khedrup's account of the history of Shartsé college of Ganden Monastery, for example, characterizes Tsongkhapa explicitly as an emanation of Mañjuśrī (*Jampal Nyingpo's Mind Ornament*, 52). Kharnak Lotsāwa, in his *History of Ganden*, also says that Tsongkhapa was "clearly of the same mind as the lord Mañjuśrī" (2a) and maintains that Tsongkhapa was born in this world specifically for the benefit of other sentient beings. Kharnak also states that Tsongkhapa was clearly an emanation of Mañjuśrī, citing sources such as the *Mañjuśrīmūlatantra* and the *Bka' chems ka khol ma* as textual support to back this claim (4b).

developed his unique philosophical outlook and ultimately achieved enlightenment.[45] The term *yidam* is used to describe a deity responsible for protecting one's spiritual practice. Often assigned by one's teacher, the yidam serves as a guide on the path to enlightenment. One's yidam is also the figure with which one identifies in visualization meditation, and it thus functions as a source of spiritual attainments.[46] In claiming Tsongkhapa to have been a disciple of Mañjuśrī, however, members of the Geluk tradition are not only saying that Tsongkhapa regarded this deity as his yidam, meditating on him and praying to him as a source of spiritual realization, but also that Tsongkhapa actually received visionary teachings on philosophical and spiritual matters directly from Mañjuśrī, who appeared to Tsongkhapa on multiple occasions.

Though they are distinct and apparently mutually exclusive, the two types of relationship with Mañjuśrī are both attributed to Tsongkhapa, even within the same work. Gyalwang Chöjé Losang Trinlé Namgyal, for example, devotes two sections of his oft-cited 1845 biography of Tsongkhapa to the issue of Tsongkhapa's divinity, arguing that Tsongkhapa was most certainly an emanation of Mañjuśrī. At the same time he maintains that Tsongkhapa was spiritually guided and mentored by the deity.[47] Tsechokling Yeshé Gyaltsen (1713–93), too, describes Tsongkhapa as an emanation of Mañjuśrī while also asserting that Tsongkhapa received revelations from the deity and had been Manjuśrī's protégé for many lifetimes.[48]

One of the few examples of a Tibetan historian noting the two distinct depictions is Gungthang Könchok Tenpai Drönmé's (1762–1823) commentary to Khedrup's work in praise of Tsongkhapa's realizations. He makes sense of the apparent incommensurability by saying it is to be explained "through the use of general and special categories. To the general assembly of followers Tsongkhapa appeared as a disciple of Mañjuśrī, while to the intimate circle

45. Such a statement is made by Paṇchen Sönam Drakpa, for instance, in his biographical sketch of Tsongkhapa embedded within his history of the old and new Kadampas (*Mind's Ornament*, 50). This is also the case with Lechen Kunga Gyaltsen's *Lamp Illuminating the History of the Kadam Tradition* (345a), in which Tsongkhapa is presented as an especially intelligent figure who had visions of various deities as a child but of Mañjuśrī in particular after his meeting with Lama Umapa Pawo Dorjé (fourteenth–fifteenth cent.).

46. For more on deity worship, see Hopkins 1987b.

47. Gyalwang Chöjé, *Wondrous Jewel Garland*, 24ff. Gyalwang Chöjé's work is unusual in that the author actually cites his sources, giving not only titles but also the names of the authors. This impressive work clearly uses a large number of both early and more contemporary historical and biographical sources to elaborate on Tsongkhapa's life. The date of the text is given as 1845 in van der Kuijp 2001, 60.

48. Tsechokling Yeshé Gyaltsen, *Biographies of the Eminent Gurus*, 655–60.

of disciples he was the deity itself."[49] Here we see a traditional hermeneutical device deployed to distinguish levels of what is, in the end, the same reality based on the perceptions and intellectual abilities of students. This is the exception, however. For many writers, the apparent discrepancy is not even noted.

Modern representatives of the Geluk tradition still depict Tsongkhapa as simultaneously a follower and an emanation of Mañjuśrī. Geshé Ngawang Dhargyey, for example, appears to have followed Gungthangpa's logic when he is reported to have said that, while Tsongkhapa appeared to the majority of his disciples as a follower and propitiator of Mañjuśrī, praying and making offerings to the deity, he appeared to his closest disciples, Gyaltsap and Khedrup, in his true form as the deity's emanation.[50] According to this account, Tsongkhapa's actions as a propitiator of Mañjuśrī are all just an act meant to inspire devotion and like-mindedness in his own followers, who due to their ignorance, cannot fathom their teacher's true divinity.[51] This account is nearly identical to the ones related to me by my own teachers Geshé Karma Sönam, Geshé Ngawang Lekden, and Geshé Losang Sopa at Sera Monastery in South India.

Nevertheless, there is strictly speaking a discrepancy between framing Tsongkhapa simultaneously as a disciple and as an emanation. If Tsongkhapa received teachings from Mañjuśrī, does this not in fact imply that the two were distinct? Given the numerous warnings in Buddhist tradition to avoid self-adoration of any kind, it would be strange indeed for Tsongkhapa to propitiate a divinity who was none other than himself.[52] Describing Tsongkhapa as Mañjuśrī's disciple emphasizes Tsongkhapa's spiritual growth: as his disciple, Tsongkhapa relies on Mañjuśrī's guidance and help in order to achieve enlightenment. As an emanation, however, Tsongkhapa is in fact already an enlightened being and no longer needs to strive to achieve enlightenment;

49. *'O na gong du rje btsun 'jam dbyang dngos yin par nan tan du bsgrub pa ma yin nam // 'dir de'i gdul byar bshad pa 'gal lo snyam na // de ni thun mong dang thun mong ma yin pa'i skabs ma phyed pa'i skyon yin pas // gdul bya thun mong ba la snang tshul rgyud tha dad dang gdul byed gtso 'khor sogs su snang yang // gnas tshod la don ngo bo gcig pa du ma yod pa'i phyir //.* Gungthang Könchok Tenpai Drönmé, *Entryway to an Array of Wonders*, 858–59.

50. Thurman 1982, 5 and 7, and Samuel 1993, 248–49.

51. According to Geshé Dhargyey, it is because both Gyaltsap and Khedrup were, in fact, themselves emanations of divinities that they could see Tsongkhapa in his true form (Samuel 1993, 248–49).

52. For an excellent discussion of problems surrounding self-praise and self-abasement in autobiographical literature, see Janet Gyatso's *Apparitions of the Self* (Gyatso 1998).

in the standard theology, he only *pretends* to do so for the good of other sentient beings.[53]

The question of Tsongkhapa's identity as Mañjuśrī's emanation and/or follower is not taken up in Western works on Tsongkhapa's life and thought.[54] But it would seem that for members of the Geluk tradition, this relationship is of utmost importance regarding both their identity and their claims of legitimacy vis-à-vis other schools. Indeed, the Geluk tradition's espousal of Prāsaṅgika over Svātantrika tenets of Madhyamaka philosophy, a stance that contributes greatly to their self-distinction from other Buddhist traditions in Tibet, is based in key respects on this relationship. According to the standard hagiographical account, it was during a retreat alongside his master Lama Umapa that Tsongkhapa had a vision of Mañjuśrī. Tsongkhapa questioned the deity and received in return key instructions on which philosophical view to espouse and which to reject.[55] That this event is considered to be one of the most, if not *the* most, important points in Tsongkhapa's life is supported by the fact that Khedrup, who wrote the earliest extant biographies of Tsongkhapa, begins his secret biography of Tsongkhapa with an account of this particular episode. For Khedrup, then, Tsongkhapa's spiritual identity would seem to begin with this encounter.[56]

By claiming that Tsongkhapa was a disciple and/or an emanation of Mañjuśrī, Gelukpas are not just establishing that their founder was an incisive and skilled teacher, which is often one of the reasons such a correspondence is made.[57] In making such claims Gelukpas also imply that the doctrines they espouse originate directly from Mañjuśrī, a divine enlightened source.[58] If Tsongkhapa's teachings are really those of Mañjuśrī, then the Gelukpas, a group that is not only centered upon these teachings but which defines who is and isn't a member of the group based on acceptance

53. The classic example of this is of course the depiction of the Buddha himself. Aśvaghoṣa's *Buddhacarita* is an early example of this pattern whereby the hero is already enlightened but nevertheless goes through the motions of a journey to enlightenment as an example to others (see Olivelle 2008).

54. One exception is Samuel, whose discussion I will consider shortly.

55. This particular teacher of Tsongkhapa is an interesting figure I take up in more detail below. His epithet, Umapa, means Mādhyamika.

56. Khedrup Jé, *Grain Tips of the Precious Story Thoroughly Discussing Certain Parts of the Ocean-Like Secret Biography of the Precious Lord Master* (hereafter *Secret Biography of Tsongkhapa*), 2b.

57. van der Kuijp 2005, 22.

58. This is indeed a claim made by Jampal Gyatso (*Supplement*, 7a).

versus rejection of these teachings, are in reality the followers of Mañjuśrī. Should the Gelukpas claim, however, that Tsongkhapa was a disciple—but not necessarily an emanation—of Mañjuśrī, this would leave room for their religious and political adversaries to claim that the philosophical and spiritual advice Tsongkhapa received from Mañjuśrī in a vision actually came from a demon in Mañjuśrī's disguise. Such an accusation is found in the writings of Gorampa Sönam Sengé (1429–89), a prominent Sakya scholar.[59] If, on the other hand, Gelukpas maintain that their views come directly from Mañjuśrī, then Gelukpas are followers not merely of Tsongkhapa but of the bodhisattva of learning and wisdom. The Geluk tradition would thus necessarily hold the true and authentic teachings that lead one to salvation.

The Geluk school is not the only Tibetan Buddhist tradition to claim that one of its members was an emanation of a deity, let alone of Mañjuśrī. Sakya Paṇḍita (1182–1251), preeminent not only as a scholar but also as a political figure, was also claimed to have been such an emanation, as were other male members of the Sakya Khön family.[60] Much later, the Kagyü tradition claimed Jamgön Kongtrul (1813–99) as an emanation of Mañjuśrī, and Nyingma tradition tells us that Longchen Rapjampa (1308–64) and Ju Mipham (1846–1912) were also emanations of Mañjuśrī.[61] Exactly when these figures came to be portrayed as emanations of Mañjuśrī is still unclear. Far more scholarly attention has been paid to the claimed emanations of another bodhisattva-deity: Avalokiteśvara. Kapstein, van der Kuijp, and Ishihama have all analyzed in some detail the belief that the Dalai Lamas were emanations of Avalokiteśvara.[62]

Similar such claims are made for the Kadam lineage founder Dromtön Gyalwai Jungné (1004/5–64), though this identification is absent from the

59. Gorampa Sönam Sengé, *Distinguishing the Views,* 32. Gorampa also composed a text refuting Tsongkhapa's theories on Madhyamaka philosophy. This text (translated in Cabezón 2007) was later challenged by Jetsun Chökyi Gyaltsen.

60. It is unclear when this claim was first made, but it was in place by at least the fifteenth century, when its traces can be found in the works of Gorampa (Samuel 1993, 486). In an oral communication, Leonard van der Kuijp informed me that figurations of Sakya Paṇḍita as Mañjuśrī are already found in the fourteenth century.

61. Philippe Cornu 2006, 353.

62. According to that research, while the cult of Avalokiteśvara as the patron deity of Tibet seems to have already existed prior to the Fifth Dalai Lama's lifetime (1617–82), it was really through the efforts of this figure and his regent, Desi Sangyé Gyatso, that the Dalai Lamas became equated with Avalokiteśvara and thereby recognized—though most likely not by all inhabitants of Tibet—as the legitimate rulers of Tibet. See Kapstein 2003, van der Kuijp 2005, and Ishihama 2003.

earliest versions of his biography and may have only appeared sometime around the fifteenth century.[63] Earlier precedents are found in the identification of members of the imperial dynasty with deities.[64] The kings portrayed by the Tibetan Buddhist tradition as having been the most influential for the propagation of Buddhism in Tibet—Songtsen Gampo (d. ca. 650), Trisong Detsen (d. ca. 797), and Ralpachen (d. ca. 838)—are said to have been emanations of Avalokiteśvara, Mañjuśrī, and Vajrapāṇi, respectively.[65] The Sakya historian Sönam Gyaltsen (1312–75) alleges the divinity of these three kings in his *Mirror Illuminating the Royal Genealogies*.[66] According to van der Kuijp, however, there are already elaborations on the motif of the "Three Protectors of Tibet" found in sources dating back to the eleventh century, and Trisong Detsen is spoken of as a bodhisattva by a text from the ninth century.[67]

Despite the many precedents, there is evidence that there was some discomfort in the Geluk tradition regarding the tension between devotional and divine ascriptions vis-à-vis Tsongkhapa.[68] As mentioned above, Dhargyey, following Könchok Tenpai Drönmé, maintained that Tsongkhapa worshipped, prayed to, and received teachings from Mañjuśrī, inspiring his followers to do likewise, and in this conventional (*kun rdzob*) sense he was distinct from the deity. But on the level of ultimate reality (*don dam pa*), Tsongkhapa *was* Mañjuśrī; he did not *really* make offerings and pay homage to the deity because he was in fact indistinct from Mañjuśrī. Of course, not many disciples realized Tsongkhapa's true identity due to the fact that their intellectual and spiritual capacities did not allow them to fathom it. Only Tsongkhapa's two leading disciples, Gyaltsap and Khedrup, directly experienced his divinity, since both were actually emanations of deities themselves. The discrepancy comes down to the difference between what the "inner" and

63. van der Kuijp 2005, 21–24.

64. See Haarh 1969.

65. van der Kuijp 2005, 22.

66. *Rgyal rab gsal ba'i me long*. See Sørensen 1994, 157–417, and also Sakyapa Sönam Gyaltsen 1996, 95–261. Kapstein notes that the portions of the Maṇi bka' 'bum that develop most elaborately Songtsen Gampo's identity as an emanation of Avalokiteśvara date, in fact, to the thirteenth century (Kapstein 2003, 528).

67. van der Kuijp 2005, 24.

68. The earliest account I have found so far in which Tsongkhapa is described simultaneously as a disciple-worshipper and an emanation is Tsechokling Yeshé Gyaltsen's *Biographies of the Eminent Gurus*.

"outer" circles of devotees were able to comprehend. Ultimately, however, there was no difference between the two visions.[69]

Geoffrey Samuel understands Geshé Dhargyey's account of Tsongkhapa's relationship to Mañjuśrī as inconsistent. He does not attribute this to a lack of logic, however, but instead to an underlying acceptance of the multiplicity of reality and the partial and delusory nature of appearances.[70] Samuel further explains that, "multiplicity of meanings is a characteristic of Tibetan symbolism."[71] In other words, the apparent inconsistency is not understood as such by the Gelukpas, due essentially to their understanding of the fundamentally flawed nature of appearances and their conception of multiple levels of reality.[72]

To ascribe such solutions to a timeless notion of the multiple levels of reality fails to take into account historical conditions for cultural negotiation and change. To be sure, it is not unheard of for Tibetans to resort to hermeneutic loopholes to relieve a tension.[73] But we can propose an entirely different account of the inconsistencies in figurations of Tsongkhapa. There is a clear temporal shift in Tsongkhapa's hagiographical tradition—historical changes that can be attributed to personal, political, and institutional forces. It turns out the earliest biographical materials for Tsongkhapa never describe him as an emanation of Mañjuśrī at all. Such a notion developed later. Given this, the attempts to reconcile the two images and keep both operational derive not so much from a vision of multiple realities as from an attempt to preserve as authoritative the manifold biographical accounts.

69. Samuel 1993, 248–49; 485.

70. Samuel 1993, 249.

71. Samuel 1993, 485.

72. For a discussion of the "two truths," see Ruegg 1981, 42–46; Lopez 1987, 192–217; Beuscher 2005.

73. The reaction to the current Dalai Lama's request that the propitiation of the deity Dorjé Shukden come to an end is a good example. The continued propitiation of the deity by pro-Shukden monks was a prime topic of discussion during my stay at Sera Monastery (1986–92). Members of the pro-Shukden community drew on the notion of two types of *buddhavacana* (Buddha speech), definitive (*nges don*; Skt. *nītārtha*) and interpretable (*drang don*; Skt. *neyārtha*). To avoid having to actually stop performing the rites, those who propitiated the deity held that the Dalai Lama's request was in fact interpretable, not definitive, and therefore did not necessarily mean that they all had to stop. There is, of course, a difference between ultimate/conventional reality and definitive/interpretable meaning. Nevertheless, both pairs of concepts are in fact grounded in the notion that appearances are deceiving. What is most pertinent here is that the resolution provided was based on a lived tension between two distinct values. For more on the Dorjé Shukden controversy, see Dreyfus 1998.

Analysis reveals that the figuration of Tsongkhapa's divinity is intimately connected to shifting agendas and circumstances. Rather than focusing on the later reconciliation of the two varying accounts of Tsongkhapa's identity with regards to Mañjuśrī, then, we will be looking to understand why the two distinct characterizations came about in the first place. In so doing we will also shed light on larger issues in the construction of major Tibetan Buddhist figures and in the use of biography as both a historical tool and a doctrinal support through which new ideas can be transformed into tradition.

We now turn to the earliest of Tsongkhapa's extant biographies. Unfortunately, none of the biographies provide exact dates for their composition. However, through comparison, these texts hint at their chronology, allowing us to order and compare them for the sake of looking at key historical developments.

Tsongkhapa's *Realization Narrative*

Before discussing Tsongkhapa's biographies per se, we first look at his *Realization Narrative* (*Rtogs brjod*) to see how Tsongkhapa himself portrays his relationship to the bodhisattva of wisdom. This rather short autobiographical account of the master's spiritual education and development was putatively composed at Ganden Monastery by Tsongkhapa himself and then written down by Kashipa Rinchen Pal (fourteenth–fifteenth cent.), who is cited as scribe in a number of Tsongkhapa's works. The text is composed entirely in verse with an interesting admixture of modesty and self-exaltation characteristic of this genre, whereby the author both proclaims his great spiritual achievements while adhering to the strong cultural value placed on humility.[74]

Throughout the body of the *Realization Narrative*, in which Tsongkhapa discusses primarily how he practiced and realized Buddhist principles, the author repeatedly thanks Mañjuśrī, referred to as Treasury of Wisdom (*mkhyen pa'i gter*), for his role as a spiritual guide throughout Tsongkhapa's life.[75] In fact, Tsongkhapa repeats the phrase "Thank you, exalted Treasury of Wisdom!" (*bka' drin che'o rje btsun mkhyen pa'i gter*) twenty times throughout the text. But Tsongkhapa never once indicates he is the deity's emanation. In light of the premium placed on humility in Tibetan Buddhism, however, we must not read too much into the absence of such a grand claim.

74. Cf. Gyatso 1998.

75. Tsongkhapa, *Realization Narrative*, 145.

Given that downplaying one's status is a highly regarded virtue, for Tsongkhapa to proclaim himself an emanation of Mañjuśrī would prove, in some senses, that Tsongkhapa *wasn't* truly the deity. Nevertheless, it seems apparent from this text that he did not see Mañjuśrī as anything but his spiritual guide. Thus Tsongkhapa's own portrayal of his relationship to Mañjuśrī provides us with a starting point by which to consider later figurations.

Khedrup's *Entryway of Faith*

The earliest known biography of Tsongkhapa is Khedrup's monumental *Entryway of Faith* (*Dad pa'i 'jug ngogs*).[76] Counting some seventy-three folios, it is also the longest early account of Tsongkhapa's life.[77] The work relates in abundant detail the various facets of Tsongkhapa's existence, beginning with a brief presentation of the subject's parents, who are depicted as extremely pious people from the extensive Mal clan.[78]

Virtually from the start Khedrup asserts that, thanks to Mañjuśrī, his subject "brought to bloom the lotus of erudition" and became blessed with the "eye of one who sees in its entirety the *maṇḍala* of all that can be known (*shes bya*)" (3a). He then moves on to describe Tsongkhapa's childhood and early education, mentioning his ordination and course of study. When only three years old, Tsongkhapa is said to have left home to study with Chöjé Döndrup Rinchen (1309–85), a friend of the family who would become his first teacher. Döndrup Rinchen, upon having been invited by Tsongkhapa's parents to their home, came bearing gifts of horses and sheep. He requested in

76. Another prominent disciple of Tsongkhapa, Jampal Gyatso, composed a supplement to this work. Since Jampal Gyatso died in 1428, his work, and therefore Khedrup's as well, must have been written prior to that date. Khedrup's work mentions the construction of a new temple at Ganden in the Mouse year, corresponding most likely to 1420, suggesting a composition date between 1420 and 1428. Jampal Gyatso's account could have been composed by some other later figure of the same name, but this seems unlikely. The text is mentioned in various lists of Tsongkhapa's earliest biographies as being by Jampal Gyatso's hand.

77. The Kumbum edition counts one extra folio, which states where the text was printed. The next relatively early biography that counts almost as many folios is that by Kunga Delek Rinchen (1446–96), allegedly counting some sixty-two folios. Unfortunately this text has yet to be found.

78. I have so far been unable to locate any supplementary information on this clan. According to Khedrup (4a), Tsongkhapa's extended family was rather large, counting up to approximately one thousand members.

exchange the privilege of educating his host's young boy, an exchange that Tsongkhapa's father gladly accepted.

Under Döndrup Rinchen's careful guidance, Tsongkhapa is said to have become very skilled in both philosophical study and esoteric ritual practices. He remained with this teacher until the age of sixteen, when he decided to go study in Central Tibet. There he met what would become the two most important figures in his development: Rendawa Shönu Lodrö (1349–1412), who taught him philosophy, particularly Madhyamaka, and Lama Umapa Pawo Dorjé, who was particularly influential for Tsongkhapa's development as a practitioner.

Though Tsongkhapa is said to have had visions of Buddhist deities and masters such as Vajrapāṇi and Atiśa prior to meeting Umapa, it was during a retreat with the latter that Tsongkhapa actually got to speak to Mañjuśrī and ask him philosophical questions (5b). Mañjuśrī is said to have responded through Umapa who acted as a "translator" (*lo tsā ba*). After the rather detailed description of Tsongkhapa's retreat with Umapa, Khedrup's text sums up the episode by saying that from the very break of dawn, Mañjuśrī directly taught Tsongkhapa on definite release from cyclic existence (*nges 'byung*), on *bodhicitta*, and on which Madhyamaka theories to espouse. Mañjuśrī also showed him the remedy for all his conflicting emotions.[79]

This event warrants careful attention since, as mentioned earlier, it is traditionally considered the watershed in the development of Tsongkhapa's

79. Khedrup Jé, *Entryway of Faith*, 29b. Khedrup goes on not only to recount Tsongkhapa's travels and retreats around Central Tibet but also discusses the teachings he gave and received; the disciples he gained; the offerings he made when he celebrated the great prayer festival in Lhasa; the monastic community he founded at Ganden in 1409; and his passing in 1419. The overall tone of the text is one of veneration for a remarkable teacher and scholar, and yet it relates Tsongkhapa's life in a very fact-oriented and largely sober style (in comparison to typical Tibetan hagiographies, which are full of incredible and seemingly exaggerated stories about their subjects' spiritual and mystical exploits). The text also gives quite a bit of interesting information on topics such as how many followers Tsongkhapa had at various teaching sessions—Khedrup says that Tsongkhapa taught to eight thousand monks at the Mönlam prayer festival in 1408 and approximately two thousand monks at Drepung during one of Tsongkhapa's teaching trips there in 1419, just prior to his death (44b and 64a). When Khedrup describes Tsongkhapa's passing, he does so in a way that is typical of sacred biography in the Tibetan Buddhist tradition. He says that he heard many stories of how Tsongkhapa's body had a fresh and youthful appearance, as though he had transformed from a normal human body to a divine one—just like the *paṇḍita* Gayādhara (d. 1103), whose body is said to have shrunk and had a fresh, youth-like appearance upon his death (66a). Ronald Davidson gives an account of Gayādhara's life and travels to Tibet and discusses his role in eleventh-century Tibetan history but gives no mention of the master retaining a youthful appearance upon his death (Davidson 2005, 178–83).

thought and teachings and thus of utmost significance to the Geluk tradition. In Khedrup's chronicle of the event, which is discussed in virtually all of Tsongkhapa's early biographies, the interaction is indirect and triangular, with Tsongkhapa's master, Umapa, serving as the intercessor.

Khedrup portrays Umapa as a particularly staunch propitiator of Mañjuśrī and as having had many visions of Mañjuśrī and having heard the deity's mantra resounding in him from early on in his childhood (28a–29a). Khedrup's Umapa is a privileged follower of Mañjuśrī, as he was able to interact directly with the deity. In fact, Umapa's relationship to Mañjuśrī is portrayed as more intimate than Tsongkhapa's, for Tsongkhapa has access to Mañjuśrī only through Umapa's mediation. Khedrup does say that Mañjuśrī actually appeared to Tsongkhapa and taught him and Umapa,[80] which allows for the experience to be shared by both Tsongkhapa and Umapa, but Khedrup also makes it clear that Tsongkhapa's interaction with the deity was not direct.

This lies in stark contrast with later accounts of Tsongkhapa's life, such as Gyalwang Chöjé's *Wondrous Jewel Garland*, the Second Jamyang Shepa's *Jewel Garland*, Tsechokling Yeshé Gyaltsen's *Biographies of the Eminent Gurus*, and even Paṇchen Sönam Drakpa's *Mind's Ornament*, all of which leave out the element of Umapa's interpretive role in the encounter between Tsongkhapa and Mañjuśrī, suggesting a more intimate connection. But in Khedrup's account, Tsongkhapa's incapacity to understand Mañjuśrī directly causes him to appear as being a step removed from the deity. Khedrup's account therefore underscores that he saw Tsongkhapa as Mañjuśrī's follower and thereby as a distinct entity. Khedrup never once hints, let alone explicitly states, that Tsongkhapa was Mañjuśrī himself.

It is worth noting that at one point in the text, Khedrup does say that Tsongkhapa addressed prayers to Mañjuśrī as though the two were indistinct (37b). This should not, however, be misconstrued as an identification of Tsongkhapa as an emanation of the deity. In the practice referred to here, *deity yoga*, one first realizes emptiness and then causes the consciousness that realizes emptiness to "appear as a divine form from within an understanding of emptiness."[81] The deity, then, is in fact a representation of one's own mind; not an actual divine being that one transforms into. It is "the appearance of a wisdom consciousness in the compassionate form of an enlightened being."[82] The practice is, in some sense, a means by which to abolish the distance that

80. *Rje btsun 'jam dbyangs kyis* (...) *dngos su 'doms* (Khedrup Jé, *Entryway of Faith*, 29b).

81. Hopkins 1999b, 132.

82. Hopkins 1999b, 139. For more information on this practice, see Hopkins 1987b.

we as human beings posit between the divine and the human spheres; it is thereby also a means by which to increase the potency of one's prayers and actions. As Berzin puts it,

> Like performing the dress rehearsal for a drama, we imagine we already possess the entire array of these enlightening faculties as a Buddha-figure, all together at the same time. Doing so acts as an effective cause for integrating these qualities and achieving such a form more quickly.[83]

Deity yoga is an important meditation technique familiar even in Indian liturgy, which maintains, "He who does not change himself into a god cannot worship a god."[84] In no way, however, does this phrase imply that Khedrup considered Tsongkhapa to be an emanation of Mañjuśrī. Khedrup never uses the term "emanation" (*sprul pa*) when describing Tsongkhapa's propitiation of Mañjuśrī, saying instead simply that he prayed strongly to him while making them (Tsongkhapa and Mañjuśrī) indistinct (*tha mi dad du byas shing gsol ba drag tu 'debs*).

Thus there is clear evidence of a discrepancy between modern portrayals of Tsongkhapa's relationship to Mañjuśrī and that given by his earliest known biographer, who was also a direct disciple. Despite the widespread Gelukpa assertion that Tsongkhapa is in reality identical to Mañjuśrī, there is nothing to support this notion in Khedrup's *Entryway of Faith*.[85]

Khedrup's *Secret Biography of Tsongkhapa*

Khedrup's second account of Tsongkhapa's life, the *Secret Biography of Tsongkhapa* (*Rje rin po che'i gsang ba'i rnam thar*), is at sixteen folios, much shorter than the *Entryway of Faith*. This biography is the second earliest of Tsongkhapa's life stories and is the premier source for Khedrup's portrayal of Tsongkhapa's relationship to Mañjuśrī; it is here that we encounter the majority

83. http://www.berzinarchives.com/e-books/kalachakra_initiation/kalachakra_initiation_1.html

84. Tucci 1980, 94.

85. That Khedrup did not see his master as an emanation of Mañjuśrī is further supported by Khedrup's *Brief Biography of Tsongkhapa* (Khedrup Jé, *Miscellaneous Writings*, 4a–6b) and his *Prayer to Bring About Tsongkhapa's Reincarnation* (Khedrup Jé, *Miscellaneous Writings*, 6b–8a).

of references to their relationship. Being a "secret" biography, one expects that this text will tell us about Tsongkhapa's spiritual experiences, describing his many wondrous visions, dreams, and meditative experiences throughout his life. More specifically, one would expect to find in this text references to Tsongkhapa's identification as an emanation of Mañjuśrī if Khedrup did indeed see his teacher in this way. But although the text does focus quite a bit on Tsongkhapa's relationship to Mañjuśrī, going on at length about their interactions, it also discusses his visions of other deities and never once suggests a relation anything more than as Mañjuśrī's propitiator and follower.

Khedrup begins this account by stating that he has already discussed the main details of Tsongkhapa's life—up to the retreat alongside Umapa—in his prior work (*Entryway of Faith*)[86] and will now focus primarily on the important aspects of his subject's "inner" (*nang*) life (2a). Khedrup begins this report with another brief biographical sketch of Umapa, telling his readers that the latter's special connection with Mañjuśrī actually began many lifetimes ago. Khedrup relates how the deity's earlier mentoring of Umapa accounts for this cowherd-turned-visionary's unexcelled aptitude in the deity's practice; his numerous mystical experiences during which he both saw and heard the deity; and his having felt the droning hum of the deity's mantra in his entire body from his most tender age (2a). Khedrup also tells us that during their retreat together, Umapa asked Mañjuśrī just who Tsongkhapa had been in his previous life and where he would reincarnate in the future. Mañjuśrī replied that in a previous life Tsongkhapa had been the son of a brahman who, upon being introduced to the Buddha by his teacher, expressed the sincere wish to fully realize emptiness in the future.[87] Mañjuśrī also said that Tsongkhapa would be reborn in Maitreya's Tuṣita heaven as the bodhisattva Jampal Nyingpo (5a). This is the only part of the text that describes Tsongkhapa's past and future lives. Tsongkhapa is not described as having descended from a Buddha realm to take birth in Tibet for the benefit of others, as many of his later biographers maintain.

In addition to the retreat with Umapa, Khedrup describes another event involving Mañjuśrī. In this case Tsongkhapa asked his contemporary and disciple, Jampal Gyatso, who is also said to have had an exceptionally close relationship to the deity, to validate one of his visions of Mañjuśrī (6a). Like Umapa, Jampal Gyatso was allegedly able to speak to and translate Mañjuśrī's

86. *De la bla ma dbu ma pa dang mjal ba yan chad kyi rnam par thar pa ni thun mong bar brjod zin pa ltar ro //*; this account must therefore have been composed after *Entryway of Faith*.

87. This story is also mentioned in Khedrup's *Entryway of Faith*, 29b.

words for those who came with questions for the deity.[88] Throughout the accounts of Tsongkhapa's retreats and interactions with Mañjuśrī, then, the deity seems to address Tsongkhapa through either his teacher Umapa or through his disciple Jampal Gyatso. Mañjuśrī addresses and instructs Tsongkhapa through these intermediaries sometimes after being invoked by Umapa and at other times appearing spontaneously. Lama Umapa and Jampal Gyatso were thus akin to oracles through whom the divinity could address human beings.

Khedrup's detailed discussion of Umapa's relationship to Mañjuśrī and the repeated mention of his agency in translating for Tsongkhapa, reminiscent of his previous work, leads me to question why the author feels it so important to stress it. Might it be a means by which to claim that Tsongkhapa's visions and interactions with Mañjuśrī, which seem to have been largely dependent upon Umapa's own relationship to the deity, are legitimate? In anticipation of challenges from rival schools, Khedrup, by repeatedly stating that Umapa himself was a fervent practitioner of Mañjuśrī who had been blessed even in childhood with visions and teachings from the deity, may have been attempting to establish that Tsongkhapa was part of an authentic lineage of Mañjuśrī practitioners. By bolstering Umapa's credentials, perhaps Khedrup means to show that the visions of Tsongkhapa he was recounting were authentic. Umapa's authenticity in turn validates the teachings and philosophical views that resulted from the meetings.[89]

By making Umapa an agent through whom Mañjuśrī interacts with Tsongkhapa, however, Khedrup diminishes the immediacy of latter's own experience. Umapa's role as interpreter indicates that Khedrup did not see his teacher as an emanation of Mañjuśrī.

In sum, Khedrup's *Secret Biography of Tsongkhapa* seems to be trying to establish above all that Tsongkhapa was destined for the spiritual greatness he achieved in his life, and that he had been blessed by many wondrous encounters with all sorts of important divinities. Not once throughout the text does Khedrup insinuate, let alone explicitly state, that Tsongkhapa was an emanation of Mañjuśrī. Although it is often the case that secret biographies are meant to inspire readers to have faith and devotion in the biograph-

88. This story is also mentioned in a later source by Tsechokling Yeshé Gyaltsen. See Willis 1995, 39.

89. An interesting passage in Gö Lotsāwa's *Blue Annals* (as translated by Roerich) mentions that Mañjuśrī had bestowed numerous teachings on Umapa, who is identified as "the transmitter of Mañjughoṣa's commands and teachings to Tsoṅ-kha-pa" (Gö Lotsāwa 1976, 1048–49n1).

ical subject,[90] Khedrup never takes the opportunity to elevate Tsongkhapa to the level of a divine bodhisattva like Mañjuśrī.[91]

Jampal Gyatso's *Supplement*

Another biography of Tsongkhapa that we will consider briefly is the *Supplement to the Great Biography of the Lord Tsongkhapa: The Biography Entitled "Treasury of Eloquent Teachings."* It is only between eleven (Lhasa edition) and thirteen (Kumbum edition) folios long, making it even shorter than Khedrup's *Secret Biography*. According to the colophon the text was composed by Tokden Jampal Gyatso, who was not only a contemporary and disciple of Tsongkhapa but also a teacher to Khedrup. His dates (1356–1428) make this an early account of Tsongkhapa's life.

Its being a "supplement" (*zur 'debs*) to Khedrup's *Entryway* implies not only that it was composed after the latter work[92] but more importantly that it has something to add to it. It might in some ways be considered a corrective. Indeed, this work stands alone as the only of Tsongkhapa's extant early biographies that hints Tsongkhapa may have been an emanation of Mañjuśrī, though it does not say so in so many words.

In contrast with Khedrup's works, Jampal Gyatso's text repeatedly tries to establish, albeit implicitly, that Tsongkhapa's exalted spiritual identity did not commence with his retreat and encounter with Mañjuśrī but was already in place even before his birth. Whereas Khedrup begins his *Secret Biography of Tsongkhapa* with an account of the retreat with Umapa, Jampal Gyatso starts his account just prior to Tsongkhapa's conception. Rather than beginning with an opening verse in praise of the subject as do most biographical works, Jampal Gyatso immediately launches into his account of the vivid and auspicious dreams that both of Tsongkhapa's parents had before his birth,

90. According to Gyalwang Chöjé, a biography (*rnam thar*) must inspire its readers and thereby become a primary cause of their enlightenment (*Wondrous Jewel Garland*, 10). Jan Willis also notes that inspiring readers (and listeners) to faith and serving as a model for conduct and progression on the path to liberation are primary functions of Tibetan hagiography (Willis 1985, 304).

91. Khedrup Jé, *Secret Biography of Tsongkhapa*, 15a–b.

92. Jampal Gyatso also refers the readers to the *Secret Biography by Changra Kachupa* (*Lcang ra Bka' bcu pa*), one of Khedrup's epithets from when he lived at Changra Monastery in Tsang, indicating that Jampal Gyatso's text comes after that work as well.

> Toward the end of the year of the monkey (1356), Tsongkhapa's father had a dream in which a monk appeared claiming he was from Mount Wutai in China.[93] He wore religious robes embroidered with multiple flower garlands and a lower garment of yellow silk with what he said were leaves from the trees in the Heaven of the Thirty-Three. He was carrying a book and said, "I would like accommodation" and disappeared into a chapel located on the upper floor of the house. As Tsongkhapa's father practiced only the *Reciting of the Names of Mañjuśrī* (*'Jam dpal mtshan brjod*) at that time, he is said to have thought "this monk must have been an emanation of Mañjuśrī."[94] His mother had a dream in which she saw herself among a thousand women lined up in a field full of flowers. From the east came a young boy clad in white carrying a water vessel, and from the west came a girl dressed in red carrying a mirror in her left hand and a peacock feather in her right. The boy pointed one by one at each of the women, asking the girl if each one was suitable, but the girl found flaws in each of them. When they reached Tsongkhapa's mother, the boy pointed to her and asked "Is she suitable?" The red-clad girl smiled and said, "Yes, she is." Then she said, "Now wash her," and the boy proceeded to wash away her impurities. Tsongkhapa's mother awoke the next morning feeling light and joyful.

The author goes on to say that from that time on, Tsongkhapa's family and their neighbors all had auspicious dreams, which continued right up until his birth,

> From that time onward, Tsongkhapa's family and the people of his region had peculiar dreams in which they say a procession of monks welcoming the Jowo (Atiśa) from Ü (Dbus). Also, there were other wondrous occurrences that took place, such as the sun, moon, and stars all visible at once, a light "rain of flowers" falling

93. Mount Wutai (the "five-terraced mountain"), revered already in pre-Buddhist China as a sacred place, had come to be identified as Mañjuśrī's worldly residence by the fifth and sixth centuries. By the eighth century it had become established as a pilgrimage site and boasted several monasteries (see Stevenson 1996, 207–8). Also, in Jetsunpa's biography of Khedrup, Jetsunpa says that Tsongkhapa told Khedrup in one of the latter's visions that he was currently residing at Mount Wutai, teaching over 800,000 monks (*Secret Biography of Khedrup*, 24a; see also appendix B).

94. Jampal Gyatso, *Supplement*, 1a–2a.

> while the sun shone, the scent of incense on the air, music emanating from the sky, and earthquakes.[95]

Jampal Gyatso's attention to the dreams of Tsongkhapa's parents signals his particular veneration for Tsongkhapa and indicates his desire to elevate him. Khedrup's *Entryway*, in contrast, gives little more than a physical description of Tsongkhapa at the time of his birth, and though he speaks of Tsongkhapa's mild and kind-hearted mannerisms as a child, he never once discusses any such miraculous dreams and events. Khedrup's accounts portray him as special to be sure, but as a human being who merely walked the path of and achieved enlightenment after receiving close spiritual guidance from deities such as Mañjuśrī. Jampal Gyatso, on the other hand, demonstrates that before he was born Tsongkhapa was already enlightened, with strong connections to many deities, and that he took birth in this world on purpose.[96]

Jampal Gyatso seems to want his readers to infer that Tsongkhapa was an emanation of Mañjuśrī. This may constitute the earliest written expression of what was later to become an inalienable part of Tsongkhapa's identity. As such, it is possible that this important shift was in fact introduced by Jampal Gyatso. Recall that Jampal Gyatso's text is a self-styled supplement to Khedrup's biography and, as such, implies that the author had been privy to certain important and sometimes secret aspects of Tsongkhapa's life and identity that Khedrup neglected to mention; he, Jampal Gyatso, is filling his readers in on this exclusive information.[97]

This novel identification of Tsongkhapa with Mañjuśrī may have something to do with a special agenda of Jampal Gyatso, who as already mentioned is said to have had a strong connection with Mañjuśrī. Like Umapa, Jampal Gyatso not only had visions of the deity and dreams in which he himself visited Mount Wutai, but he also developed such a strong connection

95. Jampal Gyatso, *Supplement*, 2a–b.

96. Jampal Gyatso's account taps into older Buddhist hagiographical conventions. Aśvaghoṣa's *Buddhacarita* describes the Buddha's appearance in his mother's dream as a glorious white elephant that approaches her from out of the heavens. Aśvaghoṣa interprets the dream as meaning that a child would be born to her and that the child would be either a universal monarch or an enlightened being (Olivelle 2008, 13).

97. Lechen Kunga Gyaltsen also informs us that Jampal Gyatso asked Mañjuśrī for Tsongkhapa's life story, which the deity then taught to him and which Jampal Gyatso committed to memory (*Lamp*, 363a). Jampal Gyatso never once says that the information he provides in his work came directly from Tsongkhapa. This stands in sharp contrast with Khedrup's works, which are cast as being based on Tsongkhapa's own words.

with this divinity that he acted on many occasions as his medium and translator for visitors and devotees, including Tsongkhapa himself. At the end of his life Jampal Gyatso is said to have fully merged with Siṃhavahana-Mañjuśrī, a peaceful two-armed form of the deity.[98]

But if we must understand the account of Tsongkhapa's father's dream to mean that Jampal Gyatso saw his master as an emanation of Mañjuśrī, which is never explicitly stated, then shouldn't we also consider Jampal Gyatso to have seen his master as an emanation of Atiśa and Avalokiteśvara? For Jampal Gyatso reports that Tsongkhapa's family dreamed of a procession of monks welcoming Atiśa from Ü, while his mother dreamed, shortly prior to his birth, that she was asked to take care of a statue of Avalokiteśvara, which eventually shrinks and disappears into her body:

> On the tenth day of the first month of the year of the hen (1357), Tsongkhapa's mother had a dream in which she saw an incredible assembly of spiritual men and women carrying victory banners, drums, and other instruments. They told her they had come to greet Avalokiteśvara. She looked everywhere, but she saw no one coming. When she looked once again, however, in front of a cloud she saw a golden statue the size of a mountain shining in all directions as brightly as the sun, emitting a melodious sound and accompanied by an excellent retinue of noble sons and daughters. As the statue descended toward her, it grew smaller and smaller until, the size of a finger, it reached the crown of her head and dissolved into her body. Seeing this, the retinue and greeters made auspicious offerings, prostrated, and circumambulated her.[99]

Given the exalted status accorded to one's teacher in Tibetan Buddhism, it is perhaps not surprising that Jampal Gyatso should want to cast his own teacher as an emanation of Mañjuśrī, especially since his own devotion toward this divinity was particularly strong.[100] Lechen Kunga Gyaltsen (1432–1506),

98. Willis 1995, 37–40. Siṃhavahana-Mañjuśrī (*seng ge nga ro*) is one of many forms of Mañjuśrī. One-headed, two-armed, golden-yellow, seated on a lion, he carries both the Prajñāpāramitā text and the sword of wisdom poised on lotuses in his left and right hands, respectively. His hands are in the gesture of turning the wheel of Dharma. (See Bunce 1994, 1:331 and 2:815; and Bhattacaryya 1993, 19–20).

99. Jampal Gyatso, *Supplement*, 2b–3a.

100. For a more detailed discussion of guru-devotion practices within the Geluk tradition, particularly relating to tantra, see Tsongkhapa 1999.

author of one of the earliest histories of the Geluk school, tells us that Jampal Gyatso had repeated visions of buddhas and bodhisattvas so often that he appeared to be mentally unstable (*yid brtan mi thub pa*).[101] Jampal Gyatso's insinuation that Tsongkhapa was an emanation of Mañjuśrī, when seen in this context, appears not to be a written expression of an idea that was already circulating among the Gelukpas for some time—one that had yet to find its way into writing—but rather an expression of Jampal Gyatso's own personal vision of Tsongkhapa, a vision highly colored by his own special relationship with the deity. Had the identification of Tsongkhapa with Mañjuśrī already been current in Gelukpa circles, we must wonder why it is completely absent from Khedrup's works and from the slightly later biography by Jamyang Chöjé discussed below.

Another divergence from Khedrup's accounts can be seen in Jampal Gyatso's discussion of Tsongkhapa's first teacher, Döndrup Rinchen. Here Döndrup Rinchen is described as a highly realized practitioner of Vajrabhairava, a wrathful aspect of Mañjuśrī, who appeared to Döndrup Rinchen in a dream and indicated, in an indirect way, that Döndrup Rinchen should care for the young Tsongkhapa. Jampal Gyatso says that Döndrup Rinchen made an offering of special ambrosia (*bdud rtsi*), other mixed pills, and a precious drawing of Vajrabhairava in request for the boy, and that he sent the gifts and request letter through a messenger. According to Khedrup's version, Döndrup Rinchen's gifts were composed of livestock, which he brought himself, and Khedrup mentions special dreams that Döndrup Rinchen may have had before asking to be Tsongkhapa's teacher. Thus Jampal Gyatso's account takes on an aspect of divine intervention by which the deity Vajrabhairava makes Döndrup Rinchen responsible for the young boy's care.

After the episode about Döndrup Rinchen's mentorship, Jampal Gyatso's biography discusses Tsongkhapa's education and intellectual exploits in a manner more reminiscent of Khedrup's works. Eventually Tsongkhapa is said to have wanted to go to India to study more. However, he was discouraged by not only his followers at the time but also by a great practitioner named Namkha Gyaltsen of Lhodrak (1326–1401), who prophesied that should Tsongkhapa go to India, he would become a great abbot but would live a shorter life and thus be of less benefit to his followers. Instead, Namkha Gyaltsen told him, he should remain in Tibet, make Mañjuśrī his tutelary deity, and teach Madhyamaka, the Stages of the Path to Enlightenment (*lam rim*), and the Kadam teachings (6b). A little later in the biography, Tsongkhapa meets Lama Umapa, who is once again said to have acted as a

101. Lechen, *Lamp*, 362b.

sort of translator between Tsongkhapa and Mañjuśrī. Mañjuśrī gives Tsongkhapa teachings and responds to his queries concerning tantra, philosophy, and his own personal practice. Jampal Gyatso then says that the tenets set forth by Tsongkhapa are actually those espoused by Mañjuśrī himself (6b–7a). Jampal Gyatso continues to speak of Tsongkhapa's education, travels, and debut as a teacher, and then a little further on states that as he was guided and blessed by Mañjuśrī, Tsongkhapa became known all over as a true scholar venerated even by the Karmapa hierarch (8b).

Compared to Khedrup's accounts of Tsongkhapa's life, Jampal Gyatso does not dwell long on Tsongkhapa's encounter with Umapa; he merely states that Umapa was an interpreter between Tsongkhapa and Mañjuśrī. This again contrasts with Khedrup, who made this event the very beginning, and therefore one of the most pivotal moments of Tsongkhapa's spiritual life.

In sum, Jampal Gyatso's account is much more supernaturally inclined. He takes pains to frame his master's biography in a way that elevates Tsongkhapa's status.[102] Jampal Gyatso's initial reference to Tsongkhapa's father's belief that the monk in his dream was an emanation of Mañjuśrī notwithstanding, however, there are no explicit remarks made by Jampal Gyatso to the effect that Tsongkhapa was an emanation of this deity. In fact, all of Jampal Gyatso's direct references to the relationship say merely that Tsongkhapa was guided and mentored by Mañjuśrī. Thus, although Jampal Gyatso's biography of Tsongkhapa is the first of which it may be said that there are hints that Tsongkhapa was an emanation of Mañjuśrī, the transformation to full-fledged identification with the divinity has not yet occurred.[103]

Jampal Gyatso's *Very Secret Biography of Tsongkhapa*

The *Marvelous Tale of Lord Tsongkhapa's Very Secret Biography* (*Rje'i rnam thar shin tu gsang ba*) is probably the shortest of Tsongkhapa's early prose

102. This is not to say that Khedrup considered Tsongkhapa to be an ordinary human being. It is evident from the list of teachings received by him and from his prayer for Tsongkhapa's rebirth that Khedrup saw his master as a wise and enlightened being (*thams cad mkhyen pa*). But even in these works, Khedrup does not qualify his master as an emanation of Mañjuśrī.

103. In a reference to Jampal Gyatso by Tsechokling Yeshé Gyaltsen in his collection of the biographies of the masters of the Ganden transmission lineage, Jampal Gyatso is said to have made a clairvoyant declaration that Tsongkhapa had been Mañjuśrī's disciple from many lifetimes, but Tsechokling never says that Jampal Gyatso saw Tsongkhapa as an emanation of the deity (Tsechokling Yeshé Gyaltsen, *Biographies of the Eminent Gurus*, 660). Part of this work is skillfully translated in Willis 1995.

biographies, counting only three folios.[104] The text is said to have been based on the words of Rinchen Gyaltsen (fourteenth cent.), one of Tsongkhapa's close and direct disciples, and to have been committed to writing by "the renunciant Jampal Gyatso" upon being presented with a golden *maṇḍala* by disciple Söshé and the Ngari ruler Namkha Sangpo (3b).[105] Thus the work is attributed to Jampal Gyatso. However, it is strangely absent from lists of early biographical works concerning Tsongkhapa by both Akuching and Chahar Geshé. This raises the question of whether the text was indeed composed by the same Jampal Gyatso as the work above or was composed by another figure. The colophon states that the text was composed in the eighth month of the hare year but does not specify any gender or element that would help identify precisely which hare year. If indeed it was composed by the same Jampal Gyatso as discussed above, the only possible date would have been 1423, but once again it is not certain. Lacking conclusive evidence, I have nevertheless chosen to include it in my discussion.

The *Very Secret Biography* was purportedly transmitted to Jampal Gyatso by Tsongkhapa himself upon Jampal Gyatso's request. The text focuses mainly on Tsongkhapa's spiritual prowess in relation to one miraculous mystical experience, though the text never says when it happened. It simply begins by saying that Tsongkhapa's main purpose in life was to increase the merit of the fortunate ones and that Tsongkhapa had been guided to the highest point of achievement on the Mahāyāna path by Mañjuśrī. Tsongkhapa thereby became unparalleled in the inner and outer sciences and developed the five sublime states of perception.[106] The text goes on to discuss an apparition of the tathāgata Indraketu (*dbang po'i thog*), who tells Tsongkhapa to quickly achieve liberation so as to selflessly expound the mantra associated with the purest view (*lta ba rnam par dag pa'i sngags*) in this impure realm. Tsongkhapa then makes the solemn wish to do just that.

The text further details the color of the deity and the place where he resides, explaining how one goes about being reborn in such a place. The

104. It is located in the first volume of the Lhasa edition of Tsongkhapa's collected works, whereas it is located near the end of the Kumbum edition, in volume dza. Scholarly attention to the significance of the varying order of texts that comprise a master's collected writings (*gsung 'bum*) from one edition to the next is lacking. Schaeffer refers to this editorial practice in his article on the publication of Jamyang Shepa's collected writings, but he does not pursue the discussion beyond that (see Schaeffer 1999, 166).

105. I have not been able to identify these two figures.

106. The five sublime states of perception (*mngon par shes pa lnga*) are clairvoyance, clairaudience, knowledge of others' thoughts, recollection of past lives, and the ability to perform miracles.

text says nothing beyond this of Tsongkhapa's life, and aside from the passage mentioned above, there is no other mention of Mañjuśrī. So even if the text were indeed written by Jampal Gyatso, it does not intimate, as did Jampal Gyatso's *Supplement*, that Tsongkhapa was Mañjuśrī's emanation. Instead it seems to follow Khedrup's lead in portraying Tsongkhapa as Mañjuśrī's disciple and worshipper.

Jamyang Chöjé's *Supplication*

The *Supplication* is a very short versified ode to Tsongkhapa, counting six folios.[107] It was composed by Tsongkhapa's disciple Jamyang Chöjé Tashi Palden (1379–1449), the founder of Drepung Monastery.[108] The vast majority of this author's works are unfortunately still unavailable, and oral tradition—related to me by the abbot of the Mé college at Sera in Tibet—has it that his works came to be considered somewhat unorthodox and were therefore removed from circulation.[109] To my knowledge, however, this story about Jamyang Chöjé is not supported by any textual evidence.[110]

In the *Supplication* the biographical sketch begins when Tsongkhapa is seven years old and has visions of both wrathful Vajrapāṇi and Atiśa Dīpaṃkara, who are said to have appeared to him and given him teachings on both tantra and the perfection of wisdom. The text then goes on to pay homage to the "Lord Lama" who had directly perceived Mañjuśrī, but there is no implication that Tsongkhapa is this deity's emanation. Further on Jamyang Chöjé pays homage to the illustrious lama whose heart was touched by Mañjuśrī's wisdom sword, thereby causing to flow into Tsongkhapa "a steady stream of immaculate ambrosia, thereby spontaneously arousing in him the *samādhi* of the highest joy."[111]

Jamyang Chöjé claims that Tsongkhapa was guided by major philosophical figures such as Nāgārjuna, Buddhapālita, Āryadeva, Candrakīrti, Asaṅga, and Vasubhandu, all of whom appeared to and taught him (3a). The text

107. *Gsol 'debs.* Found in volume ka of both the Lhasa and Kumbum editions of Tsongkhapa's collected works. A translation of this text is presented in Thurman 1982, 47–55.

108. Tsangtön Kunga Gyaltsen, *Lamp Illuminating the Wondrous Story of the Full Enlightenment of the Omniscient Jamyang Chöjé Tashi Palden as Related by Himself*, 12b–13a.

109. This was told to me during a meeting at the abbot's residence at Sera in April 2001.

110. Jamyang Chöjé was a contemporary of Khedrup, and it seems the two often debated one another at Ganden (Tsangtön, *Lamp*, 8b).

111. Jamyang Chöjé, *Supplication*, 2b–3a; Thurman 1982, 50.

goes on to mention yet more visions the subject had and even speaks briefly of the prophecy already seen in Khedrup's works that in the future Tsongkhapa would be reborn in Tuṣita. According to Jamyang Chöjé, however, this prophecy was made not by Mañjuśrī only, as Khedrup reports it, but by both Mañjuśrī and the deity Vajrapāṇi (4a).

Thus several passages specifically mention Tsongkhapa as having had a strong relationship to Mañjuśrī, but Jamyang Chöjé never characterizes the relationship as anything but master and disciple, placing his characterization of Tsongkhapa in line with that given in Khedrup's works.

Chimé Rapgyé's *Jewel Treasury*

The final work is one of four biographical sketches by Chimé Rapgyé (fifteenth cent.). As its full title—*Jewel Treasury: The Story of the Precious Lord's Endowment with the Qualities of Learning, Dignity, and Excellence* (*Nor bu'i bang mdzod*)—indicates, the text discusses Tsongkhapa's qualities as an accomplished master. Chimé Rapgyé's exact dates are uncertain, though judging by one of his statements in a separate work, it would seem that he was a disciple of Jamyang Chöjé.[112] Rakra Rinpoché, who recently rediscovered and published the text, indicates that the author must have been a contemporary of Khedrup.[113] If so Chimé Rapgyé would have to have been a younger contemporary. For in his *Golden Wick*, Chimé Rapgyé cites the *Short Biography of Khedrup* by Chöden Rapjor,[114] a text that discusses the hero's death, which occurred in 1438. The text's colophon gives the year iron-male-tiger for its composition and mentions Tashi Lhunpo Monastery, founded in 1447), placing the text's composition in 1470.[115]

Chimé Rapgyé begins his account by stating that Tsongkhapa had been mentored by great masters from Ü, Tsang, and Kham, whereby he became greatly versed in both esoteric and exoteric Buddhism. The author makes

112. *Rang gi bla ma 'jam dbyangs chos rje* (Chimé Rapgyé, *Golden Wick*, 35).

113. Chimé Rapgyé, *Jewel Treasury*, iv.

114. A translation of this work is in appendix A.

115. It is possible that there is a conflation between "tiger" (*stag*) and the homophonous "horse" (*rta*), which would place the composition in 1450, but there is little reason to believe that the date given in the colophon is in fact erroneous. Given Chimé Rapgyé's mention of Mönlam Pal (1414–91) as an upholder of the "two traditions of the seats"—implying that he was abbot (Mönlam Pal occupied the Shartsé college abbacy until 1474 and the Ganden throne from 1480–89)—that the *Golden Wick* could not have been composed earlier than 1470.

Tsongkhapa out to have been a scholar of all traditions who was knowledgeable not only in the sūtras and tantras but also in medicine and even in the life and songs of the well-known yogi Milarepa. Chimé Rapgyé says that Tsongkhapa was considered a great scholar by renowned figures from many traditions, quoting their words of praise. The text explains how Tsongkhapa rigorously kept the Vinaya discipline and inspired devotion by his exemplary conduct. The author writes that Tsongkhapa was virtuous in speech and mind too, having great compassion for all. The text then says that Tsongkhapa refused to give *mahāmudrā* teachings to women (11). Finally, the text states that even in his old age Tsongkhapa maintained a youthful appearance, and his body naturally emitted both a brilliant light and the "very sweet smell of morality" (12).

Strikingly the *Jewel Treasury* never once mentions Tsongkhapa's relation to Mañjuśrī, let alone the possibility of his being an emanation. Instead the author uses more concrete examples and evidence to portray Tsongkhapa simply as learned and virtuous.

Clearly, evidence from the earliest biographies of Tsongkhapa does not support the idea held by the later Geluk tradition that Tsongkhapa was simultaneously a disciple and an emanation of Mañjuśrī. Where and when, then, does the shift occur? Surprisingly the answer lies not in Tsongkhapa's biographies but in those of his own first biographer, Khedrup Gelek Palsang.

2. Khedrup

KHEDRUP GELEK PALSANG (1385–1438), commonly known as Khedrup Jé, is seen by the Geluk tradition as one of Tsongkhapa's two most important disciples and interpreters. The second successor to the Ganden abbacy in 1432, Khedrup was responsible for establishing the monastery's first college devoted specifically to the study of Buddhist philosophy. His status as chief spiritual heir alongside Gyaltsap is not only stressed by his biographers but is also reaffirmed by historians and numerous Tibetan thangka paintings.

Khedrup was born in the western part of Tsang in the northern Latö village of Dokshung. His father was the nobleman and government official Tashi Palsang, and his mother was Budren Gyalmo. The eldest of three sons, including the eminent Geluk figure Baso Chökyi Gyaltsen, Khedrup is said to have shown intellectual acuity from a young age. Studying and traveling to debate at a number of important institutions of his day, Khedrup quickly made a name for himself as an outstanding scholar, earning him the epithet Choklé Namgyal (*phyogs las rnam rgyal*), "victorious in all directions." At only sixteen years old he allegedly bested the renowned Bodong Paṇchen Choklé Namgyal (1376–1451) in debate, gaining the utmost respect from his peers and from Bodong Paṇchen himself.[116]

In 1405 Khedrup took full ordination from the Sakya scholar Rendawa Shönu Lodrö (1349–1412). Under this master's careful guidance he became learned in Madhyamaka (middle-way philosophy), Pramāṇa (logic and epistemology), Prajñāpāramitā (the perfection of wisdom), Vinaya (monastic discipline), and Abhidharma (taxonomy of the inner and outer worlds). A few years later, in 1407, hearing of Tsongkhapa's great qualities and intellectual acuity, Khedrup left for Ü to seek out Rendawa's former student.

At the time of Khedrup's first encounter with his master, Tsongkhapa was in retreat at Sera Chöding, a small hermitage in the hills just behind what is

116. Jetsunpa, *Secret Biography of Khedrup*, 6a–b, and Paṇchen Delek Nyima, *Delightful to the Scholar's Mind*, 3a–b.

now Sera Monastery near Lhasa. Khedrup ascended the mountain and met a gentle and simple monk of whom he asked where he might find Tsongkhapa's residence. Without uttering a word the monk disappeared inside his hut and reemerged holding a lit incense stick. He walked to a yellow building, prostrated three times holding the incense between his folded hands, stuck the incense in a pot, and said, "This is the temple in which my abbot, Losang Drakpa, resides."[117] Khedrup was impressed and humbled by this monk's appearance and conduct, which testified to his being an excellent practitioner of the Vinaya. The initial encounter between Tsongkhapa and Khedrup left quite a mark on the latter:

> On first meeting Tsongkhapa, Khedrup's hair stood on end at the mere sight of the master. Crying tears of devotion, he sang out a confused expression of reverence, and he thought to himself: "This must be my guide to freedom from cyclic existence, the virtuous friend who will protect me from the abyss of the lower vehicle."[118]

Khedrup would spend the next while learning from Tsongkhapa and a number of his disciples, particularly Gyaltsap and Dulwazinpa (Dulzin) Drakpa Gyaltsen (1374–1434). Just how long Khedrup spent with Tsongkhapa is not certain, but he eventually left for Tsang to start his own community. He founded and taught (particularly esoteric Buddhism) at a number of institutions, including Dangchen Hermitage, Changra Monastery in Upper Nyang, and Palkhor Dechen Monastery in Gyantsé, which he established in 1418 with the financial support of the Tsangpa ruler Rapten Kunsang Phakpa (1389–1442). Khedrup would later leave Palkhor Dechen due to an alleged dispute with the infamous Sakyapa scholar Rongtön Mawai Sengé (1367–1449). The dispute caused a falling out with his patron, who is said to have favored Rongtön.[119]

117. Paṇchen Delek Nyima, *Delightful to the Scholar's Mind*, 4b.

118. Jetsunpa, *Secret Biography of Khedrup*, 4b.

119. Once a chamberlain (*gzims dpon*) to the Phakmodru ruler Drakpa Gyaltsen (see Ngawang Lobsang Gyatso 1995, 149, and Wylie 2003, 484), Rapten Kunsang Phakpa had helped Khedrup establish his monastic communities of Changra and Palkhor Chödé in Tsang in 1418. Following the confrontation with Rongtön, who had been invited to Rapten Kunsang's court by the ruler himself, Khedrup became upset with his patron and left Gyantsé (Paṇchen Delek Nyima, *Delightful to the Scholar's Mind*, 19). Although a short chronology of Khedrup's whereabouts is given in Rapten Kunsang's own biography, Rongtön's presence and Khedrup's discontent are not mentioned (Jikmé Drakpa Choklé Namgyal, *Rain of Accomplishments*,

In 1432 Khedrup traveled to Nenying to greet his teacher, Gyaltsap, who was visiting his old monastery. It was on this occasion that Gyaltsap named Khedrup abbot of Ganden, thereby making him Tsongkhapa's second successor. Khedrup led the Ganden community for six years, during which he founded the monastery's first college for Buddhist philosophical study.[120]

Chöden Rapjor's *Short Biography of the Omniscient Khedrup*

As with Tsongkhapa, there are numerous biographies and biographical sketches of Khedrup's life.[121] The earliest-known extant biography of Khedrup is the *Short Biography of the Omniscient Khedrup* composed by Chöden Rapjor (fourteenth–fifteenth cent.), allegedly a disciple of Khedrup but about whom extremely little is known. A translation appears in appendix A. The work is appended in the Lhasa edition of Khedrup's collected works to a later biography by Jetsunpa that is supposedly based on it.[122] The work is also found in the first volume of the Kumbum edition, following a biography of Khedrup written by Jetsunpa's disciple Delek Nyima entitled *Delightful to the Scholar's Mind: The Biography of the Omniscient Khedrup*.[123]

Chöden Rapjor's account is only a dozen folios long. The author claims to have compiled it based on information provided by Khedrup himself, although according to Jetsunpa only part of the information came directly from Khedrup; the rest was ascertained through the power of Chöden

226). For a brief discussion of the alleged contention between Khedrup and Rongtön, see Cabezón 1992, 17–18.

120. Lechen, *Lamp*, 370b.

121. Khedrup biographies used in the present work include Chahar Geshé, *Collected Works*, 2:580–638; Chimé Rapgyé, *Golden Wick*, 14–17 (passing references); Chöden Rapjor, *Short Biography of Khedrup* (translated in appendix A); Desi Sangyé Gyatso, *Golden Vaiḍūrya*, 75–77; Jamyang Shepa II, *Biography of the Omniscient Khedrup Gelek Palsangpo*; Jamyang Shepa II, *Jewel Garland: A History of Ganden*, 5:655–56; Jetsunpa, *Secret Biography of Khedrup* (translated in appendix B); Kharnak Lotsāwa, *History of Ganden*, 10b–12a; Lechen, *Lamp*, 369a–370b; Paṇchen Delek Nyima, *Delightful to the Scholar's Mind*; Paṇchen Sönam Drakpa, *Mind's Ornament*, 67–74; Sermé Drakpa Khedrup, *Jampal Nyingpo's Mind Ornament*; and Tsechokling Yeshé Gyaltsen, *Biographies of the Eminent Gurus*, 1:877–922.

122. I wish to thank Leonard van der Kuijp for drawing my attention to this work, which is located in the last of the twelve-volume Lhasa edition published by the Library of Tibetan Works and Archives, Dharamsala, 25b–37a. The Kumbum edition counts thirteen folios.

123. *Mkhas grub thams cad mkhyen pa'i rnam thar mkhas pa'i yid 'phrog.*

Rapjor's insight.[124] The text begins much like any other Tibetan Buddhist biographical account, with a verse paying homage to Tsongkhapa and his spiritual heirs, followed by a statement, in a style reminiscent of Khedrup's *Secret Biography of Tsongkhapa*, in which Chöden Rapjor makes it clear that he has no intention of discussing Khedrup's family lineage, birthplace, or education. Instead he chooses to focus specifically on other aspects of his subject's life, such as: how Khedrup was mentored by various deities; Khedrup's meditative and visionary experiences involving Tsongkhapa and other Buddhist deities; and Khedrup's dreams and past lives. In doing so, the author makes it clear to his readers that his work is no ordinary account but a secret biography elucidating the more intimate aspects of Khedrup's spiritual life.[125]

The account begins with a discussion of Khedrup's previous lives. In a style reminiscent of Tsongkhapa's early biographies, the author tells us that his subject, Khedrup, had been a disciple of Mañjuśrī for many lifetimes, during which the deity mentored and instructed him, asking him to compose various Buddhist works. In one of these lifetimes, Chöden Rapjor says, Khedrup was even visited by the Indian philosopher Candrakīrti, who appeared to him and informed him that in the future Mañjuśrī would take birth in Tibet. Candrakīrti instructed Khedrup to go there to help in propagating the deity's teachings. Chöden Rapjor then adds, "If one reasonably reflects on this story, it is certain that Tsongkhapa is an emanation of Mañjuśrī!"[126]

While relating numerous miraculous events in Khedrup's current and past lifetimes, Chöden Rapjor repeatedly gives interpretive asides like this at key moments throughout the text. Just one such example is the author's remark that the particular tale he had just related proves that Tsongkhapa really was an emanation of Mañjuśrī. In another aside, he claims that Tsongkhapa was an incarnation of the Indian philosopher Nāgārjuna, who is equated with Mañjuśrī. These asides are unambiguous in their expression. I count eight throughout the text, nearly all of which follow stories that speak of a divinity or important figure from the past appearing to Khedrup and telling him that he should take birth in Tibet to help the spread and development of Mañjuśrī's teachings there.

In fact only one aside offers information concerning Khedrup himself, the ostensible subject of the work. On folio 27a Chöden Rapjor says that

124. Jetsunpa, *Secret Biography of Khedrup*, 1b (see appendix B).

125. We saw this tack taken by Khedrup, who distinguishes his *Secret Biography of Tsongkhapa* from his other biographical work, the *Entryway of Faith*.

126. *Yang 'di la rigs pas brtags na / rje bla ma rje btsun 'jam dbyangs kyi sprul pa yin par gor ma chag go* (26b).

Tsongkhapa was instructed to take birth in this world specifically to mentor Khedrup and Gyaltsap, who in this particular story are identified as the Shambhala kings Puṇḍarīka and Mañjuśrīkīrti. Chöden Rapjor then goes on to say that Tsongkhapa did indeed come into this world primarily for the purpose of mentoring Khedrup, and then he relates a tale meant to illustrate this point. However, at the end of this latter story, rather than claiming that the passage proves Khedrup's preeminence among Tsongkhapa's disciples, Chöden Rapjor instead adds yet another aside stating that this is further proof that Tsongkhapa was indeed an emanation of Mañjuśrī.

Given this fact that the only aside concerning Khedrup's exalted identity also speaks of Gyaltsap and that all other asides embedded in the text are used to drive home the idea that Tsongkhapa was an emanation of Mañjuśrī—including one by Tsongkhapa's own admission—the primary goal of the work appears to be not Khedrup's glorification, which would be normal for a biography of Khedrup, but the elevation of Tsongkhapa.

Thus Chöden Rapjor's biography of Khedrup is the earliest statement I have found in biographical sources declaring explicitly that Tsongkhapa was an emanation of Mañjuśrī. As such it constitutes a departure from all of the early biographies of Tsongkhapa. Chöden Rapjor's work was most likely composed only a few decades later than those discussed in the first chapter. His divergence from the early biographies appears even more marked when we consider his claims that his biography of Khedrup is actually based on words spoken directly to him by Khedrup, given that Khedrup's own works never speak of Tsongkhapa as an emanation of Mañjuśrī. It would appear, then, that Chöden Rapjor himself is adding the notion that Tsongkhapa was an emanation of Mañjuśrī, while attributing these claims to Khedrup, to multiple Buddhist deities, and even to Tsongkhapa himself.

The striking presence of Chöden Rapjor's repeated asides telling the reader how to interpret these stories makes Khedrup's life story a secondary event. Khedrup is even absent from the author's declaration of his intentions for composing the work. Usually the claim is made at the outset that the work was written to inspire faith and devotion for the hero. Immediately following his verses of praise, however, where such statements of intent are customarily found, Chöden Rapjor merely asserts that his work addresses those concerns typical of a secret biography and not those of an outer biography (26a):

> This following is a brief sketch of the life of the very being who is unparalleled in scholarship of all phenomena, the fearless one, the almighty one who is a great scholar in the five sciences, Gelek Palsangpo, as spoken directly by him. It will discuss his birth, how

> the presiding deities mentored him, and how he dreamed of the Lord Lama (i.e., Tsongkhapa). However, his birthplace, his education, his family ties, and which places he resided will not be discussed here.

It is in the colophon that the intention behind the work appears, stating that it was composed to ensure "the spread and longevity of the Buddha's teachings in general, and of the teachings of Tsongkhapa and his spiritual son in particular" (37a).[127] Interestingly there is no mention of inspiring faith in Khedrup himself, and the focus remains on Tsongkhapa's teachings. This is not to say that such information is completely absent, but had Chöden Rapjor wished to draw his readers' attention to Khedrup's greatness, one might expect his asides would concentrate on how Khedrup interpreted the experiences himself. Or else the asides might assert that the episodes from Khedrup's life are proof of Khedrup's greatness.[128] Chöden Rapjor's refusal to do this, even when a story clearly illustrates Khedrup's close relationship to Tsongkhapa, gives the impression that his primary agenda was not primarily the glorification and elevation of Khedrup but instead that of Tsongkhapa.

Of course, the hero in Tibetan biographical writing is not autonomous; his identity cannot be understood independently from his lineage and teachers. Thus Khedrup's status is intimately tied to, and in part defined by, who Tsongkhapa is said to have been. And Tsongkhapa's identity is in turn dependent upon *his* teachers and lineage. Thus, when we look back to Khedrup's discussions of Umapa's great spiritual feats and his connection to Mañjuśrī in the two biographies Khedrup wrote of Tsongkhapa, we understand that Tsongkhapa's identity is in part defined by who Umapa was. By portraying Umapa as a devoted follower of Mañjuśrī who received revelations from and interacted with the deity, Tsongkhapa's own visionary experience involving this deity is enhanced and legitimated; a legitimate master suggests a legitimate disciple. Nevertheless there is an important difference between Khedrup's and Chöden Rapjor's works. Khedrup only devotes small isolated sections to his discussion of Umapa, whereas Chöden Rapjor's repeated

127. Chöden Rapjor, *Short Biography of Khedrup*, 37a.

128. Tsangtön Kunga Gyaltsen's (fifteenth cent.) biography of Jamyang Chöjé, for instance, does this. Indeed, although the author repeatedly adds asides to his account of his hero's mystical experiences, the asides invariably explain what the experiences meant to his hero according to Jamyang Chöjé himself. The focus of the work is therefore always on Jamyang Chöjé.

insistent claims about Tsongkhapa's divinity are made virtually throughout the entire text.[129]

As far as I can tell, Chöden Rapjor's work is the earliest evidence of a definite shift in Tsongkhapa's status. We know extremely little of Chöden Rapjor and his life, and so determining his motivations for elevating Tsongkhapa to the ranks of the divine must be based on a close consideration of the biography's rhetoric and its impact on the eminence accorded both Tsongkhapa and Khedrup. It may be that Khedrup, the ostensible subject of the biography, is elevated in status by the exaltation of his teacher, as we have just seen. But for this to be true, Khedrup would need to be one of Tsongkhapa's closest disciples and not just a noteworthy follower.

Although Chöden Rapjor dedicates much of his attention to establishing Tsongkhapa's divinity, he also bolsters Khedrup's preeminence among Tsongkhapa's disciples. Chöden Rapjor depicts various deities and historical figures approaching Khedrup throughout his many lifetimes and repeatedly requesting or instructing him to take birth in Tibet to help spread Mañjuśrī's teachings there. Throughout these stories, Chöden Rapjor stresses that Khedrup was a close disciple of Mañjuśrī and thereby Tsongkhapa. Chöden Rapjor even goes so far as to say that Tsongkhapa's main purpose in this world, aside from the salvation of the Tibetan people, was to mentor Khedrup in particular:

> The victorious Kālacakra told Tsongkhapa, "Sucandra,[130] take the noble king Puṇḍarīka and Mañjuśrīkīrti[131] into your care. But especially Mañjuśrīkīrti!" This means that Puṇḍarīka is Gyaltsap Jé, and that Mañjuśrīkīrti is Khedrup Jé.[132]

And again:

> It is clear that Tsongkhapa appeared chiefly for the purpose of mentoring Khedrup exclusively, and the latter appeared for the

129. The last of Chöden Rapjor's eight asides occurs on 31b.

130. Zla ba bzang po (Skt. Sucandra) is one of the Seven Dharmarājas in the Kālacakra *skor* (see Chandra 1999–2005, 640).

131. Puṇḍarīka and Mañjuśrīkīrti are two of the twenty-five Kalkī kings of Shambhala and important figures in the Kālacakra tradition (see Chandra 1999–2005, 642).

132. Chöden Rapjor, *Short Biography of Khedrup*, 27a.

> sole purpose of upholding Tsongkhapa's teachings.[133] Indeed, Āryadeva, Śāntideva, and Buddhapālita once appeared to Khedrup and told him, "Mañjuśrī has appeared in the borderlands (Tibet) and is working to spread the teachings. As you are a specific disciple of his, worship him and whatever he says, regard it as essential for the accomplishment of practice." If one reasonably reflects on this story, it is clear and true that Tsongkhapa was an incarnation of Mañjuśrī![134]

If we recall from our discussion of Tsongkhapa's early biographies that he too is described as having been Mañjuśrī's disciple, we can speculate that Chöden Rapjor might have elevated Tsongkhapa to the status of a deity incarnate so as to facilitate Khedrup's elevation to the status of the deity's preeminent disciple. Had he not elevated Tsongkhapa in this way, then by saying that Khedrup was an important disciple of Mañjuśrī, Chöden Rapjor would be equating Khedrup's status with Tsongkhapa's. This would transgress etiquette vis-à-vis Tsongkhapa, who was after all Khedrup's teacher and therefore should rank higher than his disciple. Tsongkhapa's further elevation therefore becomes necessary in order to be able to maintain that Khedrup was himself Mañjuśrī's disciple.

It is possible that Tsongkhapa's elevation had already begun in oral tradition by Chöden Rapjor's time and Chöden Rapjor merely made use of this trend for his own purposes, consolidating Tsongkhapa's divine nature and elevating Khedrup in one and the same stroke. But Chöden Rapjor's insistence on Tsongkhapa's divine identity suggests that the master may not have been seen this way by the Gelukpa community. Were that idea already universally accepted by his readers, the need for such insistence would be lost. By reiterating over and over that Tsongkhapa was Mañjuśrī's emanation, Chöden Rapjor is likely attempting to convince his readers of something they may not have yet accepted. Later biographers of Khedrup writing in a time when Tsongkhapa's identity as Mañjuśrī-incarnate was already commonly accepted demonstrate no such preoccupation.

And this insistent equation of Tsongkhapa and Mañjuśrī goes hand in hand with the claim that Khedrup was Tsongkhapa's chief disciple—along with Gyaltsap, of course.[135] This idea too is repeated over and over, though

133. This aside is in fact the only one that speaks directly of Khedrup.

134. Chöden Rapjor, *Short Biography of Khedrup*, 27a.

135. It appears that Gyaltsap was already established as one of Tsongkhapa's closest disciples early on in Geluk history. Indeed, he is described as such by the earliest available Geluk

the emphasis is much less. Since Chöden Rapjor feels the need to repeat it, this again suggests that the idea was not commonly accepted among Tsongkhapa's followers.

Whether or not this innovation was his own or an idea that was already gaining in momentum at the time, it is not in Chöden Rapjor's biography of Khedrup that the latter is definitively immortalized as one member of the glorious triumvirate that comes to be known as the Jé Yabsé Sum. This prestigious position is conferred only later in the work of Jetsunpa.

Khedrup's Place in the Classification of Tsongkhapa's Followers

Attempts to classify Tsongkhapa's disciples appear early in Geluk historiography. Early Gelukpa historians tend to classify Tsongkhapa's followers according to their place of origin. Others do so according to each disciple's function with regard to Tsongkhapa, such as who attended him during illness, who he sent out as representatives, and who accompanied him during his retreats. The current classification according to which Khedrup holds a prominent and prized position as one of Tsongkhapa's chief spiritual heirs does not show up at all until the sixteenth century. In early sources, such as those by Lechen and Gö Lotsāwa, Khedrup's position is portrayed in a more nuanced way. Only in later histories, such as those by Paṇchen Sönam Drakpa, Desi Sangyé Gyatso, and the second Jamyang Shepa Könchok Jikmé Wangpo (1728–92), do we see Khedrup's status become more fixed.

Lechen's *Lamp Illuminating the History of the Kadam Tradition*, composed circa 1494, is one of the earliest, most extensive, and rich historical accounts of the Geluk school. It gives an account not only of Tsongkhapa's life but also of the lives of many of his followers, and even of their disciples, right down until Lechen's own time. What is most interesting for our purposes, however, is the way the text stands in contrast to many *idées reçues* of modern scholarship on the Geluk school.

One generally accepted notion is that the Geluk school, renowned for its strict doctrinal orthodoxy comprised of the writings of Tsongkhapa, Gyaltsap, and Khedrup, has always been this way. Such doctrinal orthodoxy has

histories (such as Lechen's *Lamp*), and Khedrup's biography of Tsongkhapa says that along with Dulwazinpa Drakpa Gyaltsen (1374–1434/36), Gyaltsap was one of Tsongkhapa's closest disciples. Surprisingly, however, the earliest biography dedicated specifically to Gyaltsap recorded in Akuching Sherap Gyatso's record of Tibetan biographical works is a relatively late one by Drakyap Losang Tenpa (1683–1739).

not always been paramount for Gelukpas, and that the measure of what is or is not accurate has not always been defined by the commentarial works of what is now referred to as the Jé Yabsé Sum. For there is no mention whatsoever in Lechen's text that all of Tsongkhapa's followers studied his thought only according to specific interpretations, as was to eventually become the case. Though Lechen does claim that certain figures were mandated to teach specific teachings, there seems to have been no established orthodoxy of views, especially one that included the teachings of Khedrup Jé.[136]

How then did the Jé Yabsé Sum, or the "lordly father and his two sons," come to define the limits of what is and is not orthodox for the Geluk school? The earliest occurrence I have encountered of the expression Jé Yabsé Sum in reference to Tsongkhapa, Gyaltsap, and Khedrup appears to be in the colophon of Jetsunpa's defense of one of Khedrup's commentaries on the Kālacakra cycle:

> The omniscient Khedrup clearly set down in his writings the unmistaken intended meaning of the tantra and the trilogy of commentaries by bodhisattvas, the *sādhana* of the illustrious lord Kālacakra, in accordance with the exalted speech of the Dharma-lord Tsongkhapa, who is an emanation (*'phrul pa*) of the Lord Mañjuśrī. By composing the *Kālacakra Sādhana: The Oral Instructions of Puṇḍarīka*, he accomplished an act of kindness for the fortunate ones who pursue the correct path. This coarse work entitled *Means for Eliminating Wrong Views* was undertaken by the learned monk Chökyi Gyaltsen, with the crown of his head bent toward the immaculate lotus-feet of the Lordly Father and His Two Sons (*rje yab sras gsum*). It was compiled at the supreme place of accomplishments, *Riwo Ganden Nampar Gyalwé Ling*. May the [Buddha's] teachings endure![137]

136. Dulwazinpa is said to have been mandated to teach both the Vinaya and Tsongkhapa's tantric teachings. He is also purported to have taught all of Tsongkhapa's direct disciples (Lechen, *Lamp*, 366a–369a).

137. *Bcom ldan 'das dpal dus kyi 'khor lo'i sgrub thabs // rgyud dang sems 'grel skor gsum gyi dgongs pa'i don phyin ci ma log pa rje btsun 'jams pa'i dbyangs kyi rnam par 'phrul pa // chos kyi rgyal po tsong kha pa chen po nyid kyis gsung ngag ji lta ba bzhin mkhas grub thams cad mkhyen pas gsung rab tu gsal bar bkod de // sgrub pa'i thabs padma dkar po'i zhal gyi lung zhes mdzad pas // skal ba dang ldan pa legs pa'i lam don du gnyer ba dag la bka' drin mdzad pa la // log par rtog pa sel ba'i tshul // rags pa tsam bkod pa 'di ni rje yab sras gsum gyi zhabs kyi padmo dri ma med pa gus pa'i gtsug gi yang dag par blangs pa // mang du thos pa'i btsun pa chos kyi rgyal mtshan dpal bzang pos // grub pa gnas mchog 'brog ri bo che dge ldan rnam par rgyal ba'i gling du*

This is not to say that Jetsunpa invented the expression; he could very well have been following someone else's lead. However, the term is absent from other early classifications of Tsongkhapa's disciples. Chöden Rapjor does not use the term *Jé Yabsé Sum* in his account of Khedrup's life, and it is even missing from Jetsunpa's own *Secret Biography of Khedrup*. The expression is used more explicitly and intentionally to refer to Tsongkhapa, Gyaltsap, and Khedrup in the colophon of a later Khedrup biography by Delek Nyima (sixteenth cent.), Jetsunpa's disciple and main biographer.[138] The passage states that Khedrup was succeeded on the Ganden throne in 1438 by his disciple Shalupa Lekpa Gyaltsen and that the latter, along with Yakdewa Lodrö Chökyong (1389–1463) and Khedrup's other followers, ensured and promoted the tradition of the Jé Yabsé Sum—namely Tsongkhapa, Gyaltsap, and Khedrup.[139] This would appear to be the earliest biographical work to include Khedrup in the Jé Yabsé Sum in an explicit and formal sense.[140]

Early Geluk histories in fact use a variety of locutions to refer to Tsongkhapa's closer disciples. The term *rje yab sras*, "the lordly father and son[s]," by itself is most often used to designate Tsongkhapa and his followers in general. In the earliest sources it does not designate any particular members of

---

sbyar pa 'dis kyang // bstan pa yun ring du gnas par gyur cig // (Jetsunpa, *Means for Eliminating Wrong Views*, 83a).

138. The text is entitled *Biography of the Omniscient Khedrup that is Delightful to the Scholar's Mind* (*Mkhas grub thams cad mkhyen pa'i rnam thar mkhas pa'i yid 'phrog*). The authorship of this biography is not entirely certain, as the author given in the colophon (*Delightful to the Scholar's Mind*, 14a) is simply Svasti, the Sanskrit equivalent of the Tibetan Delek (*bde legs*: "happiness" or "well being"). According to Cabezón (1992, 13), this text was composed by Kunga Delek Rinchen (1446–96), a disciple of Khedrup's younger brother Baso Chökyi Gyaltsen (1402–73). According to the Dungkar Tibetological Great Dictionary (436), however, it would seem instead that it was composed by Paṇchen Delek Nyima. There is no record of Kunga Delek Rinchen composing a biography of Khedrup, though he did write one of Tsongkhapa that is unfortunately no longer extant.

139. *Khri rin po ches thogs drangs gyag sde ba blo gros chos skyong sogs bu slob thams cad kyis rje btsun thams cad mkhyen pa tsong kha pa blo bzang grags pa // rgyal tshab dar ma rin chen // mkhas shing grub pa mchog brnyes dge legs dpal bzang po ste // rje yab sras gsum gyi mdzad pa'i rgyun rnams mi nyams par gong 'phel du mdzad pa 'di ga lags so //* (Paṇchen Delek Nyima, *Delightful to the Scholar's Mind*, 13b–14a).

140. Leonard van der Kuijp has also pointed out (van der Kuijp 1985, 98n15) that Shākya Chokden's (1428–1507) *Impartial Wisdom's Delight: Writing on How the Presentation of the Turning of the Wheel of the Dharma Is Established*, composed in 1495, contains a passage using the expression *tsongkhapa yabsé sum* (*tsong kha pa yab sras gsum*) in reference to Tsongkhapa, Gyaltsap, and Khedrup (Shākya Chokden, *Impartial Wisdom's Delight*, 472–73). This early use of the phrase occurs slightly after Jetsunpa's *Means for Eliminating Wrong Views*, composed during Jetsunpa's time at Ganden between 1492 and 1495.

his entourage and is not necessarily limited to a specific number.[141] It is also a term often used by Jetsunpa in his undated biographical work on Khedrup and in this case refers to both the general assembly of Tsongkhapa's disciples but also to Khedrup in particular when the latter is discussed in conjunction with Tsongkhapa.[142] The term *ngölop* (*dngos slob*), meaning "direct disciple," is also encountered in such works, though it is used in a very general sense to designate Tsongkhapa's direct disciples as opposed to those who did not receive teachings from him but who are nevertheless considered his followers.

Of the terms that appear the most, however, the expression *sekyi thubo* (*sras kyi thu bo*: "chief spiritual heir"), sometimes accompanied by the numeral two (*gnyis*), seems to be the most important and frequently employed.

In Lechen's *Lamp*, for example, we find *sekyi thubo* used frequently to speak of the two disciples closest to Tsongkhapa. However, contrary to later classifications which put forth Gyaltsap and Khedrup as Tsongkhapa's *sekyi thubo nyi*, this text uses the expression to refer to Gyaltsap and Dulzin, another major Gelukpa figure who was responsible for teaching all of Tsongkhapa's followers about monastic ethics (*vinaya*), something that Tsongkhapa is said to have regarded as being of the utmost importance.[143] According to Lechen, "it is said that, in general, there were no (early) disciples of Tsongkhapa who did not receive teachings from Tsongkhapa's two chief spiritual heirs,"[144] that is, Gyaltsap and Dulzin. It seems, moreover, that Dulzin was already a member of Tsongkhapa's entourage by the time Gyaltsap appeared on the scene circa 1396, giving him seniority even over Gyaltsap.[145] What's more, Dulwazinpa Drakpa Gyaltsen headed the committee responsible for appointing Gyaltsap as Tsongkhapa's successor to the Ganden abbacy. All of these points underscore Dulzin's high status within Tsongkhapa's entourage.

So, what about Khedrup? Interestingly, although Lechen does give Khedrup the epithet "Dharma king" (*chos kyi rgyal po*) and enumerates him

141. The term is used, for example, by Chimé Rapgyé in his list of Tsongkhapa's disciples (*Golden Wick*, 18), which I will discuss below.

142. *Secret Biography of Khedrup*, 7b (see appendix B).

143. Paṇchen Sönam Drakpa, *Mind's Ornament*, 63.

144. *Lar na de dus kyi rje'i bu slob thams cad kyis sras kyi thu bo gnyis la chos mi gsan pa med pa yin skad* (Lechen, *Lamp*, 366b).

145. Khedrup Jé, *Entryway of Faith*, 23b. Furthermore, Dulzin was among those close to Tsongkhapa who, following the latter's death, entreated Gyaltsap to take his place (Phurchok Ngawang Jampa, *White Lotus Garland*, 60). The date of Gyaltsap's initial meeting with Tsongkhapa is taken from Thurman 1982, 21.

among Tsongkhapa's disciples, Khedrup is invariably mentioned apart from Tsongkhapa's two chief spiritual heirs.[146] In Lechen's account then, Khedrup was not originally one of Tsongkhapa's two chief heirs. And Lechen's identification of Tsongkhapa's chief disciples is supported by Khedrup's own *Entryway of Faith*, in which Khedrup never once insinuates that he himself enjoyed the exalted status the later Geluk tradition claims on his behalf. Rather he continually refers to Dulzin and Gyaltsap as Tsongkhapa's "spiritual heirs" (*rgyal sras*).[147] Khedrup even makes it clear that it was both Gyaltsap and Dulzin, referred to as the spiritual masters or preceptors (*slob dpon*), who were entrusted with establishing and building Ganden Monastery between 1409 and 1410.[148] So according to both Lechen and Khedrup himself, Tsongkhapa's two chief disciples were not Gyaltsap and Khedrup, as the Geluk tradition would now have us believe, but rather Gyaltsap and Dulzin.[149]

It also appears that Khedrup did not even consider Tsongkhapa to be his most important teacher. In a letter to his disciple Sangyé Rinchen (dates unknown), Khedrup clearly states that, although he had around fifty different masters, his three most important teachers—the ones he considers to be his root masters (*rtsa ba'i bla ma*)—were Jampal Dorjé Nyingpo (dates unknown), Lamdrepa Yeshé Pal (dates unknown), and Tsongkhapa's own teacher, Rendawa.[150] In fact, although Khedrup did receive teachings directly from Tsongkhapa, as is clearly apparent throughout his *Gsan yig*, it would appear that Khedrup was in fact most primarily a disciple of other figures,

146. Lechen, *Lamp*, 369a.

147. Khedrup (*Entryway of Faith*, 32b) also lists eight other close disciples, all of whom accompanied Tsongkhapa during one of his important retreats at Ölka Chölung. They are classified according to their places of origin. Four disciples were from Ü: Jamkarwa Drakpa Palden Sangpo, Tokden Jangseng, Neten Rinchen Gyaltsen, Neten Sangkyong; and four from Domé. Jampal Gyatso (1356–1428), Sherap Drak, Jampal Tashi, and Palkyong.

148. Khedrup Jé, *Entryway of Faith*, 50b. Khedrup also refers to both of these figures as his teachers in his Record of the Teachings Received (Gsan yig) and extols them in separate eulogies found in his own *Miscellaneous Writings* (9a–11a and 14b–15b).

149. In contrast to Lechen's *Lamp*, the *Blue Annals* also places Khedrup as Gyaltsap's successor but mentions him only once, stating that the latter took over the office of Ganden throne holder in 1431. The text does not give him an epithet, however, and Dulzin, oddly, is not mentioned at all. Another difference is that while the *Blue Annals* (Gö Lotsāwa 1976, 1079) merely mentions that Khedrup took over from Gyaltsap, who is said to have passed away the same year, *Lamp* goes into more detail of the handing over of the Ganden abbacy to Khedrup (Lechen, *Lamp*, 365b–366a).

150. Khedrup Jé, *Miscellaneous Writings*, 174a–175a.

such as Kunkhyen Sherap Sangpo (fourteenth–fifteenth cent.) and Kunga Gyaltsen (1382–1446),[151] but also of both Dulzin and Gyaltsap.[152]

That Khedrup was Gyaltsap's disciple would also help to explain how the latter could name him as successor to the Ganden throne. Indeed, when we look at abbatial succession practices in the early Geluk school, we find that the position of abbot seems to have been handed down from teacher to disciple rather than from peer to peer.[153] The exception to this rule occurs when the benefactors of a monastery or monastic college, usually members of the Tibetan aristocracy, would intervene to entreat a particular religious figure to ascend the throne of the monastery or college of which they are patrons. This custom usually occurs, at least within the Geluk tradition, when an abbot dies before naming a successor or else has no chief students left to fill the position.[154]

According to Lechen's work, Gyaltsap was on his last journey to his home-

151. Khedrup's *Gsan yig* indeed lists these teachers frequently throughout the text.

152. Lechen (*Lamp*, 369a) names Gyaltsap as one of Khedrup's main teachers along with Dulzin and Jamkarwa Jampal Chösang (fourteenth cent.). This is further supported by Kharnak Lotsāwa's *History of Ganden*, which reports that although Gyaltsap had many learned disciples, he chose Khedrup to be his successor on the throne of Ganden (Gyalwang Chöjé, *Wondrous Jewel Garland*, 10b).

153. It was in fact possible for a fellow student to entreat a particular figure to ascend a monastery's throne, as is in some senses the case with Tsongkhapa's first successor, Gyaltsap, who is said to have been requested by a committee of Tsongkhapa's disciples headed by Dulzin to take over the Ganden abbacy in their master's stead. In this particular situation Dulzin was not the outgoing abbot, though he was entrusted with finding the monastery's first representative after Tsongkhapa. As Gyaltsap had apparently taught most of Tsongkhapa's disciples, including Dulzin himself, he seems to have been a natural choice. This does not exclude the possibility there were political considerations at play, but proving this would require more in-depth study both of Gyaltsap's life and of Geluk abbatial succession practices in general.

154. This was apparently the case with Lodrö Rinchen Sengé's successor to the abbacy of Sera Jé college, Paljor Lhundrup (1427–1514). When Lodrö Rinchen Sengé passed away, his two main disciples, Jamyang Drakpa and Chöjor Sangpo, were away teaching in Chamdo and passed away themselves before they could return to Lhasa to assume the position. The throne of Sera Jé therefore remained empty until the college's sponsors, the aristocrat Paljor Gyalpo and his consort, Butri Palzom, asked Paljor Lhundrup, who had studied briefly under Lodrö Rinchen Sengé, to ascend the throne. Eventually Paljor Lhundrup passed on the abbacy to Dönyö Palden (1445–1524), who then passed it on to Jetsunpa, who had briefly studied under both of these masters (Zongtse 1995, 238). Another such account is given in Lechen's *Lamp*, according to which the same Paljor Gyalpo asked Tsongkhapa's nephew Losang Nyima (1439–92), also a disciple of Lodrö Rinchen Sengé, to take over the abbacy of Drepung, of which Paljor Gyalpo was also a patron. Unfortunately Lechen does not mention what motivated Paljor Gyalpo's request (Lechen, *Lamp*, 373a).

land monastery in Nyangtö when he realized that his life was almost at an end and that he would not be returning. He therefore decided to hand over the Ganden abbacy to Khedrup, who had traveled to Nyangtö from his monastery in Tsang.[155] Following his decision to name Khedrup as Ganden's new abbot, Gyaltsap took Khedrup on a tour of both Drepung and Sera.

Khedrup's arrival alongside Gyaltsap seems to have caused unrest at Drepung, where as Lechen's history tells us, a group of monks approached the founder and abbot, Jamyang Chöjé, and asked him if they were obliged to bow down to Khedrup. Jamyang Chöjé answered, "You may do as you will. As for myself, I will touch my head to Khedrup's feet." The disciples followed the example of their teacher and paid homage to the new abbot of Ganden.[156]

The hesitation of Jamyang Chöjé's followers to show respect for Khedrup is indicative of Khedrup's status in the Geluk school in 1494, the time the *Lamp Illuminating the History of the Kadam Tradition* was composed. Had he been considered one of Tsongkhapa's two chief spiritual heirs and an uncontestable authority for the Geluk school, it is unlikely Lechen would portray members of this tradition asking whether they needed to pay him respect. Their hesitation indicates that Khedrup's status among Drepung's monks was an issue, and the author suggests that they did not consider themselves followers of Khedrup but primarily of Jamyang Chöjé.[157] The episode provides further evidence that Khedrup's status was in flux: his authority was not yet accepted by all members of the still young Geluk school.[158]

155. Lechen, *Lamp*, 365b.

156. Lechen, *Lamp*, 366a. At first glance, Jamyang Chöjé's willingness to bow down to Khedrup could be seen as an indication that he readily accepted Khedrup's authority as one of Tsongkhapa's chief disciples. However, when we consider the fact that he was leading a monastic community whose patronage came from the same source as that of Ganden Monastery—namely, the local Phakmodru ruler—and that Gyaltsap, Jamyang Chöjé's own teacher, was present to introduce Khedrup as his successor, then Jamyang Chöjé's actions could be seen as political.

157. There seems to have some competition between Jamyang Chöjé and Khedrup. In Jamyang Chöjé's biography by Tsangtön Kunga Gyaltsen, it is said that the two debated together often and that, upon being asked who was the more astute disciple, Tsongkhapa said that Jamyang Chöjé was the more apt at grasping and commenting on texts on first seeing them. According to this biography, Jamyang Chöjé would joke about this answer, saying that Tsongkhapa had said that he was the more intelligent of the two (Tsangtön, *Lamp*, 17b).

158. It is possible that Gyaltsap brought Khedrup to Drepung and Sera so as to present him officially as his successor to the Ganden throne. Gyaltsap's status and authority as Tsongkhapa's successor was already established throughout the Geluk school by 1431, and by accompanying Khedrup on a tour of the major Geluk institutions, Gyaltsap was officially endorsing his successor, thereby making it difficult for others to refuse or question his decision.

One of the earliest sources after Chöden Rapjor's biography of Khedrup that depicts Khedrup as one of Tsongkhapa's more important followers is Chimé Rapgyé's *Golden Wick*.[159] This work, a biography of Tsongkhapa discussed at the end of the previous chapter, gives multiple lists of Tsongkhapa's followers, sorting them by their function or by some other characteristic, and could very well be the earliest work to do so. Chimé Rapgyé's classification lists seven "prophesied heart sons," eight "retreat time renunciants," seven "great sons who aided during illness," eight "great son scholars responsible for the propagation of the two traditions in the monastic seats," three "sons who ensured the writings," three "great sons whose deeds are uncontested," four "sons endowed with the characteristics of realized persons who focused mainly on meditative practice," two "mountain hermits," two "utmost scholars of the highest tradition," two "upper and lower Sherap Sangpos," two "bodhisattvas," two "*sattvas*," two "Drakpas," six "great sons of the oral transmission lineage," three "great uncontested sons who were yogi-rulers," three "scholars of true family descent," three "great regent sons, holders of the teachings," one "ruler who was competent in liberation," and one "renunciant-yogi" (14–15). Figures are sometimes included in multiple categories. Thus Khedrup is counted along with Gyaltsap and Dulzin among the "three precious disciples" (*rin po che gsum*), who make up part of the "seven prophesied sons" (15). Khedrup is also counted in the "seven disciples who attended Tsongkhapa during his illness,"[160] and the "eight great heirs who helped the growth of the two doctrines of the monastic seats."[161] The author does not, however, use the expression "chief spiritual heirs," let alone Jé Yapsé Sum, when referring to Khedrup. Instead, he uses another term: *thuksé buchen* (*thugs sras bu chen*), or "great spiritual sons" (14). Despite the fact that Chimé Rapgyé awards Khedrup the status of one of Tsongkhapa's closer disciples, however, the classification underscores the lack of a definitive Gelukpa triumvirate composed of Tsongkhapa, Gyaltsap, and Khedrup.

Nevertheless, Chimé Rapgyé does portray Khedrup as having been an important and close disciple of Tsongkhapa, which is evident from his inclu-

159. I discussed Chimé Rapgyé's dates in the preceding chapter, where I pointed out that he could not have been writing his first biography of Tsongkhapa earlier than 1470.

160. *Bsnyung g.yog mdzad pa'i bu chen bdun*: Gyaltsap, Khedrup, Jangtsé Chöjé Namkha Pal, Shartsé Chöjé Rinchen Gyaltsen, Jamchen Chöjé Shākya Yeshé of Sera (1352–1435), Shenyen Leksang, and Chöjé Shönu Gyalchok (Chimé Rapgyé, *Golden Wick*, 16).

161. *Gdan sa'i lugs gnyis spel ba'i bu chen mkhas grub brgyad*: (list incomplete) Gyaltsap, Khedrup, Shalu Chöjé Lekpa Gyaltsen (1375–1450), and Jangtsé Chöjé Namkha Pal (Chimé Rapgyé, *Golden Wick*, 16).

sion along with Gyaltsap and Dulzin in the "three precious disciples."[162] As I mentioned in the previous chapter, Chimé Rapgyé refers to Chöden Rapjor's biography of Khedrup. He says that according to Chöden Rapjor, Khedrup received the Guhyasāmaja empowerment and teachings from Tsongkhapa just prior to the latter's death.[163] This is important not only for dating the *Golden Wick* but also for the way it shapes Chimé Rapgyé's portrayal of Khedrup. Since Chöden Rapjor's work paints his master as an important and close disciple of Tsongkhapa *qua* Mañjuśrī, and since Chimé Rapgyé's portrayal of Khedrup is based in part on Chöden Rapjor's vision, it suggests that Chöden Rapjor's elevation of Khedrup by way of his even greater elevation of Tsongkhapa had an important influence upon the growing fortunes of Khedrup himself in Gelukpa imagination.

Such an elevation of Khedrup continues in subsequent Geluk historiography. In some ways similar to *Lamp Illuminating the History of the Kadam Tradition* by his teacher Lechen Kunga Gyaltsen, Paṇchen Sönam Drakpa's *Mind's Ornament: The History of the Old and New Kadam Traditions*, composed in 1529, also uses the expression "two chief spiritual heirs" when referring to Gyaltsap and Dulzin. But Paṇchen Sönam Drakpa's work differs significantly from his teacher's portrayal of Khedrup in that it takes pains to add that, although Gyaltsap and Dulzin were indeed Tsongkhapa's two chief spiritual heirs, Khedrup was in fact Tsongkhapa's "only inner heart son" (57). Paṇchen Sönam Drakpa seems to be deliberately elevating Khedrup to an entirely new status. His casting of Khedrup Jé as "inner heart son" is the earliest such reference I have found. Paṇchen Sönam Drakpa also mentions other disciples, such as Jamyang Chöjé, Jamchen Chöjé, Jé Sherap Sengé (1383–1445), Gungru Gyaltsen Sangpo (1383–1450), and Gendun Drup (1391–1474), but they are only awarded the status of "disciples whose enlightened activities are as vast as the sky"; not as chief or even close disciples.

Paṇchen Sönam Drakpa's depiction of Tsongkhapa's most important disciples would become a point of contention. In his *Golden Vaiḍūrya*, Desi Sangyé Gyatso (1653–1705), the regent to the Fifth Dalai Lama, takes Paṇchen Sönam Drakpa to task for his ranking. The Desi argues that that Tsongkhapa's followers can be ranked in fact multiple ways depending on what qualities are deemed more important. Thus, he says, although Paṇchen Sönam Drakpa considers both Gyaltsap and Dulzin as Tsongkhapa's chief spiritual sons, if one were to rank Tsongkhapa's disciples according to who

162. It is unclear, however, as to exactly why these three were precious, for Chimé Rapgyé never explains what he means by this term.

163. Chimé Rapgyé, *Golden Wick*, 15.

was of greatest benefit to the growth and glorification of his doctrine, then there are in fact three chief disciples: the First Dalai Lama, Gendun Drup; Gyaltsap, "who was an attendant to Tsongkhapa and a philosopher in his own right"; and finally Khedrup, "who had the utmost intelligence and expansive activity."[164] Desi Sangyé Gyatso is clearly aware of a dispute concerning the classification of Tsongkhapa's disciples, suggesting that even by the Desi's time the classification of Tsongkhapa's disciples was not yet fixed.

There may be other reasons as well for Desi Sangyé Gyatso to take issue with Paṇchen Sönam Drakpa's views.[165] The Fifth Dalai Lama, Ngawang Losang Gyatso (1617–82), the Desi's teacher and a historian in his own right, also seems to have disliked this scholar's work. He makes this clear in his *History of Tibet*, where he repeatedly comments on the incorrectness of the information given by Paṇchen Sönam Drakpa, going so far as to accuse him of being an idiot who "shows his lack of erudition" by misrepresenting events related to the construction of Tashi Lhunpo.[166]

Many later authors do agree with Paṇchen Sönam Drakpa's classification of Tsongkhapa's students, though they sometimes supplement with information concerning who ranks where. Tsechokling Yeshé Gyaltsen, for example, follows Paṇchen Sönam Drakpa's classification of Tsongkhapa's followers but adds that Khenchen Ngawang Drakpa was Tsongkhapa's "heart son"; Khedrup is awarded the status of Tsongkhapa's "inner heart son" (*nang thugs sras*), implying that while both of these figures were dear to Tsongkhapa, Khedrup occupied an even dearer place in the master's heart.[167] Furthermore, the second Jamyang Shepa in his history of Ganden adds to Paṇchen Sönam Drak-

164. Desi Sangyé Gyatso, *Golden Vaiḍūrya*, 71.

165. Desi Sangyé Gyatso's animosity toward Paṇchen Sönam Drakpa was such that he allegedly ordered that Paṇchen Sönam Drakpa's works, which constituted the *yig cha* of Drepung's Loseling college, be replaced by the writings of the Fifth Dalai Lama (Chosspel 2011).

166. Ngawang Lobsang Gyatso 1995, 212. The Fifth Dalai Lama's overt animosity toward Paṇchen Sönam Drakpa could also result, at least in part, from the fact that the latter represented a rival lineage, and that his third reincarnation, Drakpa Gyaltsen (1619–56), was originally also a candidate for the position of Dalai Lama (see Dreyfus 1998, 230). According to van der Kuijp, it would seem that his animosity toward Khedrup led to the Desi's falling out with one of his teachers, the first Jamyang Shepa, over the latter's reliance upon Khedrup's interpretations in his *Pramāṇavārttika* commentary (see van der Kuijp 1985, 79). Eventually, the tension between the Desi and the first Jamyang Shepa led to the latter's departure from Central Tibet (van der Kuijp, oral conversation, September 2004). However, Desi's inclusion of Khedrup among Tsongkhapa's three foremost disciples mitigates the notion that the Desi felt such an enmity toward Khedrup. For a further discussion, see Maher 2003, 250-57.

167. Tsechokling Yeshé Gyaltsen, *Biographies of the Eminent Gurus*, 830 and 877.

pa's classification by specifying that Khedrup's elevated status is because he was very beneficial to Tsongkhapa's doctrine.[168] Both authors also use Chimé Rapgyé's classification, however, and the second Jamyang Shepa seems also to agree with Chimé Rapgyé's assessment that Tsongkhapa actually had three important disciples—Gyaltsap, Dulzin, and Khedrup—who Jamyang Shepa calls the three "regent sons who upheld Tsongkhapa's doctrine."[169] Another later author to use Paṇchen Sönam Drakpa's classification is Thuken Losang Chökyi Nyima (1737–1802) who, in his work on Buddhist philosophy, reiterates Paṇchen Sönam Drakpa's claims that Tsongkhapa's two chief heirs were Gyaltsap and Dulzin while Khedrup was Tsongkhapa's only inner heart son.[170] Interestingly, although both Tsechokling Yeshé Gyaltsen and the second Jamyang Shepa do seem to follow Paṇchen Sönam Drakpa's classification, they also quote Chimé Rapgyé's classification. For example, in his Ganden history titled the *Jewel Garland*, the second Jamyang Shepa maintains that Tsongkhapa actually had three "precious uncontested regent-sons who upheld Tsongkhapa's doctrine"—namely Gyaltsap, Dulzin, and Khedrup.[171]

So the question of precisely who got to sit alongside Tsongkhapa as his most important disciples was still at issue even by the end of the eighteenth century, several centuries after Jetsunpa's composition of the *Secret Biography of Khedrup*. However, we can also see that, despite the ongoing reconfiguration of Tsongkhapa's inner circle, Khedrup already occupied a relatively secure place among Tsongkhapa's chief spiritual heirs in the preponderance of histories and biographies.

In the nineteenth century, Khedrup is awarded an even more prestigious ranking among Tsongkhapa's disciples. Sermé Drakpa Khedrup's history of Shartsé college describes a meeting between Tsongkhapa and Khedrup during which Tsongkhapa personally asks Khedrup to compose commentaries on his works, especially regarding his theories on Madhyamaka philosophy, thereby appointing Khedrup as his chief and official interpreter.[172] This passage makes Khedrup the heir handpicked by Tsongkhapa himself to explain

168. Jamyang Shepa II, *Jewel Garland*, 647.

169. Jamyang Shepa II, *Jewel Garland*, 655.

170. Thuken refers to Dulzin as Drakpa Gyaltsen in this passage. *Commentary on Philosophical Systems*, 307. Thuken 2009, 268.

171. *Rgyal tshab bstan 'dzin gyi bu chen rtsod med rin po che* (Jamyang Shepa II, *Jewel Garland*, 655).

172. *Rje rin po ches nga'i mdo sngags kyi bstan bcos rnams kyi dgongs pa 'grel ba'i bstan bcos rnam par dag pa rtsoms // khyed par du dbu ma'i lta ba dang sngags kyi bstan pa 'di rnams rgyas par*

his teachings. Although there is mention of Tsongkhapa telling Khedrup to compose commentaries on his works in a sixteenth-century biographical account by Delek Nyima, this story is absent from most other works that mention Khedrup's interaction with Tsongkhapa.[173] And according to Delek Nyima, although Tsongkhapa's request that Khedrup compose commentaries on his works also concerned exoteric teachings, Tsongkhapa's instruction was that he especially propound tantric works.[174] In Sermé Drakpa Khedrup's story, however, Khedrup Jé is made the chosen authority concerning Tsongkhapa's Madhyamaka tenets. Also, in Delek Nyima's account, Tsongkhapa tells Khedrup to compose commentaries for the students he would later amass in his own monastic community, not necessarily for the entire Gelukpa community, as suggested by Sermé Drakpa Khedrup.[175] Delek Nyima's version of this story is further indication that Tsongkhapa's disciples were not considered to be teaching Tsongkhapa's thought to their own followers based on a predetermined set of commentaries composed by Gyaltsap and Khedrup, as has become the assumption since. The early disciples learned Tsongkhapa's thought based on their individual teachers' own commentarial works. There was no established doctrinal authority for the early Geluk school beyond Tsongkhapa himself.

Clearly attempts to classify Tsongkhapa's closest disciples begin early in Geluk history, but initial classifications varied widely. Khedrup's status, on his own account, was as mere disciple who did not consider Tsongkhapa one of his root gurus. Later biographers would variously cast him as born disciple of Tsongkhapa *qua* Mañjuśrī incarnate in Chöden Rapjor's odd biography, as one of three or seven precious disciples, as the only inner heart son and as one of three chief spiritual heirs. By the nineteenth century, however, he had assumed the position he occupies today, as one of only two chief spiritual heirs and the chief interpreter of Tsongkhapa's Madhyamaka doctrine.

---

gyis shig ces thub bstan yongs rdzogs kyi bdag por mnga' gsol (Sermé Drakpa Khedrup, *Jampal Nyingpo's Mind Ornament*, 57–58).

173. Sermé Drakpa Khedrup does not say if he relied on Delek Nyima's account.

174. Paṇchen Delek Nyima, *Delightful to the Scholar's Mind*, 15.

175. Sermé Drakpa Khedrup, *Jampal Nyingpo's Mind Ornament*, 57–58. According to Delek Nyima, Tsongkhapa is recorded as telling Khedrup, *Da khyed la man ngag rnams rdzogs par bshad yod pas nga'i sngags kyi yig cha 'di rnams kyi dka' gnad rnams la zin bris thob la / rang yang nyams su long / snod ldan gyi 'dul by are gnyis tsam byung na de rnams la shod / nga'i mdo sngags kyi yig cha'i dgongs pa 'grel ba'i bstan bcos rnam par dag pa rtsom la khyad par du nga'i sngags kyi bstan pa 'di rnams rgyas par gyis shig* (Paṇchen Delek Nyima, *Delightful to the Scholar's Mind*, 15).

There is therefore a gradual but clear ascension. It may well be the case that this ascension was initiated, at least in written sources, by Chöden Rapjor. And we have seen that Paṇchen Sönam Drakpa's work on the history of the new and old Kadampa schools was instrumental in that elevation. However, it is Jetsunpa's *Secret Biography of Khedrup* that most strongly and explicitly argues that Khedrup was one of Tsongkhapa's most important disciples.

Jetsunpa's *Secret Biography of the Omniscient Khedrup*

Jetsunpa's *Secret Biography of the Omniscient Khedrup* is the second earliest extant biography of Khedrup.[176] Jetsunpa is explicit in claiming to have based his work on Chöden Rapjor's *Short Biography of Khedrup*, and his text does use the majority of the stories reported by Chöden Rapjor.[177] But while the content of Jetsunpa's work does not differ tremendously from Chöden Rapjor's, there are significant differences in both structure and emphasis that make Jetsunpa's account distinct. Unlike Chöden Rapjor's version, Jetsunpa's *Secret Biography of Khedrup* is devoted, front and center, to the elevation of Khedrup.

Chöden Rapjor's text has no clear structure or organization—he jumps about, relating one story about Khedrup's previous life and then another concerning his meeting in this life with a deity. Jetsunpa's version, in contrast, is neatly divided into two major sections: stories of Khedrup's previous lives and a discussion of his current life. The second section is further divided into five subsections, each dealing with a particular theme or aspect of Khedrup's life, which Jetsunpa illustrates through stories of events.[178] At first glance

176. The work is found in volumes *ka* and *a* of the Kumbum and Lhasa editions of Khedrup's collected writings respectively. It varies between twenty-five folios for the Lhasa edition and thirty-nine folios for the Kumbum edition. Although both Cabezón and Hopkins refer to this text, neither have translated or analyzed it in detail, particularly with regards to its portrayal of Khedrup's relationship to Tsongkhapa (See Cabezón 1992, 13–19 and Hopkins 1989, 139–40). Another manuscript version, which I came across in Lhasa, contains twenty-nine folios and is a lovely piece of work written entirely in script with red ink used for names of important figures. As this manuscript does contain a number of spelling errors, I have referred also to the alternate printed versions for the present study.

177. I have so far found no direct, personal connection between Chöden Rapjor and Jetsunpa.

178. The five subsections are as follows: (1) the wondrous signs that occurred at the initial meeting between Tsongkhapa and Khedrup Jé; (2) the deeds Khedrup accomplished for the benefit of the Buddha's teachings by means of teaching and practice; (3) how it is asserted that the ocean of protectors performed deeds and praised Khedrup for having worked for the

this may appear to be simply a stylistic difference. After all, Jetsunpa's other writing is often similarly well structured and organized. However, as Martha Nussbaum notes, "Form and style are not incidental features...The telling itself—the selection of genre, formal structures, sentences, vocabulary, of the whole manner of addressing the reader's sense of life—all of this expresses a sense of life and of value, a sense of what matters and what does not."[179] Biographers necessarily invent through their selection and arrangement of materials; they establish cause-effect and other relationships through overall structure and form; and through inclusion and exclusion they determine what of their hero's life is most important for someone else to know.[180]

Jetsunpa, in his role as biographer, acts as representative of Khedrup by literally re-presenting him. He manipulates the information from Chöden Rapjor's work, moving some stories to the beginning of his work and others to the end, eschewing key interpretive asides, embellishing accounts of intellectual development, and organizing it all neatly into convenient subsections. In doing so, Jetsunpa plots out a path toward the glorification of Khedrup as one of Tsongkhapa's closest disciples.

From the start of the text, Jetsunpa says that Khedrup took birth as Tsongkhapa's spiritual heir to aid in the spread of his teachings, and that he was Mañjuśrī's disciple from innumerable prior lifetimes.[181] He then goes on to illustrate this point by relating the stories told by Chöden Rapjor of how Khedrup had been mentored by Mañjuśrī, thanks to whom Khedrup achieved spiritual greatness, and of how Khedrup was entreated by various illustrious figures and deities to take birth in Tibet so as to help spread the teachings of Mañjuśrī—or, in one case, Nāgārjuna—who was to take birth there as well. As we saw, Chöden Rapjor adds asides throughout his work explaining that these stories are proof that Tsongkhapa was an emanation of Mañjuśrī, thereby emphasizing Tsongkhapa's divinity rather than Khedrup's relationship to him. Jetsunpa's version, however, largely discards these asides,[182] indicating that Tsongkhapa's identity as an emanation of Mañjuśrī had already

---

benefit of the teachings; (4) the teachings Khedrup received from Tsongkhapa after the latter had passed away; (5) the miraculous omens surrounding Khedrup's departure for the Pure Realm (*Secret Biography of Khedrup*, 4a–4b; see appendix B).

179. Nussbaum 1990, 4.

180. See Backscheider 1999, 18.

181. *Secret Biography of Khedrup*, 1b–2a; for all citations of Jetsunpa's *Secret Biography of Khedrup*, see the translation of this text that I have provided in appendix B.

182. The one aside carried over from Chöden Rapjor's text (Chöden Rapjor, *Short Biography of Khedrup*, 27a) says that the story just told proves Tsongkhapa's identity as an emanation of

become settled. Jetsunpa no longer needs to convince his readers of this, and the primary emphasis of the stories is shifted to Khedrup's relationship with Mañjuśrī and thereby with Tsongkhapa. Chöden Rapjor's stories, in Jetsunpa's text, serve to stress that Khedrup really was Tsongkhapa's disciple for "uncountable earlier lifetimes" (2b).

A further shift is reflected in Jetsunpa's declared reasons for composing his work. Whereas Chöden Rapjor states that he composed his work for the benefit of Tsongkhapa's teachings, Jetsunpa claims that his work was composed not only for the purpose of preserving (*ma nyams par*) Chöden Rapjor's work, but also to inspire devotion for Khedrup (25b). Despite relating more or less the same events, Chöden Rapjor and Jetsunpa are actually doing different things.

Beyond his stated intent and his omission of Chöden Rapjor's asides, Jetsunpa harnesses the narratives he has appropriated to emphasize Khedrup's distinctive relationship to Tsongkhapa in other ways. In his first subsection dealing with the signs that occurred at Khedrup's first encounter with Tsongkhapa, Jetsunpa tells his readers that upon their initial meeting, Khedrup's hair stood on end due to his strong connection with Tsongkhapa from past lives and he developed a resolute and unsurpassed faith in his new teacher. That night Khedrup dreamed he saw Mañjuśrī, seated in a rainbow at the center of a circle of a thousand blazing swords, dissolve into him. Upon hearing of the dream the next day, Tsongkhapa told Khedrup that his vision of his new teacher as Mañjuśrī was in fact correct, and that he must be a realized tantric practitioner to have seen him in this way (5b).

Jetsunpa then breaks from the narrative to inform his readers that Khedrup was one of Tsongkhapa's three chief disciples alongside Gyaltsap and Dulzin. Jetsunpa asserts that these three were prophesied by the Nyingma adept Lhodrak Drupchen Lekyi Dorjé.[183] This is an interesting passage, for as we have already seen in Chimé Rapgyé's later work, Tsongkhapa had seven prophesied disciples, not three. According to Jetsunpa, however, Lhodrak

Mañjuśrī, to which Jetsunpa adds that one should therefore show "tremendous devotion" to Tsongkhapa (*Secret Biography of Khedrup*, 3b).

183. Jetsunpa appears to conflate Lhodrak Drupchen Lekyi Dorjé (thirteenth cent.) and Lhodrak Drupchen Namkha Gyaltsen (1326–1401), who is said by Jampal Gyatso to have prophesied that, should Tsongkhapa go to India, his life would be short (*Supplement*, 6a). Jampal Gyatso does not mention Lekyi Dorjé, nor does he speak of a prophecy of three chief disciples.

Drupchen told Tsongkhapa that he would have three chief disciples and "many other beings on the path of accumulation" (5b).[184]

Jetsunpa returns to the narrative of Khedrup's lives past and present, relating Chöden Rapjor's story that the deity Kālacakra appeared to Tsongkhapa and told him to mentor the Shambhala kings Puṇḍarīka and Mañjuśrīkīrti—who are once again identified with Gyaltsap and Khedrup, respectively—and especially Mañjuśrīkīrti (5b):

> It is said that in one of Tsongkhapa's dreams he was told, "Sucandra, take the noble king Puṇḍarīka and Mañjuśrīkīrti into your care. But especially Mañjuśrīkīrti!" That Puṇḍarīka is actually Gyaltsap Jé and Mañjuśrīkīrti is actually Khedrup Jé is found in Chöden Rapjor's biography of Khedrup Jé. Gyaltsap Jé is also identified as a manifestation of Avalokiteśvara.

While Chöden Rapjor does say that Khedrup was born to uphold Tsongkhapa's teachings, this is the only aside in Rapjor's work that mentions Khedrup Jé. He uses this event primarily to underscore Tsongkhapa's divine identity (27a):

> The victorious Kālacakra told Tsongkhapa, "Sucandra, take the noble kings Puṇḍarīka and Mañjuśrīkīrti into your care. But especially Mañjuśrīkīrti!" This means that Puṇḍarīka is Gyaltsap Jé and that Mañjuśrīkīrti is Khedrup Jé. Furthermore, it is clear that Tsongkhapa appeared for the sole purpose of mentoring Khedrup, and the latter appeared for the sole purpose of upholding [Tsongkhapa's] teachings. Indeed, Āryadeva, Śāntideva, and Buddhapālita once appeared [to Khedrup] and told him, "Mañjuśrī has appeared in the borderlands (Tibet) and is work-

184. Tsongkhapa's collected writings contain another undated account of Tsongkhapa's encounter with Lhodrak Drupchen, but it mentions no specific number of disciples; it merely says that were Tsongkhapa to go to India as he had hoped to do, then it would be an obstacle for his followers, who had all attained the paths of accumulation or preparation. It goes on to advise that Tsongkhapa himself would not return to Tibet (Tsongkhapa, *Meeting with Lhodrak Drupchen and The Gift of the Tooth to Khedrup Jé*, 3b). Since it would be odd for Jetsunpa to knowingly contradict the very text in which the prophecy he speaks of is recorded, it is unlikely Jetsunpa had access to this text; it may well be a later work incorporated into Tsongkhapa's collected writings after Jetsunpa's time. Indeed, the colophon of this short text gives the author's name as Sangyé Rinchen, which may refer to the Ganden abbot of that name (1540–1612). Jetsunpa is more likely appropriating and adapting another, possibly oral, tradition of Lhodrak Drupchen's prophecy.

> ing to spread the teachings. As you especially are a disciple of his, worship him, and whatever he says, regard it as your essential practice to accomplish." If one reflects on this [story] logically, it is clear and honest that Tsongkhapa was an incarnation of Mañjuśrī!

So whereas Chöden Rapjor uses this event to underscore Tsongkhapa's divine identity, Jetsunpa appropriates the passage to establish that Khedrup was one of Tsongkhapa's chief disciples.

In his second subsection, Jetsunpa gives information that is completely absent from Chöden Rapjor's account. He describes Khedrup's intellectual exploits, such as debates he won against other famous religious figures, accounts I have not found corroborated in earlier works. Jetsunpa here states unequivocally that Khedrup was Tsongkhapa's chief disciple. Jetsunpa then launches into a long laudatory and seemingly out-of-place explanation of the different ways in which *Tsongkhapa* proved his philosophical worth by responding to various other figures (7b–9b). This interlude is followed by a renewed discussion of Khedrup's intellectual exploits, especially his confrontation with Rongtön.[185]

Although this type of discussion of a figure's intellectual feats is more typical of an outer biography (*phyi'i rnam thar*), it is not so unusual to find it in a secret biography. Jetsunpa's inclusion of this account of his hero's prowess plays a key role in the work's overall rhetoric, for it strongly illustrates the importance that Jetsunpa places on Khedrup as a philosophical authority for the Geluk school.[186] The nature of these elaborations indicates once again that Jetsunpa wishes to encourage a sense of awe and admiration for Khedrup. This aim is evident in Jetsunpa's praise of Khedrup's morality and great compassion for all beings, two values highly regarded in Tibetan Buddhism (13a–b):

> By virtue of having practiced pure conduct throughout numerous lifetimes, in the present life Khedrup guarded his vows of higher morality. Because of this, he became the crown jewel of all those who bear the saffron victory banner. And what's more, he is the kind of being for whom the clouds of compassion move automatically, and he cannot stop crying when he merely thinks about the suffering of all sentient beings.

185. See pages 40–41 above.

186. As I will discuss in the next chapter, this is a critical issue for Jetsunpa.

Following the interlude discussing Khedrup's intellectual prowess and virtue, the text describes dreams and visionary experiences during which Khedrup is said to have been instructed by figures such as Tsongkhapa, Indrabodhi, and Sarasvatī. Jetsunpa then once again tells us that Khedrup was a key disciple of Tsongkhapa, whose teachings he helped spread. During Khedrup's previous lives in India, Jetsunpa informs us (15a),

> The gods, paṇḍitas, and siddhas all repeatedly entreated him to take birth in Tibet as the caretaker of the spread of Tsongkhapa's doctrine. He therefore took birth in Tibet a few times before this life. This was obviously in order to help Tsongkhapa's doctrine to fully mature.

In the third subsection, which deals with how the ocean of protectors performed deeds and praised Khedrup for having worked for the benefit of the teachings, Jetsunpa continues to discuss the many Buddhist deities that appeared to Khedrup, mentioning appearances by Bhairava, Six-Armed Mahākāla, Pañjara Mahākāla or Gurgön, and Four-Faced Mahākāla. All of these deities extol Khedrup—once again portrayed as one of Tsongkhapa's closest disciples—for being such an excellent and upstanding religious figure and scholar, but each interacts with Khedrup in a somewhat different way (16a–20b). Some simply appear and praise him, others demand his propitiation, while yet others tell him that they were sent by the Sakyapas to destroy him. The latter group of deities, upon seeing Khedrup and realizing his great qualities, disavow their mission, feeling it inappropriate to follow through with their orders. One such deity even says that, were it not for his previous promises to protect and serve the Sakyapas, he would have joined Tsongkhapa's entourage as their protector (18a–b).

The last two sections of Jetsunpa's work are, respectively, a discussion of the five visions Khedrup is said to have had after Tsongkhapa's death in which the latter appeared to him and gave him teachings, and an account of Khedrup's own death. The same visions are also described in Chöden Rapjor's work, where the author adds asides claiming once again that they clearly prove Tsongkhapa was an emanation of Mañjuśrī.[187] There is an aside

187. According to both Wayman (1999, 4–5) and Lamotte (1960, 35), the number five is prominently associated with Mañjuśrī. Indeed, another name for Mañjuśrī is Pañcaśīra, possibly derived from the name of the mountain chain he is said to inhabit (Pañcaśīra). By saying that Tsongkhapa appeared five times to Khedrup, Chöden Rapjor and Jetsunpa are both reinforcing the claim that Tsongkhapa is the deity.

at this point in Jetsunpa's work too, but it says that although Tsongkhapa was already dead, he nevertheless appeared as Mañjuśrī to teach and guide Khedrup. The emphasis is thus again shifted from establishing Tsongkhapa's identity as Mañjuśrī's emanation and to showing that Khedrup was Tsongkhapa's rightful heir.

All the stories in this final section describe a somewhat wistful Khedrup, saddened at the way the world is going and lamenting that his teacher is no longer around. Each time, Tsongkhapa appears and tells him not to fret. On one occasion Tsongkhapa appears dressed like a siddha, riding a fierce stallion, and brandishing a radiant sword. He encourages Khedrup, telling him Khedrup was the only thing on Tsongkhapa's mind (23b). Another tale describes how Khedrup asks Tsongkhapa about his whereabouts and what must be done in order to join him there. Tsongkhapa responds that he is in many places at once, but for the time being he has manifested on Mount Wutai in China, where he is currently teaching to over 800,000 monks. Tsongkhapa explains that although all that is required to be able to join him is to pray to him as indistinct from Mañjuśrī, there are in fact no other disciples who actually do so (24a–b). Here Jetsunpa lets the reader infer that other than Khedrup, none of Tsongkhapa's followers actually saw Tsongkhapa as Mañjuśrī, and that other than him none will therefore be able to be reborn in Tsongkhapa's presence. Khedrup is therefore shown to be a uniquely close and worthy disciple.

At the end of the text, Jetsunpa says that Tsongkhapa sent a host of *devaputras* carrying canopies and banners to escort Khedrup to him (25a). Jetsunpa makes it very clear that even Tsongkhapa—and not just Jetsunpa—considered Khedrup to be one of his most cherished followers, whom he taught and guided even from beyond the grave—or in this case, from beyond the stupa.

The addition of an entire section in Jetsunpa's biography of Khedrup dealing with his hero's intellectual prowess is indicative of the great importance Jetsunpa places on Khedrup as an authoritative philosophical figure, an emphasis that is characteristic of Jetsunpa's preoccupation with doctrinal integrity. This embellishment underscores the extent to which Jetsunpa really is building upon versus preserving Chöden Rapjor's initial intervention. As further evidenced by Jetsunpa's portrayal of Khedrup as the only one who could and did do what was necessary to be reborn in Tsongkhapa's presence, Jetsunpa is positioning Khedrup's lineage as the sole tradition that recognizes Tsongkhapa as Mañjuśrī's emanation; no other disciple appears to have seen him in this way, so no other lineage does this.

The first chapter began with a question of when, where, and why Tsongkhapa's identity shifted from disciple of Mañjuśrī to Mañjuśrī himself. In attempting to answer why that shift occurs in a biography of Khedrup, we came across the beginnings of another shift embedded within this same text—the shift in Khedrup's status from one of Tsongkhapa many disciples to his closest spiritual heir. I spoke of the interconnectedness of identities between master and disciple, and of the biographer's own personal agenda. The question now arises as to why Jetsunpa was so invested in and fixed upon transforming Chöden Rapjor's more modest picture of Khedrup. A closer look at Jetsunpa's own life may help us discern the answer. For as we have seen, not only was Jetsunpa a staunch supporter of Khedrup, but also Jetsunpa's works are now an uncontestable part of the *yig cha* of Sera's Jé college. Might Jetsunpa's *Secret Biography of Khedrup* have been instrumental in his appropriation of Sera Jé's curriculum? If so, it is an underappreciated purpose for which sacred biography has been harnessed in the Tibetan religious world.

3. Jetsunpa

SOMETIME in the first half of the fifteenth century, Lodrö Rinchen Sengé, then living at Drepung Monastery in Central Tibet, is said to have become the target of disparaging remarks and slander on the part of his fellow resident monks.[188] Although no sources report exactly what was said, their slander seems to have been serious enough that the slighted Lodrö Rinchen Sengé decided to leave Drepung altogether, taking with him over one hundred learned scholars. The group made its way to Sera Monastery, where the current abbot was Lodrö Rinchen Sengé's teacher, Gungru Gyaltsen Sangpo (1383–1450).[189]

Initially there were four colleges at Sera: Mé, Töd, Gya, and Dromteng.[190] Rather than joining one of these colleges, Lodrö Rinchen Sengé and his followers took up a somewhat nomadic existence at Sera, going from college to college to participate in rituals at each. It is said to have been for that reason that Lodrö Rinchen Sengé and his group of followers came to be known as the "errant" or "wandering" (*byes*, pronounced "jé") college of Sera Monastery.[191]

188. Lodrö Rinchen Sengé's dates are unclear. According to *Moon-Jewel Mirror*, he was born in the first part of the seventh sexagenarian cycle (*rab byung*), which in the Western calendar began in 1387 (Losang Könchok, *Moon-Jewel Mirror*, 14). He is also said to have met with Tsongkhapa and to have studied mainly under Jamyang Chöjé, Drepung's founder.

189. Zongtse 1995, 235; Drakné Kunsang Chöphel, *Ruby Necklace*, 71–72.

190. It is said to have been under Gungru that Sera's five colleges were concentrated into just two (Jé and Mé). Sera's tantric college, Ngakpa, was not founded until the early eighteenth century with the aid of the Mongol ruler Lajang Khan.

191. Zongtse 1995, 236. Though after his death Lodrö Rinchen Sengé's errant monks would build themselves an edifice, the name remained. According to a different account, the college acquired its name from the initial journey Lodrö Rinchen Sengé and his disciples made from Drepung to Sera (Losang Könchok, *Moon-Jewel Mirror*, 14). According to the account by Desi Sangyé Gyatso, however, the name comes from the fact that the Neu minister Paljor Gyalpo and his consort Butri Palzom, both patrons of Lodrö Rinchen Sengé and his disciples, decided to build an edifice at Sera that would serve as both a place for the practice of Dharma

Despite the fact that Sera Jé's physical structures were not built until after his death, Lodrö Rinchen Sengé is credited as the first abbot of Jé college and its founding father.[192] Sera Jé was his community and was known as "the college that upholds the teachings of Lodrö Rinchen Sengé."[193] Before he died, Lodrö Rinchen Sengé composed a series of texts on standard philosophical topics studied at such monastic institutions, including Pramāṇa, Madhyamaka, and Abhidharma. These works became his college's textbooks, or *yig cha*, and were considered essential to the Sera Jé curriculum.[194]

Shortly after he died both of the disciples who were expected to take Lodrö Rinchen Sengé's place also passed away while teaching in eastern Tibet in Chamdo.[195] The Sera Jé abbacy remained empty for some time until the college's benefactors, the Neu ruler Paljor Gyalpo and his consort Butri Palzom, decided to build a physical structure so that Lodrö Rinchen Sengé's followers would have their own place to pray. These benefactors asked another of Lodrö Rinchen Sengé's disciples, Paljor Lhundrup (1427–1514), to become the college's new abbot.[196]

During his fifteen-year tenure as abbot, Paljor Lhundrup seems to have

---

and as a secondary residence, for the term *byes* also means temporary or secondary residence (Desi Sangyé Gyatso, *Golden Vaiḍūrya*, 142).

192. Lodrö Rinchen Sengé later became the leader of the entire monastery as Sera's fifth grand abbot (Zongtse 1995, 50).

193. Zongtse 1995, 54 and 239.

194. Lodrö Rinchen Sengé's works are listed as part of Sera Jé's *yig cha* by Longdöl Lama (*A List of Writings by Kadampa and Gelukpa Masters*, in Chandra 1973, 1370), Thuken (*Commentary on Philosophical Systems*, 324), and Akuching (*Collected Writings*, 525; 542). Exactly how many texts he composed is not certain. The aforementioned sources refer to three philosophical texts (the *Dbu ma'i rnam bshad dgongs pa rab gsal de nyid gsal byed*, the *Rten 'bral stod pa'i bsdus don*, and the *Tshad ma'i stong thun mkhas pa'i yid phrog*) and to one biography of his teacher Jamyang Chöjé. The first philosophical text here, a Madhyamaka commentary on Tsongkhapa's *Illumination of the Thought*, has been found (Lodrö Rinchen Sengé, *Elucidation of Suchness*), and I have also located one versified ode to Jamyang Chöjé (Lodrö Rinchen Sengé, *Maṇḍala of Qualities*) and one ritual text propitiating the deity Hayagrīva (Lodrö Rinchen Sengé, *Practice Manual of Padma Wangchen*).

195. Zongtse 1995, 238.

196. The topic of abbatial succession in Tibetan monasteries has been overlooked in modern Tibetan studies, the only source on the subject being Shunzō Onoda's work "The Chronology of the Abbatial Successions of the gSang phu Sne'u thog Monastery" (Onoda 1989), which unfortunately does not discuss how abbots were chosen. To my knowledge there is no work on this topic within the Geluk monastic centers either. As I mentioned briefly in the previous chapter, it would seem that abbots were chosen not by the denizens of a monastery but by the outgoing abbot from among his own disciples. See above, note 153.

carried on Lodrö Rinchen Sengé's legacy at Sera Jé. In 1481 he rose to become the eighth grand abbot of Sera Monastery, and four years later passed on the leadership of Sera Jé to his disciple Dönyö Palden (1445–1524).[197] It was during this latter figure's tenure as abbot of Sera Jé that the seminal figure, Jetsunpa, made his first appearance at the college.[198]

Jetsun Chökyi Gyaltsen: Early Life

Born in 1469 in the Nyangtö region of Tsang in Central Tibet, Jetsunpa was to become one of the most important and influential figures in the history of Sera Jé, leading the community for nearly thirty years and authoring texts that have since become the college's principal textbooks or *yig cha*. These works, which consist mainly of philosophical commentaries based largely on Tsongkhapa's teachings, are still studied by the college's denizens today. But Jetsunpa's influence is not limited to Sera Jé. It is also felt at Sera Ngakpa, the monastery's tantric college, and at Ganden's Jangtsé college, where his works are now included among the required texts for philosophical study. It has even become the norm for monks of both Jé and Mé colleges at Sera Monastery in Tibet to study and debate Jetsunpa's works together.[199] Despite such a considerable field of influence, Western scholars of Tsongkhapa's thought and Geluk history have devoted little attention to Jetsunpa's life. Even among Jetsunpa's Tibetan readers, few read his life story.[200]

Despite his popularity and influence throughout the Geluk school, there are strikingly few Tibetan biographies dedicated to Jetsunpa. So far I have located only four.[201] Compared to the biographical traditions of Tsongkhapa

197. Zongtse 1995, 53–54.

198. Paṇchen Delek Nyima, *Rain of Accomplishments*, 9b.

199. Jetsunpa's influence did not necessarily extend so far during his lifetime; the historical outcome has much to do with later figures loyal to him implementing the study of his works in other monasteries.

200. Jetsunpa's main biography by his student Delek Nyima has yet to be published in South India and is therefore hard to come by. Although the text is easily available at Sera in Tibet, very few of the scholars or monks I encountered during my research in Tibet had read it.

201. These are: the standard biography by Paṇchen Delek Nyima (*Rain of Accomplishments*) printed at Sera in Tibet; a seven-folio biography (*Meaningful to Behold*) by Paljor Sönam Lhundrup (fifteenth–sixteenth cent.), a copy of which I found during my research in Tibet; and two (one in verse, the other in prose) by Rongpo Drupchen (1607–77). The latter of these two is largely a repetition of Delek Nyima's work. For the present biography, I have relied chiefly on Delek Nyima's work but have also consulted all other available sources.

and Khedrup, who have approximately fifteen biographies each, this is a rather small number. There are, of course, a number of short biographical sketches that can be found in more recent larger historical accounts, such as Zongtse Champa Thupten's *History of the Sera Monastery* and Losang Könchok's *Moon-Jewel Mirror*, all of which rely on Jetsunpa's primary biography written by his disciple Delek Nyima. This devotional account paints a highly hagiographical picture of Jetsunpa and his life, mixing historical events with the stories of special dreams, visions, and wondrous events that are typically found in Tibetan sacred biography.

Although his biographies do not necessarily address the exact manner or extent, Jetsunpa's life—from his childhood to his career—was greatly affected by the continuously shifting political landscape of fifteenth- and sixteenth-century Central Tibet.[202] The political stage during Jetsunpa's lifetime was dominated by the rival, though related, Phakmodru and Rinpung families. Amid this rivalry was considerable political instability, and policies and rulers could change quickly.

The Phakmodru figure Gongma (*gong ma*, "ruler") Drakpa Gyaltsen (1374–1432) and his powerful Lhasa allies had been supporters of the Gelukpas while Tsongkhapa was alive, and during the Gongma's reign, the Geluk school thrived. The Gongma, along with his minister Namkha Sangpo, who helped fund the construction of Drepung Monastery, was largely responsible financially for the establishment of Ganden Monastery and for backing Tsongkhapa's efforts to institute the Mönlam prayer festival in 1409. In 1432 the Gongma died, however, and two years later the Phakmodru house fell, marking the end of political stability for Central Tibet and steady support for the emerging Geluk school.

In 1435 the power and influence of the Rinpung family began to grow and was felt throughout the province of Tsang. Döndrup Dorjé (dates unknown), ruler of the Rinpung family, conquered Shigatsé and made it his new capital. Seeing this as open resistance to the Phakmodrupas with their seat at Nedong in Ü, now headed by the more religiously inclined Drakpa Jungné (1414–45), many of the powerful families in Tsang welcomed Döndrup Dorjé's actions and allied themselves with him. In 1445 Drakpa Jungné died and was succeeded by his younger brother, Kunga Lekpa (1433–83), who

202. Paṇchen Delek Nyima tells us that during a long period of political unrest between Ü and Tsang, Jetsunpa performed special esoteric practices in order to avert war (*dmag ldog*) at Taktsé. According to Delek Nyima, the practice was successful, and the local dignitaries (*sde pa dpon blon*) developed an unswerving faith in Jetsunpa (*Rain of Accomplishments*, 20b–21a).

unfortunately was unable to smooth over the mounting tensions between his house and his Rinpung relatives.

In 1479, Dönyö Dorjé (1462/63–1512), the son of a powerful Rinpung minister and supporter of the Karmapas, was refused permission by the Lhasa administrator to build a Kagyü temple in Lhasa. Moreover, when Dönyö Dorjé built it outside the city, monks from the neighboring Geluk monasteries razed it, and the Seventh Karmapa Chödrak Gyatso (1454–1506) narrowly escaped alive.[203] In retaliation, Dönyö Dorjé unsuccessfully led troops against Ü in 1481, advancing as far as Kyishö and capturing several districts belonging to the Lhasa administrator, who had previously opposed his father, Rinpung Kuntu Sangpo.

In 1485 Rinpung forces attempted to attack the Gyantsé district, which was under the rule of a Nedong minister, but were once again defeated with the help of the Lhasa administrator. Three years later another attempt was made, this one successful. In 1492 the Karmapa-friendly Rinpung finally invaded districts under the Lhasa administration and, in 1498, occupied Lhasa itself. The arrival of the Dönyö Dorjé and the Rinpung in Lhasa marked the beginning of a period of Gelukpa repression. Gelukpas were forbidden from celebrating the Mönlam festival, and by 1512 the pressure was such that Gelukpa monks going about in small groups in Lhasa wore red hats, making them look like members of the Kagyü tradition. It was not until 1517 that the political situation began to change, and the Rinpung forces were driven out of Lhasa.

Jetsunpa was born into an aristocratic family during these tumultuous times. His father, Sönam Pal, is described as either a prefect (*nang so* or *mi dpon*) or a governor (*rdzong dpon*), and his mother, Drölma Bum, was the daughter of "Phakpa of Gyantsé."[204]

Jetsunpa's formal religious life began in 1475 at the age of six, when he took vows with his first teacher Kunga Delek Rinchen of Nenying (1446–96), a disciple of Khedrup's younger brother and close disciple Baso Chökyi Gyaltsen (1402–73). Jetsunpa spent the next five or six years studying under Kunga Delek Rinchen, with whom he learned to read and write and to memorize texts. At the age of twelve he took novice vows and then left to study at Tashi Lhunpo Monastery in Shigatsé along with one of his brothers, Kunga Chöden.

203. See Shakabpa 1967, 277–94.

204. *Rgyal mkhar rtse ba'i sa'i bdag chen.* This could be in reference to either Rapten Kunsang Phakpa of Gyantsé, who was one of Khedrup's patrons for some time, or his stepbrother Tashi Phakpa, who replaced him on the throne at Gyantsé in 1442.

Jetsunpa was admitted into one of the colleges at Tashi Lhunpo and began his philosophical studies under Kunkhyen Chöjor Palsang (fifteenth cent.), Paṇchen Lungrik Gyatso (b. 1418),[205] and Paṇchen Yeshé Tsemo (b. 1433), the teacher responsible for introducing Jetsunpa to Khedrup's collected works.[206] By the age of eighteen Jetsunpa had become a scholar well trained in all of the main philosophical topics studied at the monastery.

In 1492, at the age of twenty-three, Jetsunpa left Tsang and journeyed for the first time to Sera Jé in Ü, meeting important religious figures on the way, such as Khedrup Rinchen Shenyen (fifteenth cent.), another disciple of Baso, who presented him with a copy of Tsongkhapa's Madhyamaka treatise, the *Illumination of the Thought* (*Dbu ma dgongs pa rab gsal*). Once at Sera, Jetsunpa received various philosophical and liturgical teachings from both Paljor Lhundrup, the abbot of Sera, and his disciple Dönyö Palden. Among the various teachings Jetsunpa received was the empowerment for the "very secret" wrathful horse-headed Hayagrīva practice that had been passed down from Lodrö Rinchen Sengé himself.[207]

During his residence at Sera, Jetsunpa undertook multiple study-retreats at which time he committed texts to memory or analyzed in detail a particular philosophical subject. Such retreats, still practiced today, are often conducted away from the monastery during times when there are no debate sessions. Jetsunpa is said to have conducted his study-retreat at Sera Chöding, the same place where Tsongkhapa is reported to have composed his work on Madhyamaka philosophy and where he first met with Khedrup.[208] During these retreats Jetsunpa reportedly committed Tsongkhapa's *Differentiating the Interpretable and the Definitive* (*Drang nges rnam 'byed*) to memory

205. Paṇchen Lungrik Gyatso was abbot of Tashi Lhunpo at the time.

206. Yeshé Tsemo was the abbot of Tashi Lhunpo when the Second Dalai Lama, Gendun Gyatso (1475–1542), was exiled from the monastery (see both Mullin 2005 and Heller 2005). Jetsunpa is recorded as saying that, had it not been for Yeshé Tsemo, Gendun Gyatso would not have gone to Drepung and would therefore have not fulfilled his greater destiny (Mullin 2005, 70).

207. Lodrö Rinchen Sengé had been a practitioner of this deity since his childhood. The practice had been passed on to him by his father, Yönten Gönpo (dates unknown), a master from the Nyingma tradition who, according to the history of the Domar Monastery of Tsang, lived in the early fourteenth century (Drakné Kunsang Chöphel, *Ruby Necklace*, 64–69).

208. Paṇchen Sönam Drakpa, *Mind's Ornament*, 68; Paṇchen Delek Nyima, *Delightful to the Scholar's Mind*, 11; Jamyang Shepa II, *Biography of the Omniscient Khedrup Gelek Palsangpo*, 704.

and understood its meaning through the aid of the auxiliary works of Lodrö Rinchen Sengé, Paljor Lhundrup, and Khedrup.[209]

Jetsunpa only remained at Sera for a short while, after which he left for Ganden, where he took full ordination with Sherap Sangpo (fifteenth cent.), who also instructed him on the monastic code and gave him tantric empowerments concerning wrathful Hayagrīva.[210] In 1495, at the end of his twenty-sixth year, Jetsunpa returned to his old monastery at Nenying to be close to his first teacher, Kunga Delek Rinchen.[211] Jetsunpa had been asked to become a teacher at Sera, but according to his biographer, he had no real desire to do so. However, Kunga Delek Rinchen strongly urged him to go, and so Jetsunpa complied with his teacher's wishes and spent the next three years teaching at Sera. He left once again after this and traveled around to various monasteries to receive teachings and to debate. At some point Jetsunpa was invited to teach at Jamchen Dewachen Monastery, an offer that he is said to have gladly accepted.[212]

During his thirteen-year tenure as a teacher at Jamchen Dewachen, Jetsunpa is said to have participated in a series of discussions between Gelukpa geshés and some prominent Sakyapa geshés from the dignitary ranks of the Rinpung court. According to Delek Nyima, Jetsunpa was unrivaled by any of the well-known Sakya scholars gathered there and defeated all of his opponents' arguments through an impeccable use of logic and scripture. After this event, Jetsunpa became known as a propagator of Tsongkhapa's doctrines.[213]

Jetsunpa did not return to Sera until around 1511, upon the invitation by Dönyö Palden to replace him as abbot of Sera Jé, a position Jetsunpa occupied until he ascended the throne of all of Sera Monastery in 1537. Delek Nyima's account of Dönyö Palden's choice of successor reads as follows:

209. Panchen Delek Nyima, *Rain of Accomplishments*, 11b. Although Jetsunpa's biographer does not specify exactly which texts by Lodrö Rinchen Sengé and Paljor Lhundrup Jetsunpa were used, he does state that he used Khedrup's Madhyamaka treatise the *Stong thun skal bzang mig 'byed* (also known as the *Stong thun chen mo*). This work has been rendered in English by José Cabezón (1992) as *A Dose of Emptiness*.

210. Paṇchen Delek Nyima, *Rain of Accomplishments*, 12b.

211. Paṇchen Delek Nyima, *Rain of Accomplishments*, 12b.

212. Paṇchen Delek Nyima, *Rain of Accomplishments*, 12b.

213. Paṇchen Delek Nyima, *Rain of Accomplishments*, 14b. This is an interesting passage. As we have seen, the Rinpung rulers are typically said to have been staunch supporters of the Karmapa, not the Sakyas. Yet this passage specifically mentions Sakya scholars acting as officials at the Rinpung court; nothing at all is said of the Kagyüpas.

> As the time came for Dönyö Palden to appoint a new abbot for Sera Jé Khenyen (*mkhas gnyen*) college, he made earnest prayers and offerings to Tārā and to the protector divinities of the omniscient Lodrö Rinchen Sengé and paid careful attention to his dreams. One night he had a dream in which he saw a young woman dressed in silk and a very white mendicant monk who said to him, "The teacher you seek is in Tsang. Invite him and his teachings will be of great benefit." Dönyö Palden thought that although there were many learned geshés who had developed the qualities of the sūtras, Jetsunpa had fully developed his qualities throughout Tsang, and although he had not relied on Dönyö Palden's teaching for a particularly long time (during his stay at Sera), he was nevertheless unrivaled in his qualities. With this and his teacher's predictions in mind, Dönyö Palden assembled the college's delegates with regards to the suitability of such a choice. Aside from one malicious teacher bent on dividing the college, all the other representatives were pleased by Jetsunpa's qualities as a learned, conscientious, and skilled teacher. Having agreed with Dönyö Palden's choice, they sent off a delegation to Tsang.[214]

Rongpo Drupchen gives a slightly different account of Dönyö Palden's dreams, saying instead that in one dream, the young woman told Dönyö Palden to select "the one from Mindruk Khyungtsé," and that in Dönyö Palden's other dream he also saw a "red person" (*mi dmar*) wearing a bracelet accompanying the mendicant. The red person told Dönyö Palden that they had been sent by Kunkhyenpa—another epithet of Lodrö Rinchen Sengé—and that the teacher presently in Tsang should be chosen as Dönyö Palden's successor.[215] It would seem that Rongpo Drupchen is attempting to justify or legitimate Jetsunpa's rule at Sera Jé by saying that Lodrö Rinchen Sengé himself sent envoys to tell Dönyö Palden to choose Jetsunpa to head his community.

Whatever the case, it is evident from the passage above that Dönyö Palden, as the outgoing abbot of Sera Jé, wanted Jetsunpa to be a new leading figure for his college. But Jetsunpa had not spent much time studying under Dönyö Palden and was not, therefore, fully established within Lodrö Rinchen Sengé's lineage, causing the abbot to hesitate in his choice. This might explain Rongpo Drupchen's additional claim that Lodrö Rinchen Sengé sent the

214. Paṇchen Delek Nyima, *Rain of Accomplishments*, 14b–15a.

215. Rongpo Drupchen, *Prose Biography of Sera Jetsunpa*, 275.

"red man" to tell Dönyö Palden to choose Jetsunpa as his successor, thereby sanctioning the decision.

Others at Sera were worthy of the position, but Dönyö Palden decided to give the job to someone who was less of a disciple but who had stronger connections in Tsang. In light of the politically charged times, this would seem a savvy move. Indeed, in a time when Sera's monks were hesitant to move about Lhasa for fear of being mistreated or even attacked due to their tradition's close ties to the Phakmodru, a closer affiliation with Tsang just might help garner some favor with the Rinpung rulers. Dönyö Palden's decision shows just how intimately connected monastic and local politics could be, and to what extent the abbots needed to be not only great scholars but also astute politicians. His hesitation to give the position to someone who had not spent a great deal of time as his student, on the other hand, suggests that this was not the norm. At least in the early stages of the school's development, as we have seen, the successor was usually chosen from among the outgoing abbot's own disciples, contrary to nowadays when such figures are elected.[216]

Jetsunpa accepted Dönyö Palden's offer. In 1511, at the age of forty-two, Jetsunpa was installed on the Sera Jé throne. Throughout his nearly thirty years as the college's abbot, and then as the grand abbot of Sera Monastery as a whole, Jetsunpa taught vastly and continued to display his skills as a scholar in debates. In particular, Jetsunpa participated in debates at the Potala and at the Neu ruler's palace in Shigatsé against Sakyapa opponents who had come to debate monks from both Sera and Drepung.[217] But Jetsunpa did not debate only against members of other schools; he also debated against the monks at Drepung, on which occasion he is said to have clarified many questions concerning the teachings of Tsongkhapa and his chief disciples:

> Many erudite geshés asked Jetsunpa to remove their doubts concerning difficult key aspects of the great commentaries of the father (Tsongkhapa) and his sons. With faultless answers he severed all their misconceptions, causing all to rejoice. It was said of him that although nowadays one who is well versed in two or three scriptures is considered a scholarly teacher, there are none

216. See above, p. 52.

217. Paṇchen Delek Nyima, *Rain of Accomplishments*, 16b. This would indicate that philosophical debate between monks of different schools still played an important role at the courts of local rulers even in the sixteenth century.

> today like the abbot of the Jé college, who is unexcelled in all the teachings![218]

At the same time that Jetsunpa was beginning to lead the Sera Jé community, a larger concentrated effort was being made from within the Geluk ranks to consolidate the school's power. This effort may also have included an attempt to create greater doctrinal cohesion among Ganden, Drepung, and Sera. At the head of this consolidation effort was Gendun Gyatso (1475–1542), better known today as the Second Dalai Lama, who held the thrones of both Drepung (1517–42) and Sera (1526–36).[219]

With the occupation of Lhasa by the pro-Karmapa Rinpung forces starting in 1498 and restrictions such as the prohibition on celebrating the Mönlam festival, Gendun Gyatso was busy making concerted efforts to take as disciples patrons who guaranteed his economic and political security. He created a support network stretching from western Tibet, through Mustang along the southern border with Nepal, to the doorstep of Kham in the east.[220] This patronage not only allowed Gendun Gyatso to ascend to positions of power within the Geluk school and, by virtue of his connection to it, extend the Geluk sphere of influence well beyond Central Tibet, this network was also instrumental in his future incarnations' rise to become the heads of the Geluk community. In 1517, the same year the Rinpung forces pulled out of Lhasa, Gendun Gyatso was chosen to ascend the throne at Drepung, and the following year the Gelukpas were once again allowed to celebrate the Mönlam festival in Lhasa under his leadership.[221]

Understanding the intricate connections between Gendun Gyatso, Jet-

218. *Rje 'di pa la dge bshes mkhas pa mang pos // rje yab sras kyi ṭik chen rnams kyi dka' gnas rnams la dogs gcod zhus pas // 'khrul med kyi lan gyis sgro 'dogs chod par mdzad pas // thams cad yi rang bas deng sang po ti gnyis gsum tsam la mkhas na yang // slob dpon mkhas pa zhig 'dug zer zhing rtsis na // byes pa'i slob dpon 'di gsung rab gang la yang thogs pa med pa 'di 'dra ba // deng sang gang na yang med zer ba byung* (Paṇchen Delek Nyima, *Rain of Accomplishments*, 18b).

219. See Heller 2005.

220. Heller 2005, 43. It should be pointed out that Heller identifies Gendun Gyatso's father as Kunga Gyaltsen and gives the dates 1432–1506. In fact, these are the dates of the Gelukpa historian Lechen Kunga Gyaltsen. Gendun Gyatso's father was actually Sektön Kunga Gyaltsen (1432–81).

221. Following Tsongkhapa's death in 1419, the privilege of presiding over Mönlam was awarded to the abbot of Drepung, Jamyang Chöjé. This was most likely due to the latter's close ties with the Phakmodru minister Namkha Sangpo, who was partially responsible for funding the construction of Jamyang Chöjé's monastery. It was subsequently a matter of tradition for the Drepung abbot to preside over the festival.

sunpa, and Paṇchen Sönam Drakpa will facilitate a more nuanced understanding of the impact of the social and political milieu on Jetsunpa's life and work. All three of these prominent figures knew and interacted with one another repeatedly, and all three held positions of political and religious power nearly simultaneously. In 1512, one year after Jetsunpa was nominated to the Sera Jé abbacy and Paṇchen Sönam Drakpa ascended the throne of Gyütö tantric monastery, Gendun Gyatso became the abbot of Tashi Lhunpo, and five years later he took over the Drepung abbacy.[222] In 1526 Gendun Gyatso took over the Sera abbacy too, and at the same time appointed Paṇchen Sönam Drakpa the head of Drepung's Loseling college. That same year, Jetsunpa became the abbot of Taktsé Rinchengang Monastery. In 1529 Paṇchen Sönam Drakpa became abbot of Ganden, a position he occupied until 1535. Then, in 1537, Jetsunpa succeeded Gendun Gyatso on the greater Sera throne. Five years later, in 1542, at the behest of Gendun Gyatso and various aristocrats, Paṇchen Sönam Drakpa took over the Drepung abbacy. Gendun Gyatso died that same year. Clearly then, these three figures had significantly overlapping spheres of activity. Furthermore, both Jetsunpa and Paṇchen Sönam Drakpa received teachings from Gendun Gyatso, and the two shared the same teacher at Sera, Dönyö Palden, under whom Paṇchen Sönam Drakpa studied for twelve years.[223] What's more, Jetsunpa and Gendun Gyatso both shared important ties to Tashi Lhunpo and Nenying monasteries in Tsang and had the same teachers—Paṇchen Yeshé Tsemo and Kunga Delek Rinchen, the latter of whom was partially responsible for Jetsunpa's composition of the *Secret Biography of Khedrup*.[224]

The intertwining of Jetsunpa with these two key figures, one of whom (Paṇchen Sönam Drakpa) was known also to have wanted to elevate Khedrup as one of Tsongkhapa's closest disciples, and the other of whom was absolutely central to the Geluk ascendancy both politically and institutionally in the Tibetan Buddhist world overall, contextualizes well Jetsunpa's own ambitions, career trajectory, and investment in Khedrup's legacy. It also underscores the importance of viewing Jetsunpa's scholarly and philosophical activity within

222. As already mentioned, Tashi Lhunpo, founded by the First Dalai Lama, was where Jetsunpa began his monastic education.

223. Zongtse 1995, 109.

224. *Secret Biography of Khedrup*, 25b (see appendix B). It appears that Gendun Gyatso did not hold a grudge against Yeshé Tsemo, despite the latter's role in his expulsion from Tashi Lhunpo. On the contrary, he seems to have always regarded Yeshé Tsemo with the utmost respect (see Mullin 2005, 88).

the context of institutional formation and competitive patronage, especially given the political climate in which he thrived.

During his thirty-year tenure as the head of Sera Jé and seven more as the abbot of the entirety of Sera, Jetsunpa appears to have been preoccupied with doctrinal coherence, critiquing and refuting what he saw as misrepresentations of or attacks on the views of Tsongkhapa and his spiritual heirs. When prominent scholars from rival schools such as Shākya Chokden (1428–1507), Gorampa Sönam Sengé (1429–89), or the Eighth Karmapa Mikyö Dorjé (1507–54) critiqued Tsongkhapa's theories, specifically concerning Madhyamaka philosophy, Jetsunpa took it upon himself to refute these attacks.[225]

Jetsunpa apparently did not hesitate to refute interpretations from within his own tradition, too. In fact, Jetsunpa was so adamant about representing Tsongkhapa's views correctly that he went so far as to refute the views of his own teacher. In his Madhyamaka commentary, Jetsunpa argues against an opponent he refers to only as "one of my masters" (*rang gi bla ma gcig*), taking him to task for his readings of Tsongkhapa's Madhyamaka teachings.[226] According to Delek Nyima, Jetsunpa is in fact referring to Kunkhyen Chöjor Palsang, one of his first teachers at Tashi Lhunpo and author of one of the texts included in Sera Jé's old *yig cha*.[227] Strikingly, Delek Nyima's account is embedded in a section of the biography in which Jetsunpa is extolled as a great being with the uncanny ability to "establish a text's true intended meaning when the author's views were correct, and to refute them using logic grounded in evidence when wrong," rather than "pretending to teach by twisting the text's words this way and that, eventually creating self-contradictions."[228] In other words, despite the fact that Chöjor Palsang was one of Jetsunpa's teachers, and therefore someone for whom the latter showed the utmost respect, Jetsunpa chose to refute his work rather than to make it falsely appear to be correct. Delek Nyima portrays Jetsunpa as a scholar who felt that doctrinal cohesion took precedence even over the highly held

225. See Jetsunpa's refutations (*dgag lan*) of Gorampa Sönam Sengé and Shākya Chokden (Khedrup Jé et al., *Compendium of Polemical Literature*, 176–518), as well as his polemical response to the Eighth Karmapa (71–173). For a brief discussion of these works, and of the genre of polemical literature, see Lopez 1996, 217–28.

226. Jetsunpa, *Garland of Fortune*, 21.

227. Paṇchen Delek Nyima, *Rain of Accomplishments*, 26b. According to Longdöl Lama, Kunkhyen's Prajñāpāramitā commentary was included among the college's debate manuals (Chandra 1973, 666).

228. Paṇchen Delek Nyima, *Rain of Accomplishments*, 26a.

Tibetan Buddhist value of deference and allegiance to one's teacher.[229] But as we will see below, there remain key ways in which Jetsunpa privileged lineage over doctrinal cohesion.

As we know, at some point during his tenure as the head of Sera Jé, Jetsunpa is said to have found fault with the writings of his forbears, in particular those of Lodrö Rinchen Sengé.[230] This is a forceful example of Jetsunpa's privileging of doctrinal purity over lineage allegiance. Lodrö Rinchen Sengé's works had been considered vital at Sera Jé, but as a result of Jetsunpa's efforts, they went out of circulation.[231] Today Lodrö Rinchen Sengé's works are virtually unknown even to the more erudite scholars. Just how and especially why Jetsunpa engineered this supersession is not entirely clear. An analysis of the processes involved, however, can shed considerable light on the place of doctrinal correctness in the Geluk monastic systems, the connection of such perceived correctness to other key social processes, and the indebtedness of Geluk power dynamics to the cult of both the text and the master.

Jetsunpa and Lodrö Rinchen Sengé

> I personally heard Jetsunpa say, "If I were to explain the words of the omniscient Lodrö Rinchen Sengé concerning Madhyamaka

229. Matthew Kapstein has remarked that it was "most unusual in Tibet to launch a broadside against one's own master" (Kapstein 2000a, 129). Oddly though, during a conversation in November 2005, Geshé Tsultrim Chöphel, ex-director of the Sera Jé Committee for Philosophical Studies, told me that it is an intellectual duty to refute any misinterpretations of Tsongkhapa's teachings, even if they come from one's own teacher.

230. Paṇchen Delek Nyima, *Rain of Accomplishments*, 21b–22a.

231. According to Desi Sangye Gyatso (*Golden Vaiḍurya*, 142), a number of philosophical works were being taught at Sera Jé in the seventeenth century by the twenty-third abbot, Hardong Ngawang Gyatso. These included Delek Nyima's Vinaya commentary (*'Dul ba'i 'grel ba legs bshad skal bzang nor bu'i phreng ba*), Jetsunpa's multiple *Abhisamayālaṃkāra* commentaries, an unspecified commentary by Sera Sharpa Gyaltsen Döndrup (seventeenth cent.), another unspecified commentary by Khönton Paljor Lhundrup (1561–1637), an Abhidharma commentary by Sera Jé Ngödrup (dates unknown), and Madhyamaka commentaries by both Jetsunpa and Gomdé Namkha Gyaltsen (1532–92). By Desi's time, however, Lodrö Rinchen Sengé's commentaries are already absent. It seems unlikely, therefore, that their disappearance from the Sera Jé curriculum would be due to a pedagogical push for greater *yig cha* consistency. Moreover, though it is possible that there was later such a push, this raises other questions, such as what were the criteria for keeping or removing texts and, more importantly, who had the authority to make such decisions?

> and pramāṇa, it would be very beneficial for Sera Jé college. However, as they contain occasional inconsistencies with the teachings of Tsongkhapa and his spiritual heirs, they must be refuted."[232]

Thus does Jetsunpa's close disciple and biographer, Delek Nyima, report his master's motivation in rewriting the *yig cha* for Sera Jé. While he extols Lodrö Rinchen Sengé's teachings as beneficial to the fame and development of Sera Jé, he is also and importantly saying that Jetsunpa felt that they contained significant inconsistencies with the teachings of Tsongkhapa and his "spiritual heirs." Although he characterizes such inconsistencies as "occasional,"[233] such an understatement belies the clear critique it implies. For not only did Jetsunpa notice such problems, he felt they necessitated refutation.[234]

As I remarked in the introduction, the stakes of philosophical accuracy in Tibetan Buddhism are high, and perhaps even more so when the topic is Madhyamaka philosophy, an accurate understanding of which is, for Gelukpas, a prequisite to direct realization of reality and ultimately buddhahood itself. Especially in the Geluk school, misrepresenting Madhyamaka teachings would be seen as having serious soteriological consequences. For Gelukpas, Tsongkhapa's presentations of these teachings are the gold standard. Saying that Lodrö Rinchen Sengé's works misrepresented Tsongkhapa's and his disciples' teachings is, therefore, a serious allegation. It implies that Lodrö Rinchen Sengé's works cannot ultimately guide his followers along the path of salvation.

But as I have also noted, Sera Jé was considered to be "the college that upholds the teachings of Lodrö Rinchen Sengé."[235] A denizen of Sera Jé would therefore have been one who considered Lodrö Rinchen Sengé's works to be authoritative and correct interpretations of Tsongkhapa's thought. To ques-

232. *Kun mkhyen rin po che'i dbu tshad kyi gsung sgros 'di rnams bshad na grwa tshang la dar rgyas shin tu che ba yong bar 'dug kyang / rje yab sras kyi gsung dang mi mthun pa re gnyis 'dug pa la dgag pa 'bul dgos pa 'byung zhes rje 'di nyid kyi gsung las dngos su thos so //* (Paṇchen Delek Nyima, *Rain of Accomplishments*, 21b–22a). Although the term *gsung sgros* can refer to oral teachings, Lodrö Rinchen Sengé's works are characterized as written texts by Longdöl Lama, Thuken, and Akuching (see above, note 194), and we have a record of Jetsunpa himself studying these works during his multiple study retreats (see above, pp. 72–73).

233. The term *re gnyis* literally means "one or two," or "a few."

234. Although he does not state it explicitly in the text, Delek Nyima's use of the term *yab sras* should be taken to refer to Gyaltsap and/or Khedrup. In the colophon of his *Delightful to the Scholar's Mind* (13b–14a), the term *rje yab sras gsum* is used in specific reference to Tsongkhapa, Gyaltsap, and Khedrup.

235. Zongtse 1995, 54; 239.

tion or deny the validity of one's own college's *yig cha* is, in a sense, to question or deny the very thing that defines the college. Far from being banished from Sera Jé, however, Jetsunpa's writings have entirely replaced Lodrö Rinchen Sengé's works, positioning Jetsunpa as the central and most important figure for the Sera Jé community. The works of other authors have come to be studied there, but Jetsunpa's commentarial works remain the largest part of the college's canon.[236] Denizens of Sera Jé must not disagree with Jetsunpa's views or else face the threat of public humiliation, punishment, or in some cases excommunication. Lodrö Rinchen Sengé's commentarial works, once at the very heart of the community, are no longer read at all.

How do Gelukpa monks today explain this? When I asked various scholars from Sera Jé both in and outside Tibet, they responded by making reference to a prophecy. According to this oft-repeated tale, during his own life Lodrö Rinchen Sengé prophesied that at some later time a great scholar by the name of Chökyi Gyaltsen would come to the college and compose new commentaries that would improve on his own more limited works. Lodrö Rinchen Sengé allegedly said that when such a time came his own works would be rendered obsolete by the sheer depth and scope of Chökyi Gyaltsen's works and should therefore be removed from circulation. In their stead, Sera Jé's inhabitants were to study the commentaries of Chökyi Gyaltsen. I have, as of yet, found no mention of this prophecy in any historical or biographical sources, which leads me to suspect that it is a purely oral tradition.

The very existence of this oral tradition indicates that there was some unrest at Sera Jé following Jetsunpa's criticisms of Lodrö Rinchen Sengé's philosophical writings. After all, the propagation of a retroactive prophecy would serve to both ameliorate internal strife and to legitimize Jetsunpa's refutation of Sera Jé's founder. As Armin Geertz remarks in his study of the role and function of prophecy in the Hopi Indian religion:

> Under the guise of precognitive authority, [prophecy] is more often than not a mechanism which incorporates contemporary affairs into the framework of traditional religious values, evaluates those affairs in terms of conceived tradition, and interprets and judges those affairs on the authority of conceived tradition. (...) Prophetic statements are told under the pretence of anterior

236. Sera Jé's *yig cha* now also include the *Lesser, Median,* and *Greater Collected Topics* by Phurbuchok Losang Tsultrim Jampa Gyatso (1825–1901), which are used during the first three years of monastic study.

> precognition (i.e., before the fact), even though in actual fact it is posterior "precognition" (i.e., after the fact).[237]

Such a postcognitive "prophecy" is set in the past and associated with some previously established traditional authority who either endorses or opposes the event. Within Buddhist cultures, prophecy, particularly when uttered by an enlightened being, serves as "one of the most potent forms of legitimation."[238] In the Tibetan context, prophecy was frequently produced in the Treasure (*Gter ma*) tradition and often served as a means by which to legitimate claims and events.[239] While most avoid making clear statements on the question, the general consensus among the few Western scholars of Tibet who have touched upon the topic seems to be that prophecy acts as a means to galvanize support for the particular actions of an individual and/or as a strategy by which an action or event, which has oftentimes already taken place, is legitimated.[240]

Thus the prophecy ascribed to Lodrö Rinchen Sengé might well be seen as a means by which to validate and legitimize Jetsunpa's suppression and replacement of the former's works. The prophecy's existence implies in turn some pressing necessity to legitimize this suppression. In other words, there was some level of resistance at Sera Jé.

Such resistance of course is to be expected, since Sera Jé, as a "textual community," defined their shared identity by their common acceptance of a specific text or texts composed by an interpreter (or interpreters) deemed by that community to be authoritative. According to Brian Stock, the interpreter is the most important element. The text itself means little without the interpreter, who uses it to direct and reform the group's thought and action.[241]

Stock's point is well illustrated by the famous Tibetan Buddhist story in which Atiśa is asked by his disciple Dromtön which is more important, the

237. Geertz 1992, 7.

238. Tun Aung Chain 2000, 133.

239. There are surprisingly few studies that deal specifically with the role and function of prophecy within Tibetan religions. See Vostrikov 1994, 27–57, and Aris 1989, 16–106. Janet Gyatso has gone further than these two in her discussions of "certificate" (*byang bu*) texts in the Treasure tradition (see Gyatso 1993, 126–30).

240. See Gyatso 1993, 126–30. The nature of prophecy in Tibet is also discussed by Holly Gayley in her article "Patterns in the Ritual Dissemination of Padma gling pa's Treasures" (2007).

241. Stock 1983, 90.

Buddhist texts or a teacher's instructions. Atiśa's response is that the teacher's instructions are more important, given that a teacher reveals a text's hidden meaning; this cannot be done by the text alone.[242] For a given textual community in Tibetan Buddhism, the authors of the authoritative interpretations of doctrine function in the capacity of the teacher in the story of Atiśa and Dromtön. That is to say, they function as the literate and skilled teacher who explains and interprets the hidden meaning of the texts to the community. Without the elucidation provided by the interpretative and commentarial corpus, the full potential of the root texts cannot be realized, and they cannot fully help to fashion and orient the community.

I am not the first to describe Tibetan Buddhist traditions as textual communities. In his work on the development of Tibetan Buddhism in the tenth to the thirteenth centuries, Ronald Davidson points out that the large influx of esoteric Buddhist rituals and texts from India, and the enormous Tibetan translation effort that accompanied it, provided Tibetans with the iconographic formulations and points of reference necessary to "reconstruct their institutions, found monasteries, and reorganize the political realities" of Central Tibet.[243] The preeminence of the tantric literature in turn affected the status of those who specialized in its translation, so that those who had not been born into aristocracy nevertheless achieved the status of society's elite as those who had "reconnect[ed] Tibetan spirituality with Indian Buddhism."[244] One of the results of this process of Tibetan cultural reformulation was the emergence of a number of communities that centered upon the esoteric texts and the literate interpreter thereof. Each of these textual communities argued its superiority above the others, claimed "ultimate sanctity for its lineages and traditions," and eventually became the major Tibetan Buddhist schools.[245]

Although the Geluk school did not yet exist during the era discussed by Davidson, it was during this very period that the Sakya tradition, in which Tsongkhapa was educated and which was to give birth to the Geluk tradition, flourished. And while Tsongkhapa's followers may not have initially seen themselves as members of a new and distinct Tibetan religious order, over time they came to distinguish themselves more and more from the Sakyas.

242. *Bka' gdams kyi skyes bu dam pa rnams kyi gsung sgros thor bu ba rnams* (160), as cited by Tucci 1980, 22.

243. Davidson 2005, 2.

244. Davidson 2005, 372.

245. Davidson 2005, 373–74. It is unclear whether or not Davidson's notion of textual community is taken from Stock.

Eventually Tsongkhapa was perceived as having diverged from the interpretations accepted by the Sakyas, for which he was greatly criticized by some of the latter tradition's foremost scholars. Consequently the Gelukpas' nascent self-identity began to solidify as a distinct religious order centered upon the acceptance of the authority of Tsongkhapa's particular interpretations.[246]

Slowly, with the creation of the major Geluk monastic centers, smaller textual subcommunities began to emerge from within the larger Geluk context. Thus, while members of Sera Jé see themselves as part of the larger Geluk school, they nevertheless consider themselves to also be affiliated to another smaller collective defined by its members' adherence to specific commentaries.

Criticism of Tsongkhapa's teachings by figures outside the Geluk tradition has often been met with a flurry of refutations by figures from within the tradition outraged at the attack on that which serves to define them as Gelukpas.[247] Gelukpas may not respond to criticism from within their own tradition the way they do to that from non-Gelukpas.[248] However, as Dreyfus has argued, failure to agree with the positions put forth by Tsongkhapa and the monastic textbooks of one's college is considered a definite sign of ingratitude or even outright betrayal. A good example is the case of the scholar Gendun Chöphel (1903–51). Although educated at Drepung, Chöphel nevertheless composed a text strongly critical of some of Tsongkhapa's key philosophical positions.[249] His actions drew a large amount of public contempt from within the Geluk community, eliciting scathing rejoinders by multiple figures including his own teacher, Sherap Gyatso (1884–1968).[250] Another, more recent, example is that of Geshé Palden Drakpa (b. 1933), also of Drepung, who was publicly admonished for failing to uphold the views of his

246. Tsongkhapa did not necessarily see his teachings as divergent. In a letter to his teacher Umapa, for example, he tells his master that he had been teaching his followers the Lamrim tradition of the Kadampas rather than his own personal views (Tsongkhapa, *Miscellaneous Writings*, 80a–82a).

247. A good example of this is the relatively recent *Dgag lan phyogs bsgrigs* (Khedrup Jé et al., *Compendium of Polemical Literature*, 1997), a compilation of works by five authors refuting non-Geluk criticisms of Tsongkhapa's Madhyamaka views. These are older works, but the history of polemical literature extends well into the twentieth century and involves all the major traditions (Lopez 1996, 218).

248. Lopez 1996, 222.

249. See Chöpel's *Dbu ma'i zab gnad snying por dril ba'i legs bshad klu sgrub dgongs rgyan.*

250. Lopez 1996, 225n10. For a more detailed discussion of Gendun Chöphel's life and activities, see Lopez 2006 and Stoddard 1985.

college (Loseling) during his geshé examination.[251] An earlier example is the story of Khedrup Jé's public reproval of Gungru Gyaltsen Sangpo for propagating views that did not correspond to Tsongkhapa's teachings on emptiness. Whether or not this event truly happened is questionable, as I will discuss shortly.[252] Nevertheless, the story clearly illustrates there was the notion that Tsongkhapa's followers must not differ from his teachings under threat of public humiliation.[253]

Gelukpa critics of Tsongkhapa's views can be, and often are, publicly reprimanded or even expelled from their monasteries and colleges. Because of this Dreyfus points out that "scholars know that any doubt they express about the orthodoxy of their school or even their monastery's manuals will be taken as attacking the overall value of these institutions and their legitimacy."[254] Although there is little indication in historical sources that the repercussions of questioning or even refuting the textbooks of one's own college were as drastic in the early stages of the Gelukpa community's history as they are now, it is nevertheless quite easy to imagine how Jetsunpa's criticism of Lodrö Rinchen Sengé's works would have upset a large portion of the community that his works helped define. It is also easy to imagine how the members of Lodrö Rinchen Sengé's textual community might have expressed their disapproval of the refutation—let alone outright suppression—of these essential works.

In all of this there remains the ineluctable question about the philosophical grounds for Jetsunpa's critique. What points in Lodrö Rinchen Sengé's works was Jetsunpa taking issue with? Moreover, in the process of establishing his own commentaries as authoritative, it is not entirely clear how much Jetsunpa was targeting Lodrö Rinchen Sengé in particular versus other *yig cha* in use at Sera Jé. There is, at least in principle, no reason to disbelieve that there was indeed an aspect of Lodrö Rinchen Sengé's work that Jestunpa judged as needing correction. The recent discovery of at least one of Lodrö Rinchen Sengé's commentarial works on Madhyamaka should in theory allow us to look into this very issue. But it also introduces new questions.

251. Dreyfus 2003, 315–16.

252. See below, page 95.

253. Criticism of those who are considered to have failed to uphold the tenets of their monastic communities is also found in Khedrup Jé own life story, when he is said to have come under fire from members of the Sakya school for repudiating the views of the very lineage that had helped him become the scholar he was (see appendix B).

254. Dreyfus 2003, 319–20.

Jetsunpa's Alleged Critique: Interpretational Authority and Lineage Loyalty

Three of Lodrö Rinchen Sengé's works are now available to us: one Madhyamaka work, an ode to Jamyang Chöje, and a ritual work on the deity Hayagrīva.[255] There nevertheless remain a number of factors that complicate an assessment of the doctrinal debate between him and Jetsunpa. First, it is unclear with which of Lodrö Rinchen Sengé's philosophical works Jetsunpa is purportedly taking issue. Jetsunpa's Madhyamaka commentary—which is where his main refutation of Lodrö Rinchen Sengé's views is likely to have been laid out—never names his opponents.[256] Instead he uses the general *kha cig, kha cig na re*, or *kho na re* ("some" or "someone"), or even *mkhas pa kha cig* ("a certain scholar"). This is not surprising. As Cabezón has pointed out in his compelling discussion of polemics, not naming one's opponent is a standard rhetorical strategy of polemical literature. In doing so, the author denies his adversary power and intellectual plausibility. "It is always easier and safer to dismiss an unattributed view than it is to reject the position of a known scholar who has a reputation."[257] If Jetsunpa does indeed engage Lodrö Rinchen Sengé's views in his Madhyamaka work, then he too denies the latter power and intellectual plausibility by not naming him directly. But he may also have been refraining from naming Lodrö Rinchen Sengé to avoid openly disagreeing with the founder of the community he now led.

These issues should be easily remedied through a comparison of Jetsunpa's presentation with that of Lodrö Rinchen Sengé. After comparing Jetsunpa's work to the one Madhayamaka commentary from Lodrö Rinchen Senge we have, however, I find no instance where Jetsunpa cites Lodrö Rinchen Sengé's commentary or takes issue with the views laid out therein. This does not mean that the refutation does not exist; only that it does not take issue with ideas in the text available to us. A number of Lodrö Rinchen Sengé's works—his Pramāṇa and Abhidharma commentaries, for example—are still unaccounted for. But in reading the work that *has* become available, does Lodrö Rinchen Sengé interpret Tsongkhapa's thought in any way that might legitimate Jetsunpa's alleged concern? His lengthy commentary on Tsongkhapa's *Illumination of the Thought* is a rich work that clearly and system-

255. See note 194 above and bibliography.

256. The late Geshé Tsulga, a scholar from Sera Jé and author of a history of Sera, told me that Jetsunpa's refutation is embedded in his Madhyamaka commentary (Geshé Tsulga, oral communication, 1999).

257. Cabezón 2007, 8.

atically explains the master's views according to multiple sources. Lodrö Rinchen Sengé clearly bases his commentary not only on the text but also on the direct teachings of Tsongkhapa himself, as well as on the oral and written explanations of Tsongkhapa's disciples. Lodrö Rinchen Sengé also frequently cites what appears to be a Madhyamaka commentary by Atiśa as translated by the latter's disciple, Naktso Lotsāwa Tsultrim Gyal (1011–64). I have yet to identify exactly which work or works Lodrö Rinchen Sengé is referring to, but it is interesting to note that Lodrö Rinchen Sengé is making direct use of a Kadam source in order to support his interpretations of Tsongkhapa's thought.[258] This tack could be attributed, in part, to an early Gelukpa understanding that theirs was in fact a continuation of the Kadam tradition, as is made evident by the titles of many of their histories.[259] Whatever the case, I have found no such source quoted by Jetsunpa in his own later commentaries.

What is certain is that Jetsunpa does not take Lodrö Rinchen Sengé to task in his own commentary on Tsongkhapa's *Illumination of the Thought*, his *Garland of Fortune*, for the latter's reliance upon such a work.[260] In fact, he does not explicitly take Lodrö Rinchen Sengé to task at all. Did Jetsunpa really did take issue with Lodrö Rinchen Sengé's "occasional inconsistencies," as is recorded by Jetsunpa's biographer, Delek Nyima? If not, then why would Delek Nyima, who was in all evidence Jetsunpa's close disciple, make such a claim? I see no reason to mistrust Delek Nyima's account. It is entirely possible that another of Lodrö Rinchen Sengé's works will surface in time and that an analysis of this work will provide the missing pieces to this puzzle. In the meantime, however, what in the Madhyamaka commentary by Lodrö Rinchen Sengé that we *do* have could be the locus of Jetsunpa's concern?

One possible avenue of inquiry is to interrogate the matter by looking at how each author engages with the interpretation of Khedrup Jé. Lodrö Rinchen Sengé's commentary on the subsection of the *Madhyamakāvatāra* dealing with selflessness of phenomena (*chos kyi bdag med*; Skt. *dharmanairātmya*) in the sixth "aspiration" (*sems bskyed*) contains one such clue. The passage, which deals with the refutation of autocognition, states that Lodrö Rinchen

258. Kevin Vose points out (2009, 193n56) that Naktso appears to have translated Candrakīrti's autocommentary on the *Madhyamakāvatāra* and that Tsongkhapa refers to this particular work in his *Illumination of the Thought*.

259. A number of Geluk histories, such as Lechen's *Lamp* and Paṇchen Sönam Drakpa's *Mind's Ornament*, refer to the Gelukpas as "New Kadampas" (*bka' gdams gsar ma*).

260. Interestingly, in his *Secret Biography of Khedrup* (2a), Jetsunpa claims that Khedrup was the reincarnation of Naktso Lotsāwa (see appendix B).

Sengé's interpretation is based on Tsongkhapa's oral instructions and the interpretations of the latter's disciples but that Khedrup interprets this matter differently.[261] This has multiple implications for our discussion. For one, it points out clearly that Gyaltsap and Khedrup were not the only of Tsongkhapa's disciples writing commentaries on their master's works, and that the works by other authors were in circulation and studied within Gelukpa circles during Lodrö Rinchen Sengé's time. The works of Gyaltsap and Khedrup were not the only sources used for understanding and interpreting Tsongkhapa's views in the early stages of Geluk history. Secondly, this statement suggests a discrepancy between Tsongkhapa's and Khedrup's interpretations, and that Tsongkhapa's other students did not necessarily agree with Khedrup. Clearly Lodrö Rinchen Sengé himself disagrees with Khedrup's interpretation, at least in this particular matter, preferring instead what he characterizes as the mainstream understanding of Tsongkhapa's thought on the subject.

Could this rejection of Khedrup's position be the source of Jetsunpa's concern? When we look at the reason Jetsunpa gives, according to Delek Nyima, for refuting Lodrö Rinchen Sengé's textbooks—the occasional inconsistency with the views of Tsongkhapa and his disciples—this same critique is equally applicable to the writings of Khedrup. And yet Khedrup remains one of the primary figures Jetsunpa cites as authoritative for correctly interpreting Tsongkhapa's thought.

For Jetsunpa, the main sources of authority for interpreting Tsongkhapa's thought are the philosophical writings of Gyaltsap and Khedrup. Although he does not cite them overabundantly and in every context, he does rely on their works in key ways for specific topics. For the subjects of Pramāṇa and Prajñāpāramitā, Jetsunpa relies on Gyaltsap's works and those of Tsong-

261. *'Di'i don ni / sngo 'dzin gyis sngon po dngos su rtogs la sngo 'dzin gyi 'jal byed ni rang rig min gyi sngo 'dzin nyid yin la / de'i dngo 'dzin gyi rnam pa shar ba'i sgo nas sngo 'dzin rtogs par mi 'jog gi / sngon pa'i rnam par shar ba nyid kyi sgo nas sngo 'dzin rtogs par 'jog pas / sngo 'dzin sngon sum gyis sngon po dang sngo 'dzin gnyis ka rtogs par 'dra ba la rnam pa shar ma shar gyi khyed par yod pas yul myong dran la myong ba zhes dang / yul can gyi myong dran la bcad pa zhes gsungs so / zhes rje thams cad mkhyen pa'i gsung sgros las 'byung la / ṭīk chen du ni de ltar myong bcad kyi khyed par las 'di thon gsung ba gsal por sbyar ba med kyang myong bcad kyi khyed par dngos su mthong ba dang / rtogs pa tsam la gsal zhing / dbang po'i mngon sum de rang rig gis mi myong bar dbang mngon rang nyid kyis rtogs la / rtogs tshul yang sngo sogs kyi rnam pa shar ba'i sgo nas gzhal bya sngo sogs grub pa nyid kyis dbang mngon de rtogs par bshad pas shugs rtogs su gsal zhing / rjes 'brang gzhan rnams kyang de bzhin du 'chad la / mkhas grub chos rjes ni gzhan du 'chad do //* (Lodrö Rinchen Sengé, *Elucidation of Suchness*, 230–31).

khapa himself,[262] and for Madhyamaka, Khedrup's commentarial works are his key authorities. Thus, while Jetsunpa's commentaries on Pramāṇa and Prajñāpāramitā are largely based on the works of *both* Tsongkhapa and Gyaltsap, his Madhyamaka commentary (*Dbu ma'i spyi don*), though purportedly a commentary on Tsongkhapa's Madhyamaka views, is chiefly a discussion of Khedrup's *Stong thun chen mo*. In fact, the only part that directly comments on Tsongkhapa's original text is a thirty-page section at the end of a work that is over three hundred pages long.[263]

Geshé Tsultrim Chöphel, ex-director of the Sera Jé Committee for Philosophical Studies and one of the college's foremost scholars today, represents the current thinking on why Jetsunpa alternated between the two interpreters. On the one hand, he explains, Khedrup's interpretations on both Pramāṇa and Prajñāpāramitā were purportedly seen as being somewhat inconsistent with Tsongkhapa's teachings, and on the other hand, he continued, Gyaltsap is considered to have either held divergent opinions on the topic of Madhyamaka or simply to have not composed extensively enough on the subject.[264] Since Gyaltsap did in fact compose multiple works dealing with Madhyamaka philosophy,[265] it seems more plausible that Jetsunpa avoided using Gyaltsap's Madhyamaka works because of perceived divergences between him and Tsongkhapa on this subject, or perhaps even between him and Khedrup. Gyaltsap's Madhyamaka texts may

262. I am referring primarily to Jetsunpa's *Eliminating Doubts Concerning the Difficult Points of the Illumination of Intent of the Pramāṇavarttika* and to his commentaries on the eight chapters of the *Abhisamayālaṃkāra*.

263. Jetsunpa, *Garland of Fortune*, 298–328.

264. Geshé Tsultrim Chöphel, personal communication, January 8, 2006. Geshé Tsultrim Chöphel is not to be confused with Geshé Tsulga cited above, who shared the same name.

265. Gyaltsap's works include: the *Elucidation of the Essential Meaning of the Madhyamaka Commentary Entitled Precious Garland* (*Dbu ma rin chen 'phreng ba'i snying po'i don gsal bar byed pa*); the *Concise Meaning of the Madhyamakāvatāra* (*Dbu ma la 'jug pa'i bsdus don*); and the *Essence of Eloquent Teachings: A Commentary on the Catuḥśataka* (*Dbu ma bzhi brgya pa'i rnam bshad legs bshad snying po*). Khedrup's two major works are the *Lessons on the View of the Middle Way* (*Dbu ma'i lta khrid*, composition date unknown) and the *Great Treatise of a Thousand Topics* (*Stong thun chen mo*, composed ca. 1424–28). Note that Khedrup's collected works also contain a number of smaller writings on Madhyamaka, such as the *Instructions on the Madhyamaka View* and a discussion of emptiness in his commentary on the *lokadhātu* chapter of the *Vimalaprabhā* (Khedrup Jé, *Elucidation of Suchness*).

have been considered to have more Sakya influence[266] than was acceptable to later Gelukpas.[267]

In any case, Jetsunpa uses Gyaltsap and Khedrup as his main authorities for interpreting Tsongkhapa's works, and more specifically, he relies heavily on Khedrup for his Madhyamaka commentary. Because of that, if Jetsunpa is refuting Lodrö Rinchen Sengé's interpretation, this implies that Jetsunpa is taking him to task not for holding interpretations that were discordant with Tsongkhapa, per se, but for holding interpretations discordant with Tsongkhapa's thought *as interpreted by Khedrup*.[268] By relying so fully on Khedrup's Madhyamaka text when he is supposed to be commenting mainly on Tsongkhapa's, Jetsunpa is insinuating that the two are so consistent with each other as to be synonymous. Since Khedrup's views are perfectly representative of Tsongkhapa's, there is no need to comment on Tsongkhapa's text directly.

As I noted above, Jetsunpa's work ceases to comment on Khedrup's Madhyamaka text in the final portion and turns primarily to Tsongkhapa's. Jetsunpa does not state his reasons for doing this. Instead he says, "Up to here the discussion is according to the system of [Khedrup's *Stong thun chen mo*] *skal bzang mig 'byed*. What follows is exactly according to the system of [Tsongkhapa's] *Dgongs pa rab gsal*."[269] Jetsunpa's use of the term *lugs* ("system" or "tradition") in speaking of the two commentaries would seem to indicate that he considers Khedrup's *Stong thun chen mo* and Tsongkhapa's *Dgongs pa rab gsal* to diverge, at least in their interpretations of the latter half of the sixth chapter of Candrakīrti's *Madhyamakāvatāra*. This implication is

266. Dreyfus (2003, 341n32) has pointed out that Gyaltsap himself considered some of his later philosophical works as being from the Sakya tradition, particularly his *Tshad ma rigs pa'i gter gyi rnam bshad legs par bshad pa'i snying po*, a commentary on Sakya Paṇḍita's *Tshad ma rigs gter*, and that he claims to follow the views of Tsongkhapa's and Gyaltsap's teacher, Rendawa, himself a member of the Sakya tradition.

267. Although, like Tsongkhapa, both Gyaltsap and Khedrup had been educated by masters from the Sakya tradition, and though it would appear that Tsongkhapa's early community of followers did not necessarily see themselves as a distinctly non-Sakya tradition, a schism between the Ganden and Sakya communities eventually caused the two to grow apart and sparked sectarian tensions between the Geluk and Sakya schools. By Jetsunpa's time, the sectarian divide had already been established. See Dreyfus 1997, 33–41, and Dreyfus 2005, 293–97.

268. A closer comparison between Jetsunpa's and Khedrup's respective Madhyamaka commentaries is necessary to determine to just what extent Jetsunpa's reliance on Khedrup causes him to diverge from Lodrö Rinchen Sengé's interpretation.

269. *'Di yan chad skal bzang mig 'byed kyi lugs so / da ni dgongs pa rab gsal gyi lugs ji lta ba bzhin brjod par bya'o //* (Jetsunpa, *Garland of Fortune*, 297).

reflected in current scholarly opinion among Gelukpa experts, who also hold that Jetsunpa's reason for shifting his discussion to focus on Tsongkhapa's work was that, at this particular point in the text, Khedrup's commentary—which presents a synthetic view of Madhyamaka philosophy based on three different works by Tsongkhapa[270]—diverges from Tsongkhapa's teachings.[271]

When Khedrup's views shift away from Tsongkhapa's teachings, Jetsunpa does not feel the need to refute him. Is there a double standard, perhaps even a show of favoritism, in Jetsunpa's handling of what he perceives to be mistaken ideas? Lodrö Rinchen Sengé's alleged divergent opinions necessitated that his works be purged and his views refuted. Khedrup's divergent opinions, on the other hand, were simply set aside for particular topics. Jetsunpa seems invested in maintaining Khedrup's authoritative position more generally and likewise in divesting Lodrö Rinchen Sengé of his. This suggests that what is really at stake is not the logic of the philosophical arguments so much as the lineage of interpretation.

Guy Newland has remarked that the three major authors of the Geluk Madhyamaka *yig cha*—Jetsunpa, Paṇchen Sönam Drakpa, and the first Jamyang Shepa—all seem to share the common goals of confirming the "fundamental coherence" of Tsongkhapa's views. In the course of their efforts, all three authors are faced with the challenge of reconciling or rebutting the views of Gyaltsap and Khedrup that are inconsistent with their own understanding of Tsongkhapa's teachings. As a result, Newland remarks, Paṇchen Sönam Drakpa "boldly overthrows the assertions of mKhas grub and rGyal tshab when they conflict with his own conclusions," while the first Jamyang Shepa attempts instead to show the inherent consistency by reconciling "apparent contradictions among Tsong kha pa, mKhas grub, and rGyal tshab."[272]

It is far from the case that there was unanimity among the very authors that Jetsunpa recognized as legitimate authorities. Khedrup certainly did not always agree with Gyaltsap's views, and Jetsunpa acknowledges such differences. In his *pramāṇa* commentary, which is a phrase-by-phrase commentary of Gyaltsap's exegesis of the first chapter of the *Pramāṇavārttika*, Jetsunpa is seen quoting an unnamed opponent who maintains that Khedrup found

270. These are the *Drang nges legs bshad snying po*, the vipaśyanā section of the *Lam rim chen mo*, and the aforementioned *Dbu ma dgongs pa rab gsal* (see Cabezón 1992, 4–5).

271. Geshé Tsultrim Chöphel, telephone conversation, January 8, 2006.

272. Newland 1996, 208–9.

fault with Gyaltsap's writings on the same topic.[273] Jetsunpa finds himself in a sort of double bind whereby if he supports the positions put forth by one source of authority, he comes under fire from the other one.[274]

In order to maintain the soundness of his positions, Jetsunpa must explain how it is that his sources of interpretive authority disagree. Jetsunpa's response is to say that although it does appear that Khedrup refutes Gyaltsap, they are really just approaching things from different angles and therefore are not in actual disagreement. Khedrup is merely pointing out, he says, that while Gyaltsap's reasoning does not *explicitly* establish what the latter had set out to establish, it nevertheless does so *implicitly*. According to Jetsunpa, this is all Gyaltsap meant. In fact Khedrup's remarks are not even a true refutation (*dgag pa*), or even an objection or criticism of a flaw (*skyon*) in the logic of Gyaltsap's position. Instead, maintains Jetsunpa, Khedrup was merely expressing doubts (*dogs pa*):

> I have offered a logical response to the doubts expressed by the Dharma lord Khedrup concerning [Gyaltsap's] *Explanation of the Stanzas of the Pramāṇavārtika*, and have thereby established that the thoughts of both the father and son [i.e., Gyaltsap and Khedrup] are, for the most part, in agreement.[275]

273. Jetsunpa, *Eliminating Doubts*, 238.

274. If we look at Khedrup's *pramāṇa* commentary, the *Ṭik chen rigs pa'i rgya mtsho*, we find that Khedrup does indeed take issue on multiple occasions with Gyaltsap's arguments and interpretations of Dharmakīrti. The particular disagreement being referred to in Jetsunpa's work (*Eliminating Doubts*, 238) concerns Gyaltsap's explanation that the words and conceptual cognitions that practically apply to an utterance are eliminative-engagers (*sel 'jug*, Skt. *apoha-parvṛtti*) because other words and valid cognitions practically apply in relation to them. The issue discussed by Dharmakīrti is complex, and space does not allow for an exhaustive discussion of Gyaltsap's comments or Khedrup's arguments (see Dharmakīrti, *Pramāṇavārttikakārikā*, 1:40). Suffice it to say that after citing Gyaltsap's reasoning (Gyaltsap Jé, *Explanation of the Stanzas of the Pramāṇavārttika that Unmistakenly Reveals the Path to Liberation*, 48b–49a), Khedrup goes on to argue that such a syllogism serves absolutely no purpose vis-à-vis establishing that words and concepts are in fact eliminative-engagers—which is exactly what Gyaltsap is trying to establish—and is therefore useless. Furthermore, Khedrup also points out that the passages cited by Gyaltsap do not help validate the latter's claims (*Commentary on the Svārtha Chapter of the Ocean of Reasoning*, 70b). For a more detailed discussion of the other instances where Khedrup takes issue with Gyaltsap's arguments and interpretations of Dharmakīrti, see Dreyfus 1997, 542–43n19. For a good discussion of Khedrup's *pramāṇa* works, see van der Kuijp 1985.

275. *Mkhas grub chos kyi rje'i zhal snga nas kyis thar lam gsal byed la dogs pa bkod pa rnams kho bos rigs lam dang mthun par lan phul te yab sras gnyis phal cher dgongs pa gcig tu bsgrub pa'o //* (Jetsunpa, *Eliminating Doubts*, 103a).

But in point of fact, when we look at Khedrup's own argument, he never uses an interrogative construction or other indication of a provisional remark. There is also no honorific wording to indicate that he was addressing his teacher in search of a response to doubts he had.[276] After paraphrasing Gyaltsap, Khedrup simply points out that the latter's arguments are faulty, just as he does with the faults found in the views of any of his other opponents. Khedrup's tone is not any different from that used in other arguments in this work.

Beyond disarming a potentially harmful attack on the consistency of his own interpretive authorities, Jetsunpa's attempt to reconcile the views of Khedrup and Gyaltsap reveals favoritism toward Khedrup. Jetsunpa struggles to maintain the notion that Khedrup's views are consistent with Gyaltsap's, even if the former in fact disagrees on occasion with the latter.

We see, therefore, that the same reason given in Jetsunpa's biography for refutating of Lodrö Rinchen Sengé's work—the presence of "one or two inconsistencies with the views of Tsongkhapa and his spiritual heirs"—also applies to Khedrup's own commentaries. But this did not cause Jetsunpa to delegitimize or supplant Khedrup's works. For he was in a very different relation with Khedrup than with Lodrö Rinchen Sengé.

Jetsunpa and Khedrup

Knowing that Khedrup did not have the same elevated status in the early days of Geluk history as he later came to have, Jetsunpa's use of Khedrup's works in the same text in which he allegedly refuted Lodrö Rinchen Sengé takes on special significance. I suggest that Jetsunpa's support of Khedrup's doctrinal authority and his usurpation of that of Lodrö Rinchen Sengé were intricately linked. Was there already a movement to crown Khedrup as a supreme interpreter of the great master Tsongkhapa? If so, associating himself with such a movement would have allowed Jetsunpa to position himself at the center of his local scholarly orbit.[277]

276. Though they are not the most frequently mentioned figures, both Dulzin and Gyaltsap are included among Khedrup's teachers in the latter's account of teachings received (Khedrup Jé, *A Record of Teachings Received*).

277. Shākya Chokden's use of the expression *yapsé sum* (see above, note 140) suggests that the term was already being used by the end of the fifteenth century to refer to Tsongkhapa, Gyaltsap, and Khedrup, but its absence from Khedrup's biographies and from early histories implies that it was not a universally accepted. What its presence does suggest, however, is that if Jetsunpa was not the one who first assigned Khedrup to this Geluk triumvirate—which

Jetsunpa's biographies all confirm that Jetsunpa's primary teachers were all descended from Khedrup's transmission lineage. Despite a brief connection to Lodrö Rinchen Sengé's lineage through a period of study under the latter's disciple Paljor Lhundrup, Jetsunpa's biographer makes it clear that his hero was educated predominantly by disciples of Baso Chökyi Gyaltsen, Khedrup's principle disciple and younger brother. Jetsunpa's primary teachers, Kunga Delek Rinchen, Yeshé Tsemo, Khedrup Rinchen Shenyen, and even Dönyö Palden, had all studied under Baso Chökyi Gyaltsen. Delek Nyima also insists that Jetsunpa's name was given to him in utero by Baso himself. The author tells a story of how Jetsunpa offered the milk from his mother's breast to honor Baso's reliquary at Ganden during a trip there at age four.[278] Delek Nyima's biographical account provides several such reasons to make us think that Jetsunpa had close kinship ties with Khedrup's family and close circle.

Another telling incident is a dream Jetsunpa is said to have had during a study retreat at Sera Chöding, the small hermitage just above Sera. This is the very spot famed as the sacred site where Khedrup met Tsongkhapa for the first time. According to Delek Nyima, Jetsunpa dreamed that Khedrup appeared to him and said, "O geshé! If you wish to obtain the particularly great view of the Madhyamaka, you must pray to Tsongkhapa as one and the same as Mañjuśrī, strive hard in purification and the accumulation of merit, and investigate the authentic doctrine." Delek Nyima also adds that because of this dream, Jetsunpa proclaimed this particular site an ideal location for study retreats, especially for achieving greater understanding of Madhyamaka.[279]

Though hagiographical, these stories do tell us something about how Jetsunpa's own tradition saw him in relation to Khedrup. It is at least plausible that the dream may have been recounted by Jetsunpa himself; we have no reason to believe Delek Nyima invented events. The dream is especially interesting for its reiteration of Jetsunpa's considerable preoccupation with doctrinal cohesion. There are multiple written and oral stories whereby Khedrup calls into question the interpretations of other disciples of Tsongkhapa. The abbot of Sera Mé in Tibet in 2001 confided to me that Khedrup argued with his fellow disciple Jamyang Chöjé over the latter's alleged espousal of

---

only further research can decide—then he was not the only one who considered Khedrup to be Tsongkhapa's chief spiritual heir and interpreter. Whatever the case, Jetsunpa's strong voice played a pivotal role in the movement to elevate Khedrup.

278. Paṇchen Delek Nyima, *Rain of Accomplishments*, 4a.

279. Paṇchen Delek Nyima, *Rain of Accomplishments*, 11b–12a.

extrinsic emptiness (*gzhan stong*).[280] According to written sources, Khedrup also publicly upbraided Sera's third abbot, Gungru Gyaltsen Sangpo, for espousing and propagating theories on emptiness that were inconsistent with Tsongkhapa's teachings.[281]

Oddly, the latter story is completely absent from older historical sources, such as *Lamp Illuminating the History of the Kadam Tradition*, and is not given in Khedrup's early biographical literature, which raises questions as to whether or not the event did in fact take place.[282] Also, although Khedrup was Gyaltsap's successor as the Ganden throne holder, it is far from certain that he actually had the authority to reproach other major Gelukpa figures for misrepresenting Tsongkhapa.[283] We should also keep in mind that the earliest mention of this incident is found in *Mind's Ornament*, a text that also attempts to elevate Khedrup as Tsongkhapa's chief spiritual heir. It is therefore entirely possible that the personal agenda of *Mind's Ornament*'s author, Paṇchen Sönam Drakpa, may in fact be casting things in a way that is favorable for establishing Khedrup's superiority among Tsongkhapa's disciples. The accuracy of the story is therefore potentially compromised, and the account should be taken with a grain of salt.[284]

Whether or not the events portrayed in the above stories about Khedrup

280. This is the view that ultimate wisdom is not empty of its own entity but is empty only of everything other than itself. It is often juxtaposed with *intrinsic emptiness* (*rang stong*), the view that all phenomona lack inherent existence, even the wisdom of emptiness wisdom itself. The former view was espoused by the Jonangpa school of Tibetan Buddhism and was vehemently opposed by leading Gelukpas. For more on *gzhan stong*, see Stearns 2010.

281. Paṇchen Sönam Drakpa, *Mind's Ornament*, 138, and Thuken, *Commentary on Philosophical Systems*, 323. The latter is translated in Thuken 2009, 273: "Not only did he destroy by reason countless thinkers who wrote critiques of the works of Jé, but he refuted the Dharma lord Gungruwa and others who, through listening to statements made by the great lord himself but failing to analyze the view fully, explained Jé's version of emptiness as an affirming negation. Moreover, he also refuted all those whose way of explaining how to maintain certainty about the view did not go along with Jé's claims. Therefore, because Khedrup Jé freed Jé Lama's unique tradition of sutra and mantra from stains, his kindness toward this teaching is matchless and unrivaled."

282. The disagreement between Khedrup and Gungru is mentioned also by Jonang Kunga Drölchok (1507–66). See Komarovski 2011, 331–32n72.

283. In a presentation at the 2003 International Association of Tibetan Studies conference held in Oxford, UK, José Cabezón suggested that Ganden was not necessarily the governing center for all Geluk monasteries in the early stages of the school's history that it would later become. It would seem that other Geluk institutions such as Sera and Drepung did not necessarily answer to the abbots of Ganden, especially on matters of education.

284. Though Paṇchen Sönam Drakpa openly disagrees with Khedrup Jé on certain points

did in fact take place, what is most pertinent to the present discussion is the fact that they *represent* Khedrup as having been concerned with doctrinal consistency and as having had the authority to reproach his counterparts. Khedrup is thereby vested with the power and responsibility of correctly interpreting Tsongkhapa's thought. Jetsunpa's dream therefore not only underscores his own penchant for doctrinal purity, it also points out how he saw himself with regards to Khedrup's lineage. Showing Khedrup talking to Jetsunpa about doctrinal authenticity and not some other figure casts Khedrup as the representative of such authenticity. Had Jetsunpa seen himself as a member of another figure's lineage, it would have been that figure and not Khedrup giving him the advice.

Delek Nyima further remarks that Jetsunpa took Vajrabhairava as his main tutelary deity specifically because Khedrup had been told to worship this same deity by Tsongkhapa.[285] Jetsunpa is also said to have had visions of the deity Damchen Chögyal, another epithet for Ganden's protector deity Yamāntaka, at important times in his life. This very deity is also said by Khedrup's biographers to have appeared to him on numerous occasions.[286]

All of these vignettes support the portrayal of Jetsunpa's strong connection with Khedrup and his transmission lineage. It is of course possible that this connection was exaggerated or even created by Delek Nyima. As little is known about Delek Nyima's life, it is for the time being impossible to determine whether or not this is the case.[287] For now, however, we can reasonably assume that Jetsunpa and Delek Nyima colluded. In light of the fact that Jetsunpa's critique of Lodrö Rinchen Sengé's views would have, and most likely did, stir up harsh resistance at Sera Jé, Delek Nyima's particular portrayal may have served to ease tensions by "proving" to his readers that it was not for reasons of personal advancement that Jetsunpa "corrected" Lodrö Rinchen Sengé, but rather out of a genuine concern for the purity and consistency—and therefore longevity—of Tsongkhapa's doctrine. Thus, while Jetsunpa did

---

regarding his understanding of Tsongkhapa's thought, this does not mean that he did not see Khedrup as superior among Tsongkhapa's interpreters.

285. Paṇchen Delek Nyima, *Rain of Accomplishments*, 21a–21b.

286. See both Chöden Rapjor's *Short Biography of Khedrup* and Jetsunpa's *Secret Biography of Khedrup*.

287. There seems to have been a movement afoot within the Geluk tradition that promoted Khedrup as one of Tsongkhapa's chief disciples and interpreters. Jetsunpa's account of Khedrup's life plays a key role in that movement, and it is to be expected that his students would follow suit. But it is also clear from Jetsunpa's own work in defense of Khedrup's *Kālacakra* commentary that Jetsunpa himself saw Khedrup in a special way.

indeed take issue with Lodrö Rinchen Sengé's *yig cha*, he did so, according to Delek Nyima's account, only for the greater good and development of both Sera Jé and the Geluk tradition.

Had Jetsunpa truly considered himself a member of Lodrö Rinchen Sengé's lineage, and Lodrö Rinchen Sengé himself to be an authentic representative of Tsongkhapa's views—as would surely be expected from a member of the early Sera Jé community—he would have made more of an attempt to reconcile Lodrö Rinchen Sengé's "occasional inconsistencies" with Tsongkhapa's views. As he felt himself to be more a member of Khedrup's lineage, he was willing to delegitimize the doctrinal works of Lodrö Rinchen Sengé, while glossing over doctrinal differences between Khedrup and Tsongkhapa or even Gyaltsap. All of this is further supported by the multiple signs of Jetsunpa's close allegiance to Khedrup, chief among which is his authorship of Khedrup's exalted secret biography.

Creating Biography, Creating Power, Creating Community

In the early years, many of Tsongkhapa's disciples, such as Dulzin Drakpa Gyaltsen, Mé Sherap Sangpo (ca. 1495–57), who founded the important Chamdo Monastery,[288] and even Khedrup himself, had established their own monasteries in and around Central Tibet and were teaching their students their individual versions of what they had learned from Tsongkhapa. Given what we know of Dulzin's status, it seems absurd to think that senior disciples such as he or even Jampal Gyatso, both of whom were Khedrup's teachers, would need to conform to the latter's interpretations in order to teach Tsongkhapa's thought. This is underscored by Lodrö Rinchen Sengé's remarks that a number of Tsongkhapa's disciples understood and explained their master's teachings differently than Khedrup. Tsongkhapa's teachings were being passed on through the writings and explanations of a multitude of direct disciples. By the time Jetsunpa was writing, Khedrup had begun his ascent up the Geluk hierarchical ladder, but his status as the inalienable third member of the Jé Yabsé Sum—the first mention of which occurs in a work in defense of Khedrup's views by Jetsunpa—and as Tsongkhapa's chief interpreter and spiritual heir were not yet set in stone. Merely maintaining that Lodrö Rinchen Sengé's and Khedrup's interpretations did not correspond

288. This was a major monastic institution, purportedly housing up to three thousand monks (Lechen, *Lamp*, 412a).

would not have been enough to support the accusation that Lodrö Rinchen Sengé misrepresented Tsongkhapa's teachings and had to be refuted.

In order for his criticism to be compelling, then, Jetsunpa would have needed first to establish indisputably the superiority and authenticity of Khedrup's interpretations. He had to somehow prove that Khedrup was in fact privy to the true intended meaning of Tsongkhapa's teachings. This is where the key tool of biography comes in. In the *Secret Biography of Khedrup* Jetsunpa can elevate his hero to the status of Tsongkhapa's chief disciple for innumerable lifetimes. In portraying Khedrup as such, Jetsunpa overtly set up Khedrup as one of the highest authorities on Tsongkhapa's thought.

Jetsunpa states that not only was Khedrup one of Tsongkhapa's chief disciples throughout multiple lifetimes, but also he took birth in Tibet for the express purpose of disseminating and developing Tsongkhapa's teachings there.[289] Khedrup, he suggests, was mandated by figures such as Nāgārjuna and Candrakīrti, and by Tsongkhapa himself in his true form as Mañjuśrī, to disseminate Tsongkhapa's teachings.[290] By legitimating Khedrup's interpretations through direct endorsement by Tsongkhapa, the *Secret Biography of Khedrup* allows Jetsunpa to make legitimating claims about Khedrup as Tsongkhapa's authentic representative, Khedrup's works as the authentic interpretations of Tsongkhapa's thought, and Jetsunpa's own preference for Khedrup's interpretations.[291]

By presenting Khedrup as the *sine qua non* in propagating the thought of Tsongkhapa, it is important to remember that Jetsunpa is casting himself in the utmost favorable light as well. As Dreyfus has remarked, for Gelukpas the composition of a text is not just a pedagogical exercise; it is a public expression of the author's allegiance and commitment to a tradition.[292] Most frequently, a biographer will have been the disciple of the biography's hero or else a descendant of his transmission lineage. Tibetan sacred biography almost always serves to tell us that the author agrees with and holds his hero's

289. *Secret Biography of Khedrup*, 1b–4a (see appendix B).

290. *Secret Biography of Khedrup*, 3a–4a (see appendix B).

291. Although Jetsunpa's *Secret Biography of Khedrup* appears to have circulated widely enough to have been included in Khedrup's collected works, it is impossible to say with any certainty how it was received at first, or even who his audience was. It is possible that it was in fact used to help establish the incarnation lineage of the Paṇchen Lamas, who came to be considered Khedrup's reincarnations (see Tucci 1980, 41–42, and Jagou 2005). However, Jetsunpa's *Secret Biography of Khedrup* does not define a reincarnation lineage for his hero as explicitly as does Delek Nyima's account (see *Delightful to the Scholar's Mind*, 2a–b).

292. Dreyfus 2003, 320.

views in high esteem, and at the same time that he sees himself as a member of his hero's lineage.[293] Thus, in writing Khedrup's secret biography, Jetsunpa is not only saying that his hero is or was a particularly wonderful and outstanding figure who is worthy of the reader's interest and respect, he is also making an important statement about himself vis-à-vis Khedrup, his lineage, and his teachings. In having set up Khedrup as an authentic interpreter and representative of Tsongkhapa's doctrine, and then claiming himself to be a member of Khedrup's lineage, Jetsunpa is also acquiring authority for his own person and commentarial works.[294]

In his analysis of the relationship between language and power, French sociologist Pierre Bourdieu has written,

> The use of language, the manner as much as the substance of discourse, depends on the social position of the speaker, which governs the access he can have to the language of the institution, that is, to the official, orthodox and legitimate speech. It is the access to the legitimate instruments of expression, and therefore

293. It is very rare that a biographer will denigrate or disagree with the views of his subject in the biography. One such striking case is found in the writings of Desi Sangyé Gyatso regarding the Tibetan medical scholar Lodrö Gyalpo (sixteenth cent.). Desi's criticism of Surkhar is striking: "His fundamental disregard of the words of Tsomé Khenchen, who is within his own teaching lineage, his over-intellectual attacks on authoritative medical works of the past such as those from the Jang tradition, and his refutations of standard poetical wisdom are a wound inflicted upon medical science. He makes the claim that the Rinpung ruler at first promised to sponsor a publication of *Four Tantras* but then failed to deliver on his promise. However, this ruler, Ngawang Jikten Drakpa, was someone who did not mistake brass for gold, and he was clearly aware of the errors of the other's twisted interpretations of the text. His corpus of medical literature, including his commentary on *Four Tantras* called *Oral Transmission of Our Ancestors*, are illustrations of his own words, 'like the crow that died, they never achieved their crowning glory'" (Desi Sangyé Gyatso 2010, 315). We must question if this type of denigration in a biography has to do with the subgenre it is situated in (medical texts) or if this is simply the exception that confirms the rule.

294. Unfortunately, Jetsunpa does not date his biographical and philosophical works. It is therefore impossible to tell whether he composed Khedrup's secret biography prior to or after writing the texts that were to become Sera Jé's new *yig cha*. Either way though, the biography would serve to legitimize his own position at Sera Jé. Indeed, if Jetsunpa composed the secret biography prior to his commentarial works, then we might speculate that he did so in preparation for his eventual doctrinal takeover. If on the other hand he composed the biography after he wrote his commentaries, then it is possible that he realized that his works lacked the necessary authority to truly supplant Lodrö Rinchen Sengé as the central figure of the Sera Jé community and that he needed to enhance his status by aligning himself with Khedrup, newly elevated for that very purpose.

> the participation in the authority of the institution, which makes all the difference—irreducible to discourse as such—between the straightforward imposture of masqueraders ... and the authorized imposture of those who do the same thing with the authority and authorization of an institution.[295]

Bourdieu's speaker must have an established social identity in order to acquire authority vis-à-vis those who hear his statement. It could be argued that, despite being the abbot of Sera Jé college, Jetsunpa did not yet have the sufficient standing in the community necessary to be able to take over Lodrö Rinchen Sengé's place as the principal intellectual authority of the college. Lodrö Rinchen Sengé's status as the college's founder already conferred upon him the "authority to speak" in Bourdieu's sense—and therefore the authority to be heard—at Sera Jé. To criticize Lodrö Rinchen Sengé's views and *yig cha* would, in these conditions, stir up too much resistance for Jetsunpa's own views to be easily accepted. Jetsunpa had to first acquire the necessary social and intellectual standing. By composing Khedrup's secret biography, presenting Khedrup as Tsongkhapa's supreme interpreter, and casting himself as a member of the inner elite of Khedrup's followers, Jetsunpa was positioning himself to be heard—and followed.

Donald Lopez points out that in the Tibetan Buddhist context, "the authority to speak is passed on through a lineage, a lineage that operates regardless of historical gaps and fissures."[296] In order for his refutations of Lodrö Rinchen Sengé's positions to be accepted, Jetsunpa needed to acquire enhanced "authority to speak." As Jan Willis has pointed out, biography was "an invaluable means for establishing a demonstrable lineage of successful ones" in Tibet.[297] In composing his *Secret Biography of Khedrup*, Jetsunpa therefore had recourse to a tried and tested method for establishing his own place in an authoritative lineage.

Evidence would seem to indicate that Lodrö Rinchen Sengé was commonly understood to have been from a completely different and possibly even rival transmission lineage to that of Khedrup.[298] What's more, two other important members of that same lineage are said to have held views that con-

295. Bourdieu 1991, 109. Although Bourdieu is dealing primarily with acts of speech, his comments are just as apt in cases of textual authority.

296. Lopez 1998, 109.

297. Willis 1985, 305.

298. Though I have found no evidence in Lodrö Rinchen Sengé's own writings to support this.

trasted with Khedrup's. Indeed, although he is said to have received teachings directly from Tsongkhapa, Lodrö Rinchen Sengé was primarily a disciple of Jamyang Chöjé and Gungru Gyaltsen Sangpo.[299] As we have seen, later oral tradition maintains that Jamyang Chöjé was somewhat of a heretic for allegedly advocating the doctrine of extrinsic emptiness and that he and Khedrup argued heatedly. We must also recall the tension that is said to have occurred at Drepung when Gyaltsap brought Khedrup there after choosing him as his successor to the Ganden throne.[300] And let us not forget the intriguingly similar story of how Khedrup publicly reproved Gungru Gyaltsen Sangpo. Furthermore, it would seem that the works of both Jamyang Chöjé and Gungru Gyaltsen were at some point removed from circulation at Drepung and Sera, just as were Lodrö Rinchen Sengé's.[301] It seems to be more than mere coincidence that three important figures from the same transmission lineage—Jamyang Chöjé, Gungru Gyaltsen Sangpo, and Lodrö Rinchen Sengé—were all accused of propounding views that did not concur with Khedrup's version of Tsongkhapa's teachings and therefore saw their writings opposed and eventually suppressed. What makes this even more intriguing is the fact that Jamyang Chöjé was a close disciple of Dulzin Drakpa Gyaltsen, whose place among Tsongkhapa's chief disciples is eventually usurped by Khedrup.

If this alleged rivalry between Jamyang Chöjé's and Khedrup's lineages did exist when Jetsunpa was writing, to simply affirm that he was a member of Khedrup's lineage would not have bolstered Jetsunpa's authority. Jetsunpa needed to elevate his hero to make him appear superior to all of Tsongkhapa's other disciples. This is what Jetsunpa does repeatedly throughout his account of Khedrup's "secret" life. By composing the *Secret Biography of Khedrup*, Jetsunpa was establishing this lineage, his own, as authentic and authoritative. And in so doing, Jetsunpa was acquiring for himself the authority necessary

299. Paṇchen Sönam Drakpa, *Mind's Ornament*, 140.

300. Strikingly, although Jamyang Chöjé's biography by Tsangtön Kunga Gyaltsen (a disciple of both Jamyang Chöjé and Lodrö Rinchen Sengé) does mention frequent debates between Khedrup and Jamyang Chöjé, and even portrays Jamyang Chöjé as being fond of saying that he was more intelligent than Khedrup, there is never any mention of animosity between the two. Nor is there any indication that the debates concerned Jamyang Chöjé's espousal of extrinsic emptiness (Tsangtön's *Lamp*, 17b). It would appear, then, that it is a later tradition that perceives Khedrup and Jamyang Chöjé as being at such odds with one another over such heretical views.

301. At present this is known largely through oral tradition. I have not come across any written records to confirm it. In any case, Jamyang Chöjé's works remain to be found, and Gungru Gyaltsen Sangpo's works, ironically, resurfaced at the same time as Lodrö Rinchen Sengé's and have been made available by the same publisher.

to be able to make himself heard at Sera Jé, debunk Lodrö Rinchen Sengé's philosophical works, and eventually supplant the founding figure at the center of his own community.

Then, by adhering to the views propounded by Khedrup—which were passed down to Jetsunpa through multiple authentic masters from Khedrup's transmission lineage—Jetsunpa's own commentarial work must also be correct representations of Tsongkhapa's teachings. This move goes a long way in making it possible for Jetsunpa to claim that Lodrö Rinchen Sengé's works misrepresent Tsongkhapa's thought. Jetsunpa's success dealt a lethal blow to the founder's identity as the doctrinal authority at Sera Jé. Such a coup makes us appreciate the far-reaching influence of Tibetan hagiography in establishing philosophical authority and curricular reform.

Conclusion

In his productive study of the hagiographical tradition of the Indian *siddhas*, James Robinson insists that religious texts need to be read on multiple levels.[302] This assessment certainly applies to Tibetan Buddhist biography. Contra earlier Tibetologists who considered such sources to contain little or no information of historical value due to their exaggerated panegyric, I have maintained that the very rhetoric these scholars dismiss has in fact much to teach us about Tibetan Buddhist institutions, lineages, philosophical tradition, and much else. I have further argued that Tibetan biographical writing is not merely a historical, inspirational, and/or instructional account, as Willis maintains, but also a powerful tool in establishing philosophical authority and legitimacy, both personally and institutionally.

This work began with a question about philosophical authority and ended up probing the rhetoric of an adulatory biography. Finding an incommensurability between a purported philosophical concern—that is, Jetsunpa's ostensible endeavor to represent Tsongkhapa's thought exactly—and what I see to be rather a concern with lineage loyalty, and perhaps even a personal aspiration for power, my turn to a close reading of Jetsunpa's *Secret Biography of Khedrup* enabled me to answer my original question. I was able to discern that Jetsunpa uses this biography at once to elevate his hero as Tsongkhapa's preeminent disciple and interpreter since countless lifetimes, and to set himself up as the legatee of Khedrup and his authentic interpretations of Tsongkhapa's thought. This newfound status as Khedrup's heir helps Jetsunpa acquire the necessary social and doctrinal position to be able to level his criticism of Lodrö Rinchen Sengé and eventually usurp Lodrö Rinchen Sengé as the central figure of the Sera Jé community. Thus looking closely at the rhetoric of Jetsunpa's *Secret Biography of Khedrup* has shed light on the important role of biography and lineage in the suppression of Lodrö Rinchen Sengé's philosophical works and their subsequent replacement by Jetsunpa's own commentaries. This procedure was grounded in a method that is somewhat reminiscent

302. That is, as history, as hagiography, and as myth; Robinson 1996, 61.

of Paul Ricoeur's "hermeneutics of suspicion" in that it not only sought to listen for what the texts had to say for and about themselves but also looked for agendas behind what on the surface posed as an idealistic concern with doctrinal purity.[303] This method included considering prophecy as a way to understand forces at work at the time the prophecy was made rather than what it purported to predict about the future. It looked at devotional biography more to learn about the author's agenda than about the glorious exploits of the hero recounted therein.

But my emphasis on lineage affiliation and the construction of personal authority is not cynical. Rather, it helps to illuminate some basic patterns both of human interrelations more generally and of social dynamics in Tibetan Buddhist religious society. The relationship between status and lineage evidenced in these biographies is akin to, and possibly even stronger than, the relationship between clan status and liturgical expertise that thrived during Tibet's renaissance period (approximately 950–1200).[304]

My discussion of the early Geluk figurations of Tsongkhapa and Khedrup has hopefully shed light not only on how the early Gelukpas perceived their founding figure, Tsongkhapa, and how that perception evolved, but also on Khedrup's shifting position in the formation of the strong orthodoxy that has come to characterize the Geluk tradition. This work has traced key historical processes by which Khedrup became so highly regarded in the Geluk hierarchy and has shown that there was a gradual shift through which he was elevated to the status of one of Tsongkhapa's two chief disciples and his chief Madhyamaka interpreter. It has also suggested reasons for why said shifts

303. As Ricoeur (1970, 27) puts it, the scholarly reader interpreting the text must maintain the balance between the "willingness to suspect" and the "willingness to listen."

304. Davidson has argued (2005, 3) that although the Tibetan clans had contributed to social instability during the Tibetan imperium (650–850), they nevertheless constituted the "primary foci for stable institution building" during the tenth through thirteenth centuries, particularly in Central Tibet. Because of the preeminent status accorded to the tantric scriptures that were brought to Tibet in the tenth through the thirteenth centuries, those who specialized in this literature were able to achieve "the *de facto* aristocratic status that some were not able to obtain by birth" (2). These specialists "put together a feudal formulation of personal charisma, clan affiliation, subtle learning, occasional sanctity, ritual virtuosity, and undeniable dedication" (372). Tibetans who wished to pursue religious or political agendas, either for themselves or communally, had to do so on the "social grid fashioned by the clan structure." It is not entirely surprising, then, that religious figures would rely so heavily on a structure similar to that of the clan. Moreover, the old Tibetan clans already constituted much of the authoritative Buddhist clergy prior to the emergence of the Geluk school, and "the aristocratic clans and regional lords became the centers for both political power and religious authority, sometimes vested in the same person" (Davidson 2005, 80).

occurred, illustrating the close interrelation that exists between the identity and status of the teacher and that of the student. My attention to a few key biographies not previously noticed, such as Jampal Gyatso's *Supplement* and Chöden Rapjor's *Short Biography of Khedrup*, has allowed me to sort out the shift in Tsongkhapa's status, when it occurred, and how later mergings of inconsistent claims masked that earlier development. I was able to discern that early accounts of Tsongkhapa's life, including the *Great Biography of Tsongkhapa* and the *Secret Biography of Tsongkhapa* by Khedrup—and even Jampal Gyatso's own *Supplement*—stand in sharp contrast with later biographies (such as the second Jamyang Shepa's hagiographical account or even Gyalwang Chöjé's, for example), particularly regarding the master's relation to the bodhisattva Mañjuśrī. I have shown that the turning point in these portrayals in fact takes place in a biography of Khedrup. Close analysis of religious histories and Khedrup's own hagiographical literature, with particular attention to his secret biographies by both Chöden Rapjor and Jetsunpa, served to provide me with a new view of Khedrup's own figuration and place among Tsongkhapa's disciples. I was thus able to sort out the history of Khedrup's elevation and shed some light on the history of the Jé Yabsé Sum triumvirate. Through an analysis of Jetsunpa's life and his role in the disappearance of Lodrö Rinchen Sengé's philosophical works, I have suggested some of the reasons and motivations behind the consolidation of Khedrup's elevation, by showing that the suppression of Lodrö Rinchen Sengé's commentaries might have had less to do with logic and doctrinal precision and more with lineage affiliation.

In short, I have attempted to provide a more nuanced vision of the early stages of the Geluk school's development. Most of all I have sought to stress the interrelatedness of philosophical authority and personal authority, which makes it only natural that biography—where personal charisma is created, constructed, and proclaimed to others—should be recognized as a key resource for research into the intellectual history of Tibetan Buddhism.

As we move forward in our study of Tibetan religion we need to take better account of biographical writing as a crucial instrument of sectarian formation. The notion of a *textual community* is particularly useful in underscoring how intellectual and educational practices of the major Geluk monasteries revolve around personal and communal relations. These relations tend to themselves revolve around religious and intellectual practices that have texts—their study, their interpretation, and their transmission—at their center. And yet those activities are as much if not more tied to the status and identity of a key figure whose authority and charisma give those texts meaning and religious significance; a significance that in turn grounds the sectarian identity and continuity of the community. This close relation between communities, texts, and expert interpreters helps us to see that, as much as being about coherence and truth claims, philosophy in Tibetan Buddhism is a social phenomenon—a matrix of practices inextricable from personal status and allegiance.

Appendix A
Chöden Rapjor's *Short Biography of the Omniscient Khedrup*

I bow down with the crown of my head to the unconditionally compassionate Losang Drakpa and his heirs! (26a)

I bow to the feet of the exalted master
arisen as the disciple of Losang Drakpa,
the great unsurpassed scholar
of the infinitely profound teachings!

The following is a brief sketch of the life of the very being who is unparalleled in scholarship of all phenomena, the fearless one, the almighty one who is a great scholar in the five sciences, Gelek Palsangpo, as spoken directly by him. It will discuss his birth, how the presiding deities mentored him, and how he dreamed of the Lord Lama (i.e., Tsongkhapa). However, his birthplace, his education, his family ties, and which places he resided will not be discussed here.

Countless lifetimes ago this master was mentored by Mañjuśrī. Indeed, during his life as Abhayākaragupta, Mañjuśrī appeared to him and told him, "Compose the *Ocean of Sādhanas*," which he composed, among many other texts.

Another time, during his life in India as the paṇḍita Vidyākokila the Elder, Candrakīrti helped free him from the fetters of the extremes.

Yet another time, Candrakīrti said to him, (26b) "In the future, the lord Mañjuśrī will take birth as a *bhikṣu* in the borderlands (i.e., Tibet). At that time, you must take birth there too, carry out his wishes, and spread his teachings wide." If one reflects on this logically, it is certain that the Lord Master (i.e., Tsongkhapa) was an emanation of Mañjuśrī![305]

Khedrup also took birth as Kamalaśīla, a novice monk under Mahākāśyapa.

305. This is the first of eight interpretive asides given by Chöden Rapjor.

Later, the Lord Master (Tsongkhapa) is said to have appeared to Khedrup in a dream and recited the *Kāśyapa Chapter* to him.[306]

Also, during his life as Vidyākokila, Nāgārjuna appeared to him and taught him on some very subtle key points [of Madhyamaka philosophy]. As a result, Khedrup freed himself from the delusion of reification (*dngos 'dzin*). "The Indian siddhas serve Mañjuśrī. For this reason, when I encountered very subtle and difficult key points in the teachings, I entreated him and analyzed the deeper meaning. You too should serve him!"

He then said, "Mañjuśrī is the utmost of supreme deities. By serving him, I achieved the unmistaken realization of dependent origination."

Nāgārjuna also said, "I pray that in the future I may bring about the welfare of beings in the borderland (*mtha' khob*—i.e., Tibet). At that time, (27a) you will be the principal student in my entourage." If we ponder this logically, it is clear that the Lord Master (Tsongkhapa) was an incarnation of Nāgārjuna![307]

Also, Tsongkhapa appeared for the sole purpose of mentoring Khedrup. Indeed, the Victorious Kālacakra told Tsongkhapa, "Sucandra,[308] take the noble kings Puṇḍarīka and Mañjuśrīkīrti into your care. But especially Mañjuśrīkīrti!" This means that Puṇḍarīka is Gyaltsap Jé and that Mañjuśrīkīrti is Khedrup Jé. Furthermore, it is clear that Tsongkhapa appeared for the sole purpose of mentoring Khedrup, and the latter appeared for the sole purpose of upholding [Tsongkhapa's] teachings.[309] Indeed, Āryadeva, Śāntideva, and Buddhapālita once appeared [to Khedrup] and told him, "Mañjuśrī has appeared in the borderlands (Tibet) and is working to spread the teachings. As you especially are a disciple of his, worship him, and whatever he says, regard it as your essential practice to accomplish." If one reflects on this [story] logically, it is clear and honest that Tsongkhapa was an incarnation of Mañjuśrī![310]

In yet another previous life, Mañjuśrī appeared to him and said, "It is a pity! In the borderlands, beings are deluded. (27b) They do not know what is to be accepted or rejected and are ignorant of the fact that they are wan-

306. The Buddha's disciple Mahākāśyapa is the principal interlocutor in the *Kāśyapaparivarta* mentioned here, an early sutra in the Ratnakūṭa collection. Kamalaśīla (*Pad ma'i ngang tshul*) here, then, is not the scholar of that name who came to Tibet at the end of the eighth century.

307. Aside 2.

308. Sucandra (Tib. *Zla ba bzang po*) is one of the Seven Dharmarājas in the Kālacakra *skor* (see Chandra 1999–2005, 640).

309. This interpretive aside is in fact the only one that speaks directly of Khedrup.

310. Aside 4.

derers in cyclic existence. They have thus embarked on the wrong path. In order to set them on the road to liberation and omniscience, I will go there and take the commonly accepted form of a monk. As you are my disciple, you must also come there!" If one reflects on this [story] logically, it is certain that Tsongkhapa was an emanation of Mañjuśrī![311]

In yet another previous life, the great brahman siddha Saraha appeared [to Khedrup] and said, "In the obscured borderlands, the victorious Vajrabhairava has truly appeared and is working for the benefit of sentient beings. Go there and follow him, thereby benefiting sentient beings!" He said, "All of us Indian siddhas have made an oath to keep Vajrabhairava as our secret tutelary deity."

Khedrup then asked, "Is it not contradictory that you worship Bhairava since you are the main siddha of the Cakrasaṃvara tradition?"

[Saraha] said, "Ha ha! Lalitavajra and I are friends and siblings. We have mutual Dharma connections. Generally speaking, we Indian paṇḍitas serve Mañjuśrī, but it is important for mahāsiddhas to serve Bhairava. For if one is without such a tutelary deity, (28a) is it really possible to subdue the practices of the five degenerations, the three poisons, and the four demons?"[312] If one analyzes this logically, then one understands that Tsongkhapa was indeed Mañjuśrī![313]

Further, it is clear that Khedrup is the incarnation of Lord Gö (Khukpa Lhetse). While in Ngari, Atiśa said to him, "You are a man of great intelligence, one of great intelligence who is mentored by Mañjuśrī. Had you been born in India, you would have been equal to Śāntipa."

Tsongkhapa himself told Khedrup, "Because you are the incarnation of Lord Gö, you have become well versed in the Guhyasāmaja tradition of Nāgārjuna."

In a dream, Heruka appeared and said, "Of all the *yig cha* that have been established in both India and Tibet, I have not seen a better one than Tsongkhapa's."

Khedrup then exclaimed, "Well, may I too achieve realizations based on Tsongkhapa's *yig cha*!"

Heruka replied, "There is no difference between Tsongkhapa and myself.

311. Aside 5.

312. The five degenerations (Skt. *kaṣāya*; Tib. *snyigs ma*) are the degenerations of lifespan (*āyu, tshe*), defilements (*kleśa, nyon mongs*), sentient beings (*sattva, sems can*), the cosmic age (*kalpa, dus*), and view (*dṛṣṭi, lta ba*). The three poisons are desire, anger, and ignorance. The four negative influences (*māra, bdud*) are the negative influences of the aggregates (*skandha, phung po*), the defilements (*kleśa, nyon mongs*), the lord of death (*mṛtyu, 'chi bdag*), and the divine son (*devaputra, lha'i bu*).

313. Aside 6.

Those stuck in the Blistering Hells will see Vajradhara as a mere common being."

Khedrup said, "I admit I am unable to see the Master as the Buddha!" Heruka rejoiced, and the Master and Heruka merged into one and gave him instructions on Cakrasaṃvara.

Then Heruka said, "I am presently in my maṇḍala on Mount Wutai.[314] Should one perform my practice on the tenth day of the waxing and waning moons, I will truly come to him. Although it is easier than going to the celestial realms, few actually do this."

On another occasion (28b), a beautiful azure-colored girl came and said, "O son of a noble tradition, compose a maṇḍala visualization and a commentary on the essential Hevajra tantra!" So he composed a commentary on the *Two Segments*[315] complete with maṇḍala visualization, an offering litany (*pūjamālā*), prayers, verses of auspiciousness, and all the other necessary ingredients. Once he had finished this, there were many auspicious omens, such as Hevajra appearing directly to him and conferring on him empowerments and blessings. Hevajra told him, "It is truly wonderful that, having completely realized the key points of the creation and completion phases of my [tantric cycle], you have produced such an eloquent elucidation!"

The night the two lord masters (Tsongkhapa and Khedrup) first met, Khedrup dreamed he was disoriented and dizzily wandering about for a long time on a road, surrounded by a black fog. Then from the east came a circle of one thousand swords at the tips of which blazed one thousand suns. In the center of this circle was a lattice of multicolored light, like a five-hued rainbow. At the center of this lattice sat Orange Mañjuśrī, holding a sword and a text and bedecked with many precious gems. His appearance was that of a young boy with long locks held by a solitary pearl necklace. He was bright and beautiful, and it was nearly impossible to take one's eyes off him. Then he dissolved into Khedrup, the light dispersed all the darkness, (29a) and the lattice spread throughout the ten directions.

The next day, when he met with [Tsongkhapa], he asked about his dream. Tsongkhapa replied, "It is good! You have seen the master and the tutelary deity as undifferentiated. You must be a unique practitioner of tantra, a being like a precious gem. Though the way you saw me as Lord Mañjuśrī is indeed accurate (*don la gnas mod*), other more feeble-minded people see me in an ordinary way. You may be very beneficial to many disciples!" If we look at this

314. Both the Sherig Parkhang and the Kumbum editions of this work mention Mount Wutai. The Zhol edition, however, reads, "I am currently atop the central mountain of my maṇḍala" (475).

315. This is the shorter version of the *Hevajra Tantra*.

[story] logically, we see that Tsongkhapa is, by his own admission, an emanation of Mañjuśrī. What more textual or philosophical proof need be provided to produce certainty?[316]

Tsongkhapa then asked him, "What tutelary deity do you worship?"

Khedrup replied, "Since the master nowadays worships Mañjuśrī as Vādisiṃha (*smra seng*) and Raktayamāri (*gshed dmar*), I too take Vādisiṃha and Raktayamāri as my tutelary deities."

Tsongkhapa then said, "In general, whichever you take as your tutelary deity—Raktayamāri, Kṛṣṇayamāri, or Bhairava—as they are increasingly wrathful aspects of Mañjuśrī, it is thus as though you take him as your lord. Nevertheless, you must understand that my lineage is looked after and blessed by Mañjuśrī. You should therefore also worship Bhairava as your tutelary deity. (29b) As Mañjuśrī showed himself at the moment of both the causal and fruition phases of practice, this must be of great significance. Unfortunately, others do not at all understand its importance. One must know how to practice both peaceful and wrathful aspects of Mañjuśrī combined! No other Indian or Tibetan scholar was given this particularly special, secret, and exclusive essential teaching. But Mañjuśrī saw me alone as the right disciple for this practice and so he directly bestowed it upon me. There are some who do not consider this practice so essential and maintain that it is so profound that it is difficult to bring about the associated experiences. Based on this assumption they strive day and night practicing with blatant disregard for life and limb. I pity them! There are those who do not endeavor to complete the core of the philosophical and tantric paths or follow the supreme and qualified masters who teach it or the tutelary deities who swiftly bestow true ordinary and extraordinary siddhis, but instead hope to achieve the state of Vajradhara based on counterfeit instructions and groundless [practices concerning] the channels, winds, and severance (*gcod*)! I pity them even more! Without you requesting it, I will give you teaching on Vajrabhairava." Tsongkhapa happily gave him teachings, and from then on, Khedrup faithfully performed practice and self-empowerments on this tutelary deity. (30a)

On another occasion, the victorious Vajrabhairava appeared directly to Khedrup and said, "I praise you, Lord, as the utmost of those who strive for the fulfillment of the tantra and *samaya* of the great Vajradhara!"

Another time, the tutelary deity appeared to him and said, "Praise to you who sound the Dharma conch of the great Vajradhara!"

On another occasion, King Indrabhūti appeared to him and said, "This great master, the *vajradhara*, is very skilled and highly realized in the Guhyasāmaja father tantra. You too should place his feet on the crown of your head!"

316. Aside 7.

Another time, the Dharma protector Pañjara Mahākāla[317] appeared to him and said, "Do not abandon Sakya! Stay at Sakya!"

Khedrup thought, "If there is one person here with pure views and conduct, I may stay. However, the tenets of the spiritual forefathers no longer exist, and their descendants have gone too. The temples are filled with women, donkeys, cows, and barmaids. Who could remain in such a sorry place? The mind grasps but the body will not remain. Especially since this life is short, I will stay wherever the Lord Master is." He said, "I offer cakes to you, the ḍākinīs and protectors of Sakya."

He was told, "You must stay where the Dharma is in decline! New things will come. I too remain here not because there is someone here who has pure views and conduct but because I was commanded to do so by the spiritual forefathers. (30b) Otherwise, my retinue and I also follow your teacher (i.e., Tsongkhapa). The Sakyapas definitely don't like you. They gave me ritual cakes and told me to harm Tsongkhapa and his spiritual heirs, particularly you! Unable to resist their entreaties, and remembering the commands of the forefathers, I donned a wrathful countenance and made it as far as Kharak (*kha rag*), but then I retreated."

Another time, Four-Faced Mahākāla came to him and said, "Do the Sakyas no longer merit my protection?" If you choose to leave, I will follow you wherever you go!"

Another time, two Sakya *bhatraputras* (*bha tra spu tra*)[318] and a female subterranean spirit (*bstan ma*) appeared and said, "You keep high company! Who does not know that Tsongkhapa is really Vajrabhairava? Have you forsaken your own lineage to keep high company? I thought 'the Sakyapas have become the kind of people that steal from the poor and give to the rich, and Sachen Kunga Gyaltsen,[319] who was an emanation of Lord Mañjuśrī, is no longer with us. Will you (i.e., Khedrup) uphold [the tradition]?' But you have forsaken it like a stone used for wiping one's ass! Who will uphold the Sakya tradition now?" and they began to cry.

Khedrup Jé replied, "Do not cry, you two.[320] I will uphold the Sakya tenets. I will worship the deity Hevajra and make cake offerings to the lesser and greater Dharma protectors. I will even offer cakes to your local deities!" (31a)

317. Pañjara Mahākāla (*gur mgon*) is a protector deity particular to the Sakya school.

318. I am uncertain what this term refers to. According to Monier-Williams a *bhaṭa* is a serpent demon in Buddhist literature, but it is not clear whether this bears any relation to Chöden Rapjor's reference here.

319. Sakya Paṇḍita Kunga Gyaltsen (1182–1251).

320. Oddly, although three figures are said to be addressing Khedrup, he only responds to two.

Then they said, "What use is a promise that is not backed by action? There is nothing left for us to do." And they returned [to Sakya].

Another time, Sarasvatī appeared to him and said, "I am Mañjuśrī's consort. If you wish to be skilled in poetry, you must worship me!"

Sarasvatī again said, "Much is known to me. You are the most skilled in poetry of those studying under the Lord Master. There are none better than you elsewhere, and though your adversaries are numerous, your pride is not great."

Yet another time, the lord of wisdom, Six-Armed Mahākāla, appeared with his host and, reciting the śāsana mantra, circumambulated and said, "Compose my *yig cha* complete in every detail."

On yet another occasion, the lord of death appeared to him surrounded by eight boys and eight girls and said, "We follow the orders of Yamāntaka to protect Tsongkhapa's teachings. All those who uphold his doctrine must practice and worship me and my entourage."

More specifically, though, Antarasādhana Dharmarāja appeared to him with his retinue of four buffalo-faced beings and said, "I was instructed by the fearsome Yamāntaka to protect the Lama's (i.e., Tsongkhapa's) teachings. Make me your personal deity!" Then Bāhyasādhana Dharmarāja placed his staff in Khedrup's hands. (31b)

In one previous life, the Invincible One (i.e., Maitreya) appeared to Khedrup and said, "In this southern land of Jambudvīpa, a graceful emanation of Mañjuśrī who is like the very heart-essence of the buddhas and bodhisattvas will come to illuminate the Buddha Śākyamuni's doctrine like the sun. Spread his teachings wide!" If one analyzes this [story] logically, it proves that even Maitreya said that Tsongkhapa was an emanation of Mañjuśrī![321]

Yet another time, Four-Faced Mahākāla appeared and said, "The Sakyapas have been entreating me, hurling cakes night and day, to destroy you. The master commands that calamity befalls you. But when I approached you, I thought: 'Alas, here is a practitioner of the Dharma; what will we do if he is no more? If I harm Tsongkhapa and his spiritual heirs, who adhere to the tenets of Nāgārjuna, who will I protect?' So I went back. But take care not to remain here!" Then he left.

On yet another occasion, Four-Faced Mahākāla once again appeared and said that the omniscient Losang Drakpa was a pillar supporting the doctrine, particularly since no one else really understood Nāgārjuna's thought. He said he was somewhat upset, however, because although he was the protector of Nagarjuna's teachings, [Tsongkhapa] offered not a single ritual cake to him.

321. Aside 8.

After having gone off to benefit other beings (i.e., passed away), Tsongkhapa appeared (32a) repeatedly to Khedrup in his dreams and taught him. One day, after a teaching session, Khedrup went inside and thought to himself:

> Sentient beings still fail to accumulate merit, and there are no more true spiritual guides. When one teaches that all compounded things are impermanent, they concentrate on permanence; if one teaches that the nature of all phenomena is empty, they take things as truly existing; if one explains to them that riches are not essentially stable, they strive harder to acquire more; when one teaches them that fame is like an echo, they make it their ultimate goal. In short, as extremely rare as the *uḍumbara* flower[322] are those who are one with the great practitioners, and who have reached the ultimate expression of the 84,000 heaps of Dharma—the very essence of the teachings—and who thus fully embrace the eloquent philosophical and tantric elucidations of the lord *vajradhara* so that there are no longer any delusions whatsoever.
>
> Day and night I earnestly teach the subtle path that can lead one to the state of Vajradhara in this lifetime in accordance with [Tsongkhapa's] quintessential teachings and oral instruction. Still, the unfortunate do not see the feast of nectar that are his teachings. They have abandoned the perfect teacher, who is like Vajradhara, for spiritual friends who are foolish and ignorant, with nothing to say, who teach nothing and learn nothing, ignorant of what is to be maintained and what is to be rejected. (32b) Lacking pure uninterrupted instruction, they get carried away by misguided idiosyncratic fabrications. Devoid of the wisdom of one skilled in the five sciences, they fall into the ravines of perversion. No longer following the gods, they are led down the mistaken path by demons and other hindrances. Abandoning the goal of enlightenment and omniscience, they fall into the three lower realms. They pursue worldly riches in this life and have turned shame and impropriety into qualities. They spend their entire life in the presence of bestial spiritual friends who cultivate ignorance or practice nothing at all, listening to self-praise and disparaging speech—talk of theft and war, vicious gossip, and words of fame and glory, riches and

322. *Ficus glomerata* or *Ficus racemosa*, a non-flowering fig tree. In Tibet, it was said that it only blooms when a supreme Buddha or cakravartin is born in the world.

> fortune, self-praise and vilification of others—while morality and meditative experience rot like a dog or a pig.
>
> If only the knowledge of such things remained unchanged, how wonderful it would be! See how a person with the knowledge of what is to be maintained and what is to be rejected finds his mind at ease! And should honest words be spoken, they touch the hidden weaknesses of charlatans! Should dishonest words be spoken, then they were spoken out of overwhelming loving kindness and compassion, so as to prevent people from following such beings. Think of all the beings who are on the wrong path, who are carried away by the *gongpo*[323] demons of worldly pleasures, who are distracted by fame and glory and do not think about death!

Saddened, (33a) he wept. Then, having prepared good offerings, he prayed earnestly to the Lord Master and cried. Tsongkhapa appeared to him riding on a superb white elephant, apparently sixty years old, with seven limbs and six tusks. Its hairs were white like a glacier, its body covered with a golden mesh, and it was bedecked with a wondrous gold bell and a precious saddle. Tsongkhapa appeared as himself and said, "Do not be upset my son. By remembering your master, some very potent earlier misdeeds will be purified. You will be able to accumulate a great deal of merit. We have a strong teacher-student bond. The great yogi Milarepa, too, composed songs in memory of his teacher. Spread my teachings wide!"

Another time, Khedrup Jé had questions concerning some key points of the teachings, particularly on the generation and completion stages [of the tantric path]. He thought: "Were my teacher still alive, I could ask him, but my teacher is no longer here. I have no other sources of certainty. Oh, how happy I would be if only my master were still alive! Where is my precious master now?" Saddened, he made some good offerings, including a maṇḍala, lamenting, "O precious father, Lama Tsongkhapa!" (33b) Tsongkhapa then appeared to him seated on a golden throne adorned with pearl water lilies and so on and carried by *devaputras*. He proceeded to clarify all the difficult points and gave Khedrup Jé many teachings and empowerments. He also instructed him vastly on the Dharma.

Another time, Khedrup was studying Tsongkhapa's works, principally the two *Stages*.[324] He also studied many other texts. He thought:

323. A *'gong po* is a type of evil spirit, often used to symbolize ego-clinging.

324. The *Great Stages of the Path* (*Lam rim chen mo*) and the *Great Stages of Secret Mantra* (*Ngag rim chen mo*).

> Tsongkhapa taught the three collections of scripture and the four classes of tantra; the philosophical scriptures on implicit and explicit meaning; proper order; the commentaries and autocommentaries by each author; and texts on the way major philosophers analyze the meaning of the teachings through reasoning based on facts. He taught on subtle points such as the illusory body and clear-light samādhi, the precious [union] of bliss and emptiness that result when accomplished yogis tap subtle points on the body; everything, all the way up to the Vinaya section dealing with washing one's mouth before meals. He wrote and taught the very simple yet unexcelled tantra so as to inhibit one from falling into lower realms and put in place the conditions necessary for the salvation of even one sentient being.
>
> Furthermore, he did not simply teach but explained things as one who truly knows how to both teach and listen, so that if contemplated, his teachings were easily assimilated by all, be they of lesser, middling, or greater intellectual capacity. Being thus suited to the intellect of each, everyone's mind was tamed.
>
> In short, (34a) by training the mind according to all the paths—starting with the way in which one honors a spiritual friend—he entered the Mahāyāna, becoming a suitable recipient by means of discipline in holding the vow of entering [the path to becoming a bodhisattva] (*'jug sdom*), by means of the six perfections that bring one to spiritual maturity, and by means of the four ways of gathering disciples which bring others to spiritual maturity.[325] Other than my teacher, the Lord Tsongkhapa, an emanation of Mañjuśrī, there has never been such a one who has completed the core of the Vajrayāna path through which one achieves the state of Vajradhara in one life with one body. Neither in the saintly land of India nor in Tibet—even in the Kadampa and Mahāmudrā traditions.

Reminded of all his teacher's qualities, he developed an immense faith and shed so many tears his clothes were thoroughly soaked. Then, praying fervently, he exclaimed, "O benevolent and precious father! All the beings in the world could not repay your great kindness. O Lord Tsongkhapa!" Tsongkhapa then appeared to him, riding on a ferocious, bejeweled snow lion, and he was just like a bodhisattva. His appearance was that of a young

325. *Bsdu ba bzhi*. The four ways of gathering disciples (*catvāri saṃgrahavastu*): generosity, pleasant speech, skillful conduct, and personal example.

boy, orange-hued, with jewels holding his long hair, and he carried a sword in one hand and a book in the other. He said,

> Do not cry, my son. (34b) I will teach you some Dharma.
>
> In unfortunate times in general, there are many different types of beings. In these times in particular, there are people who do not reflect on death and impermanence or the suffering of the three lower realms. They crave wealth, fame, easy living, and so on. Constantly focusing on their worldly activities for this life, they accomplish nothing for the next.
>
> Look around! Few reflect on what their next life will be. And even if they have some small wish to do so, they spend the next few years accumulating Dharma as if it were provisions, and thinking about battling enemies and protecting loved ones. They fill up their future, always procrastinating. And even if they do make preparations, then too, it is hard to find a true spiritual friend. Even if one teaches them using eloquent teachings and examples, they do not understand. And when they do understand, those who actually renounce the violence of this life and go into solitary retreat and practice day and night are more rare even than the stars that shine during the day.
>
> I pray wholeheartedly to the lamas and meditation deities for you. Accumulate merit and purify your obscurations! Look to the eloquent teachings that bring certainty, and traverse the expanse of the great scriptural traditions! Rest confident, secluded, and remain in single-pointed meditation in the palm of the Buddha's hand! Those who do so are rare. There are still some worthy followers. Help them! (35a) And specifically, spread wide my tantric teachings! We will see each other again in the next life.

Another time, Khedrup is said to have been recalling Tsongkhapa when the thought arose, "I wonder where my master is. If only I could see him again!" Hair on end and distraught, he wept uncontrollably and prayed fervently, saying, "O Lord Master Tsongkhapa, look at me! Witness the conduct of unruly beings! Will your teachings quickly dissolve into themselves like light in space or the [illusory] city of the gandharvas? Will I again be in your presence one day?" Then Tsongkhapa appeared to him riding a fierce tiger and dressed in yogic attire. He was red, with bulging eyes and a prominent nose. In the sky his right hand brandished a radiant sword, while at his heart his left hand held a skullcup overflowing with nectar. His hair was red and in his topknot was stuck a red flag, and he wore ornaments made of bone. He was surrounded by an entourage of eighty fearsome mahāsiddhas, and he smiled brightly, saying:

> Son, do not let your mind sway! I think of nothing but you. Who else do you think of but me? I have not gone off and left you alone. Remember me! (35b) As the *yig cha* that focus on the philosophical and tantric *Stages* are my testament and my proxy, rely on them! In general, the virtue of sentient beings has diminished, and the afflictions are strong. The conclusion to the teachings has been written. Abandon your desire to join the celestial beings!

Yet another time, Khedrup thought, "Maybe it is better that I stay in the presence of sentient beings. If I make offerings and pray to my master, he will appear." So he made good offerings, including an unimaginably [great] golden maṇḍala, and thought, "Where are you, my master? I have some more questions." He prayed long and fervently from the heart, saying, "O father, buddha of the past, present, and future, Mañjuśrī, sole protector of those who are helpless, peerless Vajradhara!"

Tsongkhapa then appeared to him amid a massive fresh white cloud, dressed as he was prior to ordination, and said, "Son, prepare to join me! I will send you an escort."

Khedrup Jé asked him, "O Master, may I come to where you are?"

Tsongkhapa replied, "I have emanations in many places, such as the celestial realms, Tuṣita, and Jambudvīpa. Right now, however, (36a) I am on Mount Wutai in China, instructing 800,000 *vajradhara* monks on Madhyamaka and the *Stages of the Path* in the morning, and on the generation and completion stages of Cakrasaṃvara, Guhyasāmaja, and Vajrabhairava in the evening. Pray long and fervently to come here, and before long we will meet again."

Khedrup then asked, "But your other disciples who pray likewise, will they too be reborn there and experience the nectar of your speech if their prayers are strong?"

Tsongkhapa said, "If they pray to me as being indistinct from Mañjuśrī, then they will be born here. But there is none so worthy of being born here and mentored, none who prays so fervently."

Then Khedrup asked, "What is required to be mentored by you and Mañjuśrī?"

Tsongkhapa answered, "To be nurtured by myself and Mañjuśrī, the special requirements are the development of and dedication to disenchantment [with cyclic existence], altruism, and [maintaining] a pure view."

"Is there anything else?" asked Khedrup.

Tsongkhapa replied, "Create representations of the body, speech, and mind of Mañjuśrī and myself, and pray fervently to us as undifferentiated and inseparable.[326] Do not only pay lip service! Your practice of devotion must flow from certainty about cause and effect, and aided by the four remedial strengths, you must promise to avoid sins and downfalls. With these, you will (36b) no doubt be born here and nurtured."

Khedrup then prayed in the presence of [Tsongkhapa], saying, "O Lord, Master Losang Drakpai Pel! I respectfully entreat you from the bottom of my heart: please grant me your blessing that I may quickly join you wherever you now reside!"

Then, as Khedrup had strongly expressed the wish to go benefit other beings (i.e., to die), the protector of wisdom appeared and impatiently said to him, "If you, caretaker of the doctrine, are no longer, who will uphold the pure teachings of Tsongkhapa?"

There were many other miraculous events. One time, Four-Faced Mahākāla appeared. "If you are no longer, then who will uphold the pure views of Tsongkhapa, which are Nāgārjuna's legacy? There are so many who scandalize them!" he said, turning his face skyward. He continued, "I am Nāgārjuna's Dharma protector; I favor those who uphold the Madhyamaka view; I favor the Guhyasāmaja teachings; there is no difference between Tsongkhapa and Nāgārjuna. Views that misconstrue cause and effect and that do not encourage the upkeep of vows and sacred commitments are misunderstandings."

Then, on the evening of the twentieth day of the year, a host of *devaputras* bearing canopies and banners came to escort [Khedrup away]. He manifested in many different ways. (37a) To some, he appeared to enter Tuṣita riding a white elephant, while to others he appeared to go north to Shambhala. And one saw him riding a snow lion and going to Mount Wutai.

By this merit, may all beings be cared for by you, O pure spiritual guide who teaches the profound and vast Dharmas!

[Colophon]

326. Such supports representing the enlightened body, speech, and mind are, respectively, statues, religious texts, and stūpas.

This brief biographical sketch was composed by the monk Chöden Rapjor, who, having heard many teachings directly from Tsongkhapa and by placing the dust of the master's feet on the crown of his head, practices chiefly detachment from this life and has achieved the realization that all appearances are illusory like the city of the gandharvas. It was compiled at the hermitage of Rendawa known as the "jewel pendant of Mount Bulé" for the purpose of ensuring the spread and longevity of the Buddha's teachings in general and of the teachings of Tsongkhapa and his spiritual heirs in particular. May they guide us, and may all wishes in accord with the Dharma come true!

Virtue!

Appendix B
Jetsun Chökyi Gyaltsen's *Secret Biography of the Omniscient Khedrup*

(1b) Homage to Lord Mañjughoṣa!

With great reverence I prostrate myself at the feet of the venerable lamas
endowed with unconditional great compassion.
I remain inseparable from the lotus heart of the three:
the great treasure of knowledge, the lord *muni*;
his regent, the omniscient Tsongkhapa;
and his chief spiritual heir, Khedrup Gelek Pal.

I bow down to Khedrup, the moon of speech,
who by his immaculate erudition fully completes the circle,
whose moon of unconditional compassion
shines white beams of benefit and well-being in the ten directions.

Despite having already achieved the highest state of buddhahood,
assuming the form of the heir of the second king,
you performed many actions to increase the Victor's teachings.
O Khedrup, Dharma king, please grant me your protection!

Even though this lord's exceedingly great life
cannot be fathomed in this realm of lesser minds,
nevertheless, out of faith and to inspire sincere devotion,
I praise this truly great being.

Our illustrious and pure teacher, the omniscient Khedrup Jé, well known throughout the three lands, was from numerous past lives spiritually mentored by Mañjuśrī. (2a) He studied extensively and meditated on all the principles of the Dharma, thereby completing the realization of the paths and stages (*sa lam*). Both intellect and scriptural authority establish that he was one who had truly achieved the status of Vajradhara.

The life to be explained here is implicitly clear, but as those of weaker intellect still find it hard to comprehend, I will present it briefly from the standpoint of the ordinary disciples.

The basis of this work is the work known as the *Secret Biography* composed by Chöden Rapjor, who studied the path of sūtra and tantra throughout many previous lives, and in whom was thus born both the awakened mind that takes others to be more important than oneself and the special primordial wisdom of blissful emptiness realized through generation and completion. By virtue of this, he was endowed with many great qualities, such as unparalleled insight and the ability to remember his own and others' past lives. It is said that he himself recognized he was the reincarnation of Naktso Lotsāwa.[327] The biography that he composed was, for the most part, directly spoken to him by Khedrup Jé, (2b) though some of the information was acquired through his insight and then written down.

There are two parts to the present biography: first, the stories of Khedrup Jé's previous lives, and second, a brief explanation of the more important aspects of his present life.

How Khedrup Jé Remembered His Previous Lives

Back when the Buddha was in this world, Khedrup Jé took birth as Kamalaśīla, a novice monk of Mahākāśyapa. He was endowed with the great courage for liberation and the intelligence to teach, and he possessed the three *piṭakas*. This is why in this life Tsongkhapa is said to have appeared to him in a dream and recited the *Kāśyapa Chapter*, by which Khedrup Jé achieved special realization. But I will discuss this later.

Furthermore, throughout uncountable earlier lifetimes, Khedrup Jé studied under Lord Mañjuśrī. Indeed, when he took birth as Abhayākaragupta, he studied under the guidance of this lord and thus became an unparalleled scholar of all the teachings. Moreover, he composed the *Ocean of Sādhanas* at Mañjuśrī's request.

At the Ganden hermitage there lived an accomplished practitioner who propitiated Four-Faced Mahākāla, and he was asked by some people who were mistaken about Khedrup's prior incarnation. When the yogi asked the Dharma protector, he was told that Khedrup Jé was the reincarnation of

327. Naktso Lotsāwa Tsultrim Gyal (1011–64).

Abhayākaragupta. (3a) This story, despite having a sound basis, does not in itself prove that Khedrup was the reincarnation of Abhayākaragupta, but this was also affirmed by Khedrup Jé himself.

Nevertheless, Khedrup Jé took birth as the great paṇḍita Vidyākokila. At that time, he studied under the illustrious Candrakīrti and thereby cast off the limiting bonds [of cyclic existence]. Once Candrakīrti said to him, "In the future Lord Mañjuśrī will take birth as a monk among the barbarians (i.e., Tibetans). Take birth at that time too, follow his words, and spread his teachings!"

Another time, Nāgārjuna appeared to him and taught him on some very subtle key points [of Madhyamaka philosophy]. As a result of that, Khedrup Jé freed himself from the delusion of reification. "The Indian siddhas serve Mañjuśrī. For this reason, when I encountered very subtle and difficult key points in the teachings, I prayed to him and analyzed the deeper meaning. You too should serve him!" Nāgārjuna told him, "Mañjuśrī is the utmost of supreme deities. By serving him I achieved the unmistaken realization of dependent origination. I pray that in the future I may bring about the welfare of beings in the borderland. At that time you will be the principal student in my entourage."

Another time, Āryadeva, Śāntideva, and Buddhapālita all appeared to him (3b) and said, "Mañjuśrī will come to the borderland to spread the teachings there. As you are his follower, honor the dust of his feet and accomplish what is essential!"

In sum, it is clear from these stories that Tsongkhapa is of the same mindstream as both Mañjuśrī and Nāgārjuna. These are the oral traditions that maintain that Khedrup Jé incarnated in India as very famous paṇḍitas and upholders of the baskets of scripture.

In yet another lifetime, Mañjuśrī appeared to him and said, "I have compassion for all the beings in the borderlands who do not realize that they lack discernment. Ignorant of the fact that they are wanderers in cyclic existence, they go down the wrong path.[328] In order to establish them in the state of freedom and omniscience, I will take birth there as a fully ordained monk, in accordance with the merit of these feeble-minded beings. Since you are my follower, come there too!" This firmly establishes that Tsongkhapa was an incarnation of Mañjuśrī. One should therefore have tremendous devotion for him.

In another life, the Invincible One (Maitreya) appeared to Khedrup Jé and said, "In order that Śākyamuni's teachings may shine like the sun in this

328. The block print version says *log pas* ("mistaken") while the manuscript version uses *legs pas* ("excellent"). The former seems to make more sense in the present context.

southern land of Jambudvīpa, an incarnation of Mañjuśrī who is as beautiful as the very heart-essence will come. Spread his teachings widely!"

In an earlier lifetime (4a), the great brahman Saraha appeared and said, "Lord Yamāntaka will come to Tibet and will work for the benefit of beings there. Go be of benefit to sentient beings through becoming his disciple and upholding his instructions! Moreover, myself and all the Indian siddhas worship Vajrabhairava as our secret tutelary deity."

To this, Khedrup Jé asked: "You are the main siddha of the Cakrasaṃvara tradition! Is it not contradictory for you to worship Yamāntaka?"

Saraha laughed: "Ha! Ha! Lalitavajra is my spiritual brother and companion. We share mutual spiritual connections. Generally speaking, Indian paṇḍitas and siddhas serve both Mañjuśrī and Yamāntaka. This is very important, for if one does not have such a personal deity, then how is one to subdue the five degenerations and the four negative influences?"[329]

These stories are of the unsurpassable lives of both Tsongkhapa and Khedrup Jé. Keeping them in the center of their hearts, fortunate ones should strive to practice devotion to the Mahāyāna teachers.

This concludes the first part concerning the Dharma king Khedrup Jé's previous lives.

Part 2 is a brief presentation of the important events of Khedrup Jé's present life. This has five sections:

1. The wondrous signs that occurred at the initial encounter between Tsongkhapa and Khedrup Jé. (4b)
2. The deeds he accomplished for the benefit of the Dharma by means of teaching and practice.
3. How it is asserted that the ocean of protectors performed deeds and praised him for having [worked for the benefit of the teachings].
4. The teachings Khedrup Jé received from Tsongkhapa after the latter had gone to Tuṣita [i.e., had passed away].
5. The miraculous omens surrounding Khedrup Jé's departure for the pure realm.

The Wondrous Signs that Occurred at the Initial Encounter

On first meeting Tsongkhapa, it was as like the bodhisattva Sadāprarudita meeting Dharmadgota. At the mere sight of his physical appearance, Khed-

329. See above, note 312.

rup Jé's hairs stood on end. Crying tears of devotion, he sang out a confused expression of reverence. He thought to himself: "This must be my guide to freedom from cyclic existence, the virtuous friend who will protect me from the abyss of the lower vehicle." It is said that due to their latent connection, at that moment Khedrup Jé developed an unexcelled and resolute faith in Tsongkhapa.

That night Khedrup Jé dreamed that he was wandering around for a long time, aimless and dizzy, in a thick darkness. Then from the east appeared a circle of hundreds of swords. At the tip of each sword shone hundreds of suns, and in the middle of the circle was a five-hued rainbow. At the center of the rainbow sat Orange Mañjuśrī, holding a sword and a text and bedecked with unimaginable precious gems. (5a) His appearance was that of a young boy, glowing and incredibly attractive, with strings of pearls in his hair. He smiled and dissolved into Khedrup Jé. The light from the sun circle lifted all his obscurities and suffused the entire world.

The next day, when he again went to meet with Tsongkhapa, Khedrup Jé asked what his dream meant. Tsongkhapa told him: "You saw the teacher and the personal deity as one and the same. You must be a precious practitioner of the tantras! Your vision of me as Mañjuśrī is accurate. Most others see me simply as a regular being. You will greatly benefit many beings in the future!" Then he asked him, "What personal deity do you worship?"

Khedrup Jé replied, "My personal deities are Orange Mañjuśrī and Raktayamāri."

Tsongkhapa said, "In general it is good to worship either Raktayamāri, Kṛṣṇayamāri, or Bhairava as your personal deity. But as each is an increasingly wrathful aspect of Mañjuśrī, it is fitting to make Mañjuśrī your lord. Since my tradition is under the guidance and blessings of Mañjuśrī, we must in any case worship Bhairava as our personal deity, particularly since he has Mañjuśrī's countenance at both the causal and resultant phases [of the fulfilment stage]. Many do not understand how important this is." (5b) Then, without Khedrup Jé formulating the request, Tsongkhapa bestowed on him the Bhairava transmission. From then on Khedrup Jé upheld and unceasingly practiced this tradition.

Gyaltsap Jé, Dulzin, and Khedrup Jé are chief among Tsongkhapa's disciples. Indeed, Lekyi Dorjé,[330] in his predictions concerning Tsongkhapa's lifespan and entourage, said, "You will have three exalted disciples in your entourage and many others on the path of accumulation." These are the three mentioned above. There is no doubt that these three were superior beings.

330. Lhodrak Drupchen Lekyi Dorjé (thirteenth cent.).

Indeed, it is said that in one of Tsongkhapa's dreams he was told, "Sucandra, take the noble king Puṇḍarīka and Mañjuśrīkīrti into your care. But especially Mañjuśrīkīrti!" That Puṇḍarīka is actually Gyaltsap Jé and Mañjuśrīkīrti is actually Khedrup Jé is found in Chöden Rapjor's biography of Khedrup Jé. Gyaltsap Jé is also identified as a manifestation of Avalokiteśvara. As for Khedrup Jé, when he passed away, some of his pure disciples saw him appear to be going to Shambhala. This is very much connected to the story mentioned above. As separate biographies of Gyaltsap Jé and Dulzin are available, one should read them.

This concludes the section concerning Khedrup Jé's meeting with Tsongkhapa.

Khedrup Jé's Actions to Benefit the Buddha's Teachings

The following is a brief description of Khedrup's deeds of teaching and practice. (6a)

Throughout many earlier lifetimes Khedrup Jé trained in the five sciences, and by virtue of having had Mañjuśrī as his teacher, he became unexcelled from a young age in this life in his understanding of the scriptural collections and the four classes of tantras. He became a great champion who, through a garland of speech, brought respite to all the scholars of Tibet.

How so? When Khedrup was sixteen, the paṇḍita Jikmé Drakpa Choklé Namgyal[331] challenged the Sakya monks, saying, "Who among the Sakya monks can best me in debate?" Everyone was reluctant, and none responded to the challenge.

Then the northern lord gathered all the scholars of Ngamring together and said, "As [Choklé Namgyal] is refuting Sakya Paṇḍita, I will give a large reward to anyone who can uproot his blasphemous views like plucking an [unwanted] hair."

331. A.k.a. Bodong Choklé Namgyal (1376–1451). Gene Smith notes (2001, 180) that many Gelukpa writers mistakingly conflated Bodong with Jonang Choklé Namgyal (1306–86), the founder of Ngamring Monastery and a partisan of extrinsic emptiness (*gzhan stong*). The physical proximity of the Bodong and Jonang (Ngamring) seats as well as the overlap in lay patronage may have added to the confusion. Given the mention in this story of Ngamring, a Jonang institution, it is possible that Jetsünpa is also conflating the two figures. Jonang Choklé Namgyal would have been dead for fifteen years by the time the debate is said to have taken place, whereas Bodong would have been twenty-five years old. But Bodong, as Gene notes, was decidedly not a proponent of extrinsic emptiness, and neither was he associated with Ngamring.

Choklé Namgyal sat on a seat amid the assembly of Ngamring scholars, while upon a throne sat the patron surrounded by [Sakya] scholars. First, renowned figures such as Dönsang Gyaltsen (6b) debated against him but were bested within two or three logical consequences (*thal 'gyur*), making them contradict their own tenets.

The patron, feeling very uneasy, scolded them: "Who among you can best his arguments?" They discussed and decided that the Kachupa (*bka' bcu pa*) Gelek Pal (Khedrup Jé) was the greatest scholar among them and would therefore be the best suited for the task.

So the next day they set up a seat as before, and the scholar blocked all [challenges]. This great being (Khedrup Jé) destroyed his opponent's arguments one after the other and made him undermine his own tenets by means of faultless logic. At that point, all Choklé Namgyal could do was to make statements that contradicted the Sautrāntika tenets. The details are clearly related in the debate report (*rtsod yig*).

Another time, during the rainy season retreat, Khedrup Jé engaged and bested Chöjé Yakpa in a debate.[332] It was said that he (Khedrup Jé) had a special deity as his master and that he had studied for many lifetimes, thereby becoming naturally unexcelled [in knowledge].

Later on, Khedrup Jé came to be Tsongkhapa's chief disciple. By the continuous flow of the nectar-like teachings, he attained the state in which his understanding of the scriptural collections and the four classes of tantras were unaffected by delusions. (7a) By his great compassion, through which he loved all sentient beings as though they were his own children, his fortunate followers received many great teachings on the Vinaya. In general he composed many commentaries on the intended meaning of the Buddha's teachings in order that future disciples, too, might understand that the perfect path of Tsongkhapa's teachings is indeed the road upon which previous kings have gone, the difficult path that leads to omniscience and enlightenment. Specifically, however, he composed many treatises on Tsongkhapa's vajra-like teachings, thereby rendering them as clear as a gooseberry (*skyu ru ra*) in the palm of one's hand. In Tibet he spread not only the sūtras and tantras but more specifically the thought of Nāgārjuna as presented by Tsongkhapa—the teachings particular to the Prāsaṅgika school. The minds of fortunate ones are fulfilled by experiencing this unprecedented festival of eloquence, while the tenets of those who brag about their sophistication are nothing but *chang bu* made from sand.[333] The demons of falsehoods are

332. Possibly Yaktön Sangyé Pal (G.yag ston Sangs rgyas dpal, 1350–1414).

333. *Chang bu*, a sort of ritual cake made from dough squeezed in one's fist that is typically

thoroughly quashed, and the Buddha's teachings are made to bloom like a lotus in water.

Around that time, the teacher known as Rongtön Shākya Gyaltsen,[334] (7b) unable to contain in his mind Khedrup Jé's unsurpassed eloquent sayings, took them to stand in contradiction to the views of Candrakīrti, implying that he should take on the burden of defending Tsongkhapa's teachings. However, he could not argue directly with Tsongkhapa or his disciples, and hoping to become famous, said, "Let us debate each other! I will uphold the doctrines of the Sakya school!" While at Nyangtö, Rongtön continuously nagged Khedrup Jé, saying, "Come on, let us debate together." At that time, all the fools at Sakya who were skilled in magical incantations, blind to what are Dharma activities and what are not, spread the rumor out of competitiveness, attachment, and aversion that Tsongkhapa and his followers had criticized the tenets of the Sakya school. They even performed rituals such as casting out ritual cakes to send evil their way. I will discuss this in more detail later.

Also, Ngorpa Kunsangpa,[335] who was treated like Vajradhara himself by the Sakyapas, out of attachment to worldly fame and riches and disregarding his precepts and promises, slandered Tsongkhapa despite having received Vajrayāna teachings from Tsongkhapa himself. The scathing rejoinders to the self-damaging argument texts (*rtsod yig*) composed by the so-called Kunting Gushri geshé of Sakya[336] are clearly given in Tsongkhapa's collected works. (8a) Thus indeed, how could [these Sakyapas] be anything but idiots who have never heard the essence of the teachings?

I heard from my teacher, a most reliable source, that when Tsongkhapa was residing in Nyel, [Gyaltsap] Darma Rinchen, the omniscient one of the age of strife and utmost in debate of all the seven disciples of the great Dharma-eye-possessing Rendawa, who had mastered countless teachings, went to debate against Tsongkhapa. He paid Tsongkhapa much respect and asked him many questions. As Tsongkhapa's responses were vast, Darma Rinchen's heart filled with joy, and he developed an unfaltering faith in Tsongkhapa. Then he bowed down before him and received teachings. That night, although he tried, he could not sleep. He therefore went to do prostrating rounds and to meet with Tsongkhapa. He remained there for a time.

---

offered to the hungry ghosts.

334. This is another name for Rongtön Mawai Sengé.

335. Ngorpa (or Ngorchen) Kunga Sangpo (1382–1456), founder of Evaṃ Chöden.

336. Kunting Gushri Namkha Sangpo (dates unknown).

In response to Chöjé Yakpa's questions regarding provisional and definitive meaning, Tsongkhapa composed the work on distinguishing the two truths also known as the *Essence of Excellent Explanation* (*Drang nges legs bshad snying po*) and had it sent to him at Sakya. This greatly pleased Chöjé Yakpa, and he decided he wanted to receive teachings from Tsongkhapa. But when he was about to leave, his disciples, who had great attachment for him, stopped him, therefore preventing his journey.

Furthermore (8b), the great scholar Choklé Namgyal, too, felt great joy at having seen Tsongkhapa's teachings, and in the many poetic letters addressed to Tsongkhapa, he wrote:

> O excellent Losang, great king of erudite geese,
> who possesses the resounding drum of renown,
> at the feet of the lord of the waves of elegant speech,
> this fearless young bee addresses these words.
>
> The sun of the Dharma falls on the peak of the western mountain.
> The suffering of the bees and of those endowed with knowledge is vast.
> In these times of wandering and the collected activity of evil slanderers,
> the sun of speech, Losang Drakpa, shines brightly.
>
> Though the sky of that which can be known is limitless,
> you are surrounded by scholars like billions of polar mountains.
> In this age when countless rays of the Dharma are sent off,
> you bring rest to the hundreds who are weary and have strayed from the path.

In yet another letter it was written:

> There is no one like you, let alone above you, so skilled at using the beacon of scripture and reason to expel the darkness of misunderstanding of those, such as myself, who impute happiness where there is none. Without this, teaching and practice are [tenuous] like water bubbles.
>
> If one desires an end to constant births, one must know and practice discipline, and one must know the teachings from their roots. If one is disciplined but has not heard many teachings, then practice is like a show for the blind. Those with direct realization

> of both views and behavior sever inflated claims by means of study, contemplation, exposition, and debate.
>
> Without correct views, hindrances cannot be dispelled. Without vast conduct, progress cannot be made. Without the direct realization of the stages of meditation, the end cannot be reached. (9a) Therefore follow the teachings through your body, speech, and mind. For one who seeks liberation, there is no other path but this in either Tibet or the entire world. Scattering the lesser paths in all directions, this system is thus the only one worth holding.

Sasang Lotsāwa Ngawang,[337] too, wrote in a letter addressed to Tsongkhapa:

> In this realm of the Dharma king, the powerful *muni*, your enlightened activity illuminates the Buddha's doctrine. What [is there left for me], a representative of the Buddha, to do? Is Maitreya not jealous? For a long time I wondered whether your mass of qualities and the knowledge that is the great treasure of understanding of Mañjuśrī actually existed. But now my understanding is placed on a palanquin.
>
> You in whom all the volumes of the teachings are united, you fulfill all of a disciple's hopes. Gradually, the great burden of hope is shouldered. How marvelous is the silk of the ocean!

And at the end he wrote:

> I cry to the bodhisattvas every day and implore all spiritual friends that I may be able to see you someday soon.

At that time the discriminating scholars who had heard the teachings of Tsongkhapa and his disciples developed faith in him, and those who had experienced directly the nectar of his speech found themselves to have grown physically stronger. (9b) At that time the only Tibetan teachers who did not pay homage to Tsongkhapa were Karma Könchok Shönu and so on, out of arrogance, and three madmen. Aside from them everyone paid respect to Tsongkhapa. Such was told to me by my teacher.

The great refuge-lord, [Khedrup Gelek] Palsang, the great scholar, came to consider Tsongkhapa's great tradition as amazing, encouraged the compo-

337. The identity of this figure is uncertain.

sition of the *Great Exposition of the Stages of the Path* (*Lam rim chen mo*) for both sūtra and tantra, and put them into practice.

Moreover, Denö Sumpa Shönu Lodrö (i.e., Rendawa), the incarnation of the great paṇḍita Amoghavajra[338] and the utmost of Tsongkhapa's teachers, practiced both the sūtras and tantras in general, but more particularly he practiced the key points of the tenets of the Prāsaṅgika school as they are presented by Tsongkhapa's tradition. There is no need to speak of other conceited persons! However, these are merely further points; now the ordinary meaning will be explained.

As it has been explained, although the great Chöjé Rong(tön) met with Tsongkhapa at Tashi Dokha and the Kyishö palace and on those occasions received teachings from him, he nevertheless maintained that he was the greatest of Sakya geshés. Abandoning whatever Dharmic connections he had [with Tsongkhapa], he appears to have developed his own independent tradition. (10a) On multiple occasions, while Khedrup Jé had gone into retreat with some followers on Mount Dangchen[339] and was giving teachings on the sūtras and tantras, he heard that Chöjé Rongtönpa and his disciples had been invited to Gyalkhar Tsé by Dakpo Rapten.[340] Thinking that now was his chance to debate him, Khedrup Jé cut short his teachings and at once set off to meet him in Palkhor Dechen.

One day, while circumambulating the main living quarters, Khedrup Jé let off a debate cry,[341] and his mind seemed to buzz. At that point a devoted disciple asked him why he had done this, to which he replied, "As I am now analyzing the meaning of the scriptures, a black figure appeared and said, 'Debate me!'" That black figure was Six-Armed Mahākāla. Indeed, this was expressed directly to Jé Draksam by the scholar Chögyal.[342]

Then, Khedrup Jé left Palkhor Dechen with his disciples. While touring at Sangphu Monastery, he remembered a fine reception Rongtön had given him and felt the gesture should be returned. And so Rongtön and his disciples were invited to tea in Khedrup Jé's quarters. But Rongton felt uneasy and

338. Amoghavajra (Don yod rdo rje, 705–74), sixth patriarch of esoteric Buddhism in China.

339. Ri bo mdangs can Monastery (founded in 1412), near Shigatsé.

340. Dakpo Rapten Kunsang Phakpa (1389–1442). Gyalkhar Tsé (Rgyal mkhar rtse) is the expanded name for the fortress at Gyantsé. Kunsang Phakpa founded Palkhor Dechen (Dpal 'khor bde chen) monastery at Gyantsé in 1418.

341. *Thal skad* refers to the opening exclamation in a debate, consisting of the seed syllable *dhiḥ*.

342. Jé Drakpa Samdrup (fifteenth cent.) and Baso Chökyi Gyaltsen (1402–73). The connection between Rongtön and Mahākāla is unclear.

thought, "This must certainly be the time he will debate me." (10b) Flustered, Rongtön could not go for tea and could not return the invitation either.

Khedrup Jé then invited renowned scholars from Nenying and Shalu to assist a debate and requested the presence of a patron in accordance with custom. Seats of equal status were placed between the right and left pillars of Palkhor Dechen for Khedrup Jé and Rongtön, respectively. When tea had been offered and the debate was to be decided upon, Rongtön became quite agitated. He pretended to have no upper garment in his quarters and ran around violently. He repeatedly behaved as though he wanted to go home. This is no exaggeration on our part; it is confirmed by all the students who were present.

As Rongtön had previously challenged Khedrup Jé, shouting, "Let's debate!" he could not refuse to debate him now. When the debate began, Rongtön knew he himself was versed only in the works of Maitreya and not in all the scriptural traditions, and that Khedrup Jé was unparalleled at explaining the intended meaning of the sūtras and tantras. Thus, when Khedrup Jé pressed him harder, Rongtön thought, (11a) "If Khedrup Jé could defeat the likes of Choklé Namgyal when he was but a child, who could best such a scholar? Paṇchen Choklé Namgyal even shut me up! Now is the time to use cunning so as to avoid having to debate him."

He said to Khedrup Jé, "As I have already defeated your teacher Gyaltsap [in debate], it is pointless that I debate you now."

Khedrup replied, "I have seen the debate records that discuss whether or not Gyaltsap was defeated. You did not defeat my teacher! Come now and see if I do not defeat you! Have you forgotten that I defeated Yakpa before the entire Ngamring assembly? You repeatedly sent me messages when I was far away saying 'Debate me! Debate me!' Why can you not debate now [that we are face to face]? Don't be a disgrace! Come debate me right now!" and he turned to prepare the debate grounds.

Then, when the conch shells sounded [calling everyone to] the assembly, Rongtön and his followers became all flustered. He sent a disciple in first, but that idiot disgraced the debate grounds with his harsh language, saying that Khedrup Jé would not debate against Rongtön, and trying to make it unnecessary for the two to confront one another. But Khedrup Jé sent another message [to Rongtön], "Were all your earlier challenges to debate meaningless? If not then call on the scholars to witness the debate and meet me here in the great assembly hall! (11b) We have set up a seat for you there; will you come debate or not? If you truly cannot debate me, then you must cease denigrating Tsongkhapa and the tenets of Nāgārjuna and his disciples! Moreover, you must burn all of the *yig cha* that you have composed!"

[In the end] Rongtön backed down, saying, "You and I will not debate," proving by himself that all of his previous challenges were empty.

Then the seats and other preparations that had been made for the debate in the great assembly hall had to be taken down. Khedrup Jé went there and began letting out debate cries and reciting [texts] from atop the temple. Then he proceeded to give explanations of verses by Choklé Namgyal. This is clearly mentioned in his collected teachings. This embarrassed Rongtön and his followers, and though he tried, he could not do Khedrup Jé any harm.

He therefore once again figured that he would have to use cunning. So when Khedrup Jé was reciting the dedication prayer in the assembly, he sent in a disciple who grabbed what looked like a text and began to compose something of a refutation. At that time the assembly was chanting, and when Khedrup Jé made a gesture to stop reciting, everyone quieted immediately. The filthy-hearted one (i.e., Rongtön's disciple) was nervous and thereby blurted out his response all wrong. (12a) Khedrup Jé then asked, "What is this idiot trying to say?" However, [Rongtön's disciple] was extremely nervous and afraid, and he dropped his response and ran out. It was a real embarrassment.

Thus Rongtön and his followers were very much humbled in Khedrup Jé's presence, and it is said in this region of Tsang that he subsequently took the oath never to speak again. In this region, all those who are conceited and proud are cowed, and it is said that henceforth there is no longer anyone who carelessly shoots his mouth off. This has been an account of Rongtön's defeat by Khedrup Jé.

Khedrup Jé performed countless actions for the Dharma by means of exposition, debate, and composition. And he was also one who had the inconceivable quality of direct realization through meditative experience of the meaning as it is heard. And even during the periods when he was concentrating on teaching his disciples, he was filled with thoughts of serving the Dharma and other beings. At that time he only taught, debated, and wrote about the faults of cyclic existence so as to put his followers on the right path. Whatever wealth he received, he considered pointless and deceptive. (12b)

In his own realization narrative, Khedrup wrote:

> If the unerring continuous flow of nectar
> that is the Buddha's rare and supremely precious advice
> is offered to an unfortunate being with no capacity for trial and
> hardship,
> he refuses it like poison.

But when guided over the waves of the great ocean
of textual traditions in the boat of scriptural and logical explanations,
these immature and small minds
are rid of their fear and listlessness.

I have disseminated explanations of the teachings like grass
and meticulously taught garlands of comprehensive arguments,
yet I see this has little purpose, as karma is eating away at life.
In the end, I must let it all go.[343]

He also wrote:

Though I act like it is a golden age by my elegant speech
and by donning the armor of erudition,
the teachings, which are like an empty butter votive,
are still hidden underground like a treasure by the unfortunate.

Time can never remain still,
and the luster of youth drifts away like the autumn clouds.
Seeing how most beings are unfortunate,
a scholar like me thinks only of the meaning of the Dharma.

In this life, in saṃsāra, my one hope is that I may have the opportunity
to transcend the seduction of attachment and aversion.
To rush into dispute on the few words spoken here,
a scholar like me views such as though it were vomit.[344]

At another point, he wrote:

Now,[345] having guided the mind that comprehends properly
the master's teachings on the unexcelled sūtras and tantras,
a scholar like me only thinks of
putting their meaning into practice. (13a)

343. Khedrup Jé, *Story of My Own Realizations*, 36b.

344. Khedrup Jé, *Story of My Own Realizations*, 37b.

345. Jetsunpa's work slightly misquotes Khedrup, saying "now" (*da ni* or *der ni* in the manuscript version) whereas the Kumbum edition of Khedrup's realization narrative gives "therefore" (*de phyir*).

Cherished is the glimmer from the jewels of a king's crown,
and beloved is the dust from the soles of his feet.
The very dewdrops on the tips of the blades of grass by his toes are
worshipped.
These are of no benefit to a scholar like me.

Wealth and pleasures are like the riches in a dream.
Having seen them as inferior to both intelligence and the Victorious
One,
a scholar like me views them as an offering of soda,
as of no great value.

One cannot be proud of an echo,
and timeless fame is a demonic messenger.
A scholar like me trusts no one
who says otherwise.[346]

In brief, let it be known that this is taken from his realization narrative. When read by the great trailblazers, it reveals to them all the secrets to the Buddha's teachings, but for those whose mind's eye is obscured, it seems whatever they do is left unrealized.

In other words, with regard to the verses on personal gain and honor, with one vision Khedrup Jé thinks of [safeguarding] both the teachings and other beings, thereby accomplishing uncountable acts for the teachings by means of explanation, debate, and composition. This is the most important aspect of this great being's life. Moreover, by virtue of having practiced pure conduct throughout numerous lifetimes, in the present life he guarded his vows of [monastic] discipline. (13b) Because of this, he became the crown jewel of all those who bear the saffron victory banner (i.e., the Gelukpas). And what's more, for a being like him, the clouds of compassion move spontaneously and tears fall irrepressibly when he so much as ponders the suffering of all sentient beings.

The sons of buddhas past, present, and future acclaim him greatly as one worthy of praise who has the unexcelled quality of true realization. I will describe below the ways in which he was acclaimed for his great compassion. In brief, this great being was always crying in accordance with the noble Dharma, and he greatly pleased Tsongkhapa with the offering of his spiritual attainment. By the uninterrupted flow of his nectar-like speech, he achieved

346. Khedrup Jé, *Story of My Own Realizations*, 38a.

the realizations particular to the paths and stages. Indeed, one night when he had very subtle doubts concerning key theories, he prayed eagerly to Tsongkhapa. That night Tsongkhapa appeared to him in a dream and recited the *Kāśyapa Chapter* once. From that point the illusion that takes things as having true existence was uprooted, and he attained the realization from direct experience of the true nature of phenomena. It is said that Gendun Drup too saw Tsongkhapa in a dream in which he recited the *Kāśyapa Chapter*. At that moment, removing the stains of delusional views, he prayed for a direct experience of emptiness. (14a)

Furthermore, many deities and mahāsiddhas appeared to Khedrup Jé, heaping unfathomable blessings on him. One time, Heruka appeared to him and said, "Of all the *yig cha* that have been established in both India and Tibet, I have not seen a better one than Tsongkhapa's."

Khedrup replied, "Well, then, may I too achieve realizations based on Tsongkhapa's *yig cha*!"

Heruka rejoiced, and the two merged into one, and Heruka gave him Cakrasaṃvara instruction. Then he said, "You are now on the central mountain of my maṇḍala. If you keep your promise, then I will truly come to you on the tenth day of both the waxing and waning moon. Although it is not difficult to travel in space, few do it."

Another time, a beautiful azure lady appeared to him and said, "O son of a noble tradition, compose a commentary on the essential Hevajra tantra!" Because of this, when he composed his work entitled *Commentary on the Two Segments*, complete with maṇḍala visualizations, offering chants, and auspicious supplications, Hevajra appeared directly to him and gave him unbelievable empowerments and blessings. Hevajra said to him, "Having utterly realized the generation and completion phases of my practice, you have attained the path. It is wonderful!"

Another time, the goddess Sarasvatī appeared to him and said, "I am Mañjuśrī's consort. If you wish to be skilled in poetry, then you must venerate me! (14b) Many claim to know me, but under Tsongkhapa none is more skilled in poetry and grammar than you. But do not be vain about it, as vanity is your enemy!"

On yet another occasion, Lord Indrabhūti appeared to him and said, "This great master, the vajra bearer (i.e., Tsongkhapa), is very skilled in Guhyasāmaja and is also highly realized. Go be his disciple and place his feet on the crown of your head!"

There is a very important connection here, as Tsongkhapa told Khedrup Jé directly, "As you are an incarnation of Lord Gö (Khukpa Letsé), you are naturally very skilled in the noble system of Guhyasamāja." Thus let it be known that the life stories of Lord Gö are also the life stories of Khedrup Jé! But Khedrup Jé was also said to be the reincarnation of Khedrup Lhawang Lodrö.[347] Indeed, as he clearly and perfectly recalled his previous lives when he was but a youngster, he was truly the reincarnation of Khedrup Lhawang Lodrö. To be sure, Lhawang Lo was unparalleled in his understanding of the meaning of the vast textual traditions but was also a great yogic master blessed by many deities. Also, when Khedrup was in Dölchung,[348] a war broke out and he could not go anywhere. He was stuck there for some time and at one point prayed to Tārā. She appeared to him in the sky and said, (15a) "O noble one, come up here!" and his arms carried him up into the sky and took him to wherever he desired to go.

Khedrup took various different births in Tibet, but the main one was as the omniscient Gelek Palsang. Indeed, in that life he performed incalculable actions on behalf of Tsongkhapa's teachings. Furthermore, when he was in India [in a previous life], the gods, paṇḍitas, and siddhas all repeatedly entreated him to take birth in Tibet as the caretaker of the spread of Tsongkhapa's doctrine. He therefore took birth in Tibet a few times [before this life]. This was obviously in order to help Tsongkhapa's doctrine to fully mature.

Although these have been tales of Khedrup Jé's past lives as an addendum, I have focused mainly on his past lives in India. In brief, for many lifetimes the gods and other deities taught and blessed Khedrup Jé. As he had the direct realization of emptiness—the true nature of phenomena—he won the battle against misery and suffering. He had unceasing compassion for all, holding others dearer than himself, and because of this he loved all beings, considering them to be like his own children. (15b)

This great yogi, Gelek Palsang, by virtue of having attained the state of one who is supremely victorious in battle against the afflictions, could not be harmed by evil external elements. Indeed, when he was the abbot of Palkhor Dechen, at the end of a summer session, he went into the mountains accompanied by a group of disciples for a holiday. Having stopped for tea in a meadow, they were all seated together in a line when suddenly the sky became clouded, a heavy rain began to fall, and a lightning bolt abruptly struck nearby. Khedrup Jé lifted his finger into the air, and the rain immediately ceased. This was witnessed by all those sitting with him, and I myself heard it directly from Jamyang Kunga Delek Rinchen.

Another time, while Khedrup Jé was overseeing renovations at Baso

347. Dharmakīrti's disciple Devendramati (ca. 630–90).

348. Dol po lu chung Valley in Lho brag.

Lhundrup Dechen, a volatile *rgyal po* spirit entered the shrine hall. Khedrup Jé therefore made thread-crosses and other such wards and performed a profound exorcism ritual. (16a) Everyone around the temple, humans and animals alike, suddenly fell unconscious. This is one of the more minor events of his life and is only mentioned as a point of interest.

In brief, Khedrup Jé had complete and direct realization of the generation and completion stages of the tantras, as was mentioned, and as the Dharma protectors followed his advice as though they were his servants, the elemental spirits could not harm him. Merely seeing him physically or paying homage to his clothing, which are supports for blessings, one would surely be automatically liberated. The way Khedrup Jé mastered the particular realization of the generation and completion stages as explained in the tantric treatises has already been signaled for those of a higher intellect. However, this must remain secret to all those who are not true practitioners of the tantras.

How the Ocean of Worldly Protectors are Believed to Have Performed Deeds and Praised Khedrup Jé

I have heard it said that while Khedrup Jé was accomplishing deeds for the welfare of the Victorious One's teachings by means of teaching and practice, he was greatly extolled not only by the gods, the nāgas, and the yakṣas who protect virtue, but also by special personal deities and Dharma protectors. (16b) Indeed, one time Yamāntaka himself appeared to him and said, "Praise to you, O excellent one, who have fully completed the body of the path of Vajradhara!" This is most certainly a true story.

Another time, a personal deity appeared to him and said, "Praise to you who blows the great Dharma trumpets of Vajradhara!"

On another occasion, Six-Armed Mahākāla appeared with his host and, reciting the śāsana (practice) mantra while circumambulating, said, "You will correct my *yig cha*, making it complete in every last detail."[349]

On yet another occasion, Lord Yama appeared to him along with his entourage of eight sons and eight daughters. They said, "We follow Yama's orders. As he is the protector of Tsongkhapa's teachings, all those who uphold his doctrine must practice and worship him and his entourage."

349. *Khyod kyis nga'i yig cha las kha tshar dang bcas 'chos.* Jetsunpa differs by his use of the word *'chos* ("correct" or "improve") rather than *rtsom* ("compose"), as was the case with Chöden Rapjor (see appendix A).

More specifically, though, the Antarasādhana Dharmarāja appeared to him with his retinue of four buffalo-faced beings and said, "I was instructed by Yama the terrible to protect the Lama's (i.e., Tsongkhapa's) teachings. Make me your personal deity!" Then Bāhyasādhana Dharmarāja placed his hand on Khedrup Jé's head.

Although Khedrup Jé had mastered all the tenets in his studies with the Sakyapas, he became a true Mahāyāna spiritual friend under Tsongkhapa, the second Buddha, and took birth in order to expound Tsongkhapa's pure teachings in this world. (17a) Thus Khedrup Jé followed Tsongkhapa just like Ānanda followed the Buddha.

While he was serving the teachings through explanation, debate, and composition, some arrogant people claiming to be Sakyapas became upset and, out of jealousy and without reason, removing their shoes at the mere sound of water,[350] spread the rumor all over that Khedrup Jé had criticized the Sakya tenets. But none of these arrogant persons could ever measure himself in debate against this great being. They cast ritual cakes and performed all sorts of black magic. All those skilled in magical incantations were brought together at Sakya, and they repeatedly threw ritual cakes in whatever direction Khedrup Jé was staying. By that time Khedrup Jé had already taken Pañjara Mahākāla and Four-Faced Mahākāla as his main Dharma protectors. Also, as there were signs that a Six-Armed Mahākāla hex-protection needed to be done, it was. According to a reliable source, it was effective.

Later, when Khedrup Jé went to Ganden [i.e., ascended the throne], the Sakyas once again sent black magic to Ganden. This utterly disgusted the holy one, but aside from opening the doorway to their own rebirth in the lower realms, how could they possibly have harmed this great yogi? (17b) During that time, Khedrup Jé told the monks in the assembly: "The Sakyapas have for one year been throwing ritual cakes here toward Ganden, but in that time they have been unable to harm even one young monk. This is my doing!" Indeed, there were absolutely no signs that their magic was at all effective. It appears, furthermore, that among other signs, cracks appeared on the main temple at Sakya as a result of the counter hex.[351] It is [the way of the] Dharma that powerless aspirations should backfire.

350. *Chu'i sgra kho nas lham 'bud pa'i rtsom pa*. In other words, acting precipitously before fully understanding a situation, such as while walking down a path, one removes one's shoes at the mere sound of water before even coming to a stream.

351. The manuscript uses the term *sdib pa* ("to stammer"), whereas the blockprint gives the term *rdib pa* ("to crack or crumble"). The latter makes more sense, given that the author is referring to the temple itself.

Around that time, Ngorpa Kunsang was the bearer of the Sakya tenets, and he sent a letter to both Rongtön and Chöjé Sönam Lo[drö][352] saying, "Since Khedrup Jé has criticized the Sakya tenets, I will debate him on Mantra! Rongtön, you are known for debating Prajñāpāramitā, and Sönam Lo for debating Pramāṇa. It is not good that you were ineffective [against him]!"

Then, relying on the Sakya tenets, Ngorpa composed a critique of the views of Tsongkhapa and his followers and had it delivered to Khedrup Jé. In this text, he misunderstood the teachings, writing that, "Earth, water, fire, and wind are the *five* types of form"! Furthermore, having misunderstood Jñānagarbha's discussion of the two truths, he [misquoted the texts] saying, (18a) "According to the self-commentary by Śāntarakṣita on the two truths," and so on. In short, he did not even understand the general language of the texts and succeeded only in shaming himself. Nevertheless, to refute this nonsensical argument, Khedrup Jé composed a rejoinder entitled *Wheel of Thunderbolts* and disproved all his erroneous views.[353]

At that time, the Dharma protector Pañjara Mahākāla appeared to him and said, "Do not abandon Sakya! Stay at Sakya!"

Khedrup Jé thought, "If there is one person here with pure views and conduct, I will stay! However, the tenets of the spiritual forefathers no longer exist, and their descendants have gone too. The temples are filled with women, donkeys, cows, and barmaids. Who could remain in such a sorry place? The mind grasps but the body will not stay. Especially since this life is short, I will stay wherever Tsongkhapa is."

He was told, "You offer cakes to the ḍākinīs and protectors of Sakya. You must stay where the Dharma is in decline! New things will come. I too do not remain here because there is someone here who has pure views and conduct; I remain because I was commanded to do so by the spiritual forefathers. Otherwise my retinue and I also follow your teacher (i.e., Tsongkhapa). The Sakyapas definitely don't like you, and they offered me cakes and told me to harm Tsongkhapa and his followers. Their request was not enough [to make me do it], but I remembered the instructions of the forefathers [to serve them]. (18b) So with a wrathful countenance I made it as far as Kharak but then returned [to Sakya]."

Another time, Four-Faced Mahākāla appeared and said, "The Sakyapas have been entreating me night and day to destroy you, but I will not. I heard

352. Possibly Khewang Sönam Lodrö.

353. The full title of this text is *Phyin ci log gi gtam gyi sbyor ba la zhugs pa'i smra ba ngan pa rnam par 'thag pa'i bstan bcos gnam lcags 'khor lo*. See Khedrup Jé et al., *Compendium of Polemical Literature*, 1–69.

the lamas' commands, but when I got near you I thought: 'What will we do if this practitioner of the Dharma is no more? If I harm someone who is a disciple of Tsongkhapa and who adheres to the tenets of Nāgārjuna, who will protect them?' So I went back. Because I did not do their bidding, I was no longer welcome [at Sakya], so I left."

On yet another occasion, Four-Faced Mahākāla appeared to Khedrup Jé and said, "The omniscient Tsongkhapa was a supporting pillar of the doctrine, especially as no one else really understood Nāgārjuna's thought. My request to give me cakes has gone unheeded. I am so upset!" There appears to be a story related to this one. Once, when Shartsé Rinchen Gyaltsen was in Tsongkhapa's presence, Tsongkhapa said to him, "Four-Faced Mahākāla just appeared to me boastfully demanding that I offer him cakes. (19a) Go inside. If there is food set aside for the gods, make it into a substitute for the cake and offer it to him. Go now!" He thereby did not offer the cake himself, instead entrusting the task to Rinchen Gyaltsen. There was a specific reason for this, but I will not get into it here. I heard this story directly from Jamyang Kunga Delek [Rinchen].

Tsongkhapa instructed his followers to worship both Six-Armed Mahākāla and Damchen Chögyal (i.e., Yamāntaka), and these two were told to properly look after those followers. These two are thus the main guardians of the teachings of this tradition (i.e., Geluk). However, Tsongkhapa did give instructions on Nāgārjuna's Guhyasāmaja tradition. Since Tsongkhapa was without a doubt the incarnation of Nāgārjuna, he automatically was part of this [divine] entourage too.

It is just as I explained earlier, how Tsongkhapa appeared in his physical state according to the needs and hopes of his older and closest disciples such as Khedrup Jé. Later on Gendun Drup too beheld an apparition of Four-Faced Mahākāla moving around in the sky and saying, "An upholder of the doctrine such as yourself must worship and practice the Dharma protectors," and so on. It is said that from the time of his birth, he was already under the protection of Four-Faced Mahākāla. (19b) It is said that Dulzin Lodrö Bepa[354] was also protected by this deity from the time he was born. Indeed, as it says in the biography composed in verse by Jé Rokchö,[355] "Four-Faced Mahākāla showed many signs of protecting him since his childhood." And in the words of my illustrious teacher, Kunga Delek Rinchen: "I automatically had the protection of Four-Faced Mahākāla, even though I did not particularly do the practice." This teacher also became a great repository for the

354. A.k.a. Dülkarwa (*'dul dkar ba*, 1400–1475), a student of Tsongkhapa.

355. Identity unknown.

Guhyasāmaja tradition of Nāgārjuna, and there is no question that he had the power that comes from the transmission of perfect theories. There are many other stories I will not include here.

So as I said, Tsongkhapa's followers naturally acquired the protection of Four-Faced Mahākāla, but in accordance with his instructions, they keep both Six-Armed Mahākāla and Damchen Chögyal as their main personal deities. My teacher said that they are greatly blessed by them, though many have fallen short of the accumulation [of the mantra].

How could this lama (i.e., Khedrup Jé) willfully criticize the Sakya tenets? (20a) As it was said, "When elucidating to the world the exact intended meaning of Tsongkhapa's eloquent teachings, the commentaries by the two utmost charioteers among the six ornaments,[356] the three collections of scripture, the four classes of tantra, there is no wrong in taking apart other systems." He thus prevented blindness on various issues that were due to mistakes within the Sakya tenets. The problem is with their tenets; how could Khedrup Jé be faulted for this? Let those endowed with intelligence think this over.

Another time, two Sakya *putras*[357] and a female subterranean spirit appeared to Khedrup Jé and said, "You keep high company! Who does not know that Tsongkhapa is really Vajrabhairava? Did you not forsake your own lineage [in order to] keep high company? I thought, 'the Sakyapa's have become the kind of people that steal from the poor and give to the rich, and Sachen Kunga Gyaltsen, who was an incarnation of Lord Mañjuśrī, is no longer with us. Will you (i.e., Khedrup Jé) uphold [the tradition]?' But you have forsaken it like a stone used for wiping one's ass! Who will uphold the Sakya tradition now?" and they began to cry.

Khedrup Jé replied, "Do not cry, you two. I will uphold the Sakya tradition. I will worship the deity Hevajra and will make cake offerings to the lesser and greater Dharma protectors. I will even offer cakes to your local deities."

Then they said, "As you did not do this before, your promise is worthless to us. There is nothing left for us to do." And they left. (20b)

This has been the account of how it is believed that the Dharma protector gods and deities praised and performed deeds in honor of Khedrup Jé.

356. The six ornaments *(rgyan drug)* are Nāgārjuna, Asaṅga, Āryadeva, Vasubandhu, Dignāga, and Dharmakīrti. The two utmost charioteers are Nāgārjuna and Asaṅga.

357. The context of the story implies that this is a type of spirit. Chöden Rapjor gives *bha tra spu tra*. See note 318 above.

The Teachings Khedrup Jé Received from Tsongkhapa After the Latter had Gone to Tuṣita

The praiseworthy regent who had great faith in Tsongkhapa, the great Khedrup Jé, was one who could make the buddha realms tremble. Thus, after passing away, Tsongkhapa appeared both in his dreams and in person and gave him many teachings. On one occasion, following a teaching session, Khedrup Jé went back to his quarters and thought:

> Sentient beings still fail to accumulate merit, and there are no more true spiritual guides. When one teaches that all compounded things are impermanent, they concentrate on permanence; if one teaches that the nature of all phenomena is empty, they take things as truly existing; if one explains to them that wealth is not essentially stable, they strive harder to acquire more. If one teaches them that fame is like an echo, they make it their ultimate goal. In short, rarer even than the *uḍumbara* (21a) flower are those who are one with the great practitioners, and who have reached the ultimate expression of the 84,000 heaps of Dharma—the very essence of the teachings—and who thus fully embrace the eloquent philosophical and tantric elucidations of the lord *vajradhara* so that there are no longer any delusions whatsoever.
>
> Day and night I earnestly teach the subtle path that leads to the state of Vajradhara in this lifetime in accordance with [Tsongkhapa's] quintessential teachings and oral instruction. Still, the unfortunate do not taste the nectar of his teachings. They have abandoned the perfect teacher for spiritual friends who are foolish and ignorant, with nothing to say, who teach nothing and learn nothing, ignorant of what is to be maintained and what is to be rejected. Lacking pure uninterrupted instruction, they get carried away by misguided idiosyncratic fabrications. Devoid of the wisdom of one skilled in the five sciences, they fall into the ravines of wrong views. No longer following the gods, they are led down the mistaken path by demons. Abandoning the goal of enlightenment and omniscience, they fall into the three lower realms. They pursue worldly riches in this life and have turned shame and impropriety into qualities. They spend their entire life in the presence of bad spiritual friends who cultivate ignorance or practice nothing at all, listening to self-praise and disparaging speech—talk of theft and war, vicious gossip, and words of fame and glory, riches and

> fortune, self-praise and vilification of others—while morality and meditative experience play like a dog or a pig.
>
> If only the knowledge of such things remained unchanged, how wonderful it would be! See how a person with the knowledge of what is to be maintained and what is to be rejected finds his mind at ease! (21b) And should honest words be spoken, they touch the hidden weaknesses of charlatans! Should dishonest words be spoken, then they were spoken out of overwhelming loving kindness and compassion, so as to prevent people from following such beings. Think of all the beings who are on the wrong path, who are carried away by the *gongpo* demons of worldly pleasures, who are distracted by fame and glory and do not think about death!

Khedrup Jé shed tears of sadness. Then he made good offerings and prayed earnestly to Tsongkhapa and cried. Tsongkhapa appeared to him, riding on an elephant white like a glacier, with six tusks and eight limbs and appearently sixty years old.[358] Its body was covered with a golden mesh, and it was bedecked with a wondrous gold bell and a precious saddle. Tsongkhapa appeared as his normal self and said, "Do not be upset, my son. By remembering your master, some very potent earlier misdeeds will be purified. You will be able to accumulate a great deal of merit. We have a strong teacher-student bond. The great yogi Milarepa, too, composed songs in memory of his teacher. Spread my teachings wide!"

Another time, Khedrup Jé had questions concerning some key points of the teachings, particularly on the generation and completion stages [of the tantric path]. He thought: "Were my teacher still alive, I could ask him, but my teacher is no longer here. (22a) I have no other sources of certainty. Oh how happy I would be if only my master were still alive!" Saddened, he made some good offerings, including a maṇḍala, and then prayed, lamenting, "O precious father, Lama Tsongkhapa." Then he cried. Tsongkhapa then appeared, seated on a golden throne adorned with pearl water lilies and carried by gods and goddesses. He proceeded to clarify all the difficult points and gave Khedrup Jé many teachings and empowerments. He also instructed him vastly on the Dharma.

On yet another occasion, Khedrup Jé repeatedly studied the teachings of Tsongkhapa that focused on the two *Stages* texts. Khedrup Jé thought,

358. In the manuscript version of this text, the elephant's age is sixteen.

> Tsongkhapa taught the proper order of the esoteric and exoteric teachings along with their commentaries, such as the three collections of scripture and the four classes of tantra; the explanations of each particular author; the methods used by the major philosophers for analyzing the meaning of the teachings by means of reasoning through fact. He taught on the illusory body and clear-light samādhi and so on that result when accomplished yogis tap the subtle points on the body. He taught [all stages] of the *vinaya*, from washing one's mouth before meals right up to the sprinkling of water, and everything up to the extremely unelaborated unsurpassable tantra, reuniting the conditions necessary for even one single being to achieve enlightenment. (22b)
>
> Not only did he simply teach these things but explained it as one who knows how to teach would to one who knows how to listen. And if contemplated, then it is possible for anyone [to understand], be they of lesser, middling, or greater intellectual capacity. As they are suited to everyone's intellect, one's mind is tamed.
>
> In short, there has been no one either in the saintly land of India or in Tibet, in either the Kadam or the Mahāmudrā traditions, like my teacher the Lord Tsongkhapa, an emanation of Mañjuśrī who taught [everything] from the means by which one attends to a spiritual friend, to the method by which one purifies oneself and becomes a perfect vessel, [to topics] such as the complete body of the path of the means by which to enter into the Vajrayāna, which is the profound path by which to realize the state of Vajradhara in one lifetime and one body.

Reminded of all his teacher's qualities, Khedrup Jé developed an immense faith and shed so many tears his clothes were thoroughly soaked. Then, praying fervently, he exclaimed, "O benevolent and precious father! All the beings in the world could not repay your great kindness. O Lord Tsongkhapa!" Tsongkhapa then appeared to him: young, orange-hued, bejeweled, and carrying a sword in one hand and a book in the other. He was riding a snow lion and was just like a bodhisattva. He said to him,

> Do not cry, my son. I will explain some Dharma.
>
> In unfortunate times in general, there are many different types of beings. In these times in particular, there are people who do not reflect on death and impermanence or on the suffering of the three lower realms. (23a) They crave wealth, fame, easy living, and

> so on. Constantly focusing on their worldly activities for this life, they accomplish nothing for the next.
>
> Look around! Few reflect on what their next life will be. And even if they have some small wish to do so, they spend the next few years accumulating Dharma as if it were provisions and thinking about battling enemies and protecting loved ones. They fill up their future, always procrastinating. And even if they do make preparations, then too, it is hard to find a true spiritual friend. Even if one teaches them using eloquent teachings and examples, they do not understand. And when they do understand, those who actually renounce the violence of this life and go into solitary retreat and practice day and night are more rare even than the stars that shine during the day.
>
> I pray wholeheartedly to the lamas and meditation deities for you. Accumulate merit and purify your obscurations! Look to the eloquent teachings that bring certainty, and traverse the expanse of the great scriptural traditions! Rest confident, secluded, and remain in single-pointed meditation in the palm of the Buddha's hand! Those who do so are rare. There are still some worthy followers. Help them! And specifically, spread wide my tantric teachings! We will see each other again in the next life.

Thus, even though Tsongkhapa had passed on (23b), he nevertheless appeared to Khedrup Jé as Mañjuśrī and gave him teachings.

Another time, Khedrup Jé cried, thinking, "Where is my master? When will I see him again?" Distraught, he began to tremble. His hair on end, he prayed saying, "Tsongkhapa, look at me! Witness the conduct of unruly beings! Your teachings are dissolving quickly like the light in space and the illusory city of the gandharvas. When may I come join you?"

Then Tsongkhapa appeared to him riding a fierce tiger and dressed as a yogi. He was red with bulging eyes and a prominent nose. In the sky his right hand brandished a radiant sword, while at his heart his left hand held a skullcup overflowing with nectar. His hair was red and in his topknot was stuck a blue[359] flag, and he wore ornaments made of bone. He was surrounded by an entourage of eighty fearsome mahāsiddhas, and he smiled brightly, saying:

> Son, do not let your mind sway! I think of nothing but you. Who else do you think of but me? I have not gone off and left you alone.

359. In Chöden Rapjor's version, the flag is red.

> Remember me! As my philosophical and tantric *yig cha* are my testament and my proxy, rely on them! In general, the virtue of sentient beings has diminished, and the afflictions are strong. The conclusion to the teachings has been written. (24a) Abandon your desire to join the celestial beings!

Yet another time, Khedrup thought, "Maybe it is better that I stay in the presence of sentient beings. If I make offerings and pray to my master, he will appear." So he made good offerings, including an unimaginably [great] golden maṇḍala, and thought, "Where are you, my master? I have some more questions." He prayed long and fervently from the heart, saying, "O father, buddha of the past, present, and future, sole protector of those who are helpless, peerless Mañjuśrī, Vajradhara!"

Tsongkhapa then appeared to him amid a white cloud, dressed as he was prior to ordination, and said, "Son, prepare immediately to join me! I will send you an escort."

Khedrup Jé asked him, "O Master, may I come to where you are?"

Tsongkhapa replied, "I have emanations in many places, such as the celestial realms, Tuṣita, and Jambudvīpa. Right now, however, I am on Mount Wutai in China, instructing 800,000 *vajradhara* monks on Madhyamaka and the *Stages of the Path* in the morning, and on the generation and completion stages of Cakrasaṃvara, Guhyasāmaja, and Vajrabhairava in the evening. Pray long and fervently to come here, and before long we will meet again."

Khedrup then asked, "But your other disciples who pray likewise, (24b) will they too be reborn there and experience the nectar of your speech if their prayers are strong?"

Tsongkhapa said, "If they pray to me as being indistinct from Mañjuśrī, then they will be born here. But there is none so worthy of being born here and mentored, none who prays so fervently."

Then Khedrup asked, "What is required to be mentored by you and Mañjuśrī?"

Tsongkhapa answered, "To be nurtured by myself and Mañjuśrī, the special requirements are the development of and dedication to disenchantment [with cyclic existence], altruism, and [maintaining] a pure view."

"Is there anything else?" asked Khedrup.

Tsongkhapa replied, "Create representations of the body, speech, and mind of Mañjuśrī and myself, and pray fervently to us as undifferentiated and inseparable. Do not only pay lip service! Your practice of devotion must flow from certainty about cause and effect, and aided by the four remedial strengths, you must promise to avoid sins and downfalls. With these, you will no doubt be born here and nurtured."

Khedrup then prayed in the presence of [Tsongkhapa], saying, "O Lord, Master Losang Drakpai Pal! I respectfully entreat you from the bottom of my heart: please grant me your blessing that I may quickly join you wherever you now reside!"

This concludes the section on how Khedrup Jé received teachings from Tsongkhapa, who appeared to him even after Tsongkhapa's departure for Tuṣita.

The Miraculous Omens Surrounding Khedrup Jé's Departure for the Pure Realm

(25a) Khedrup Jé himself had already worked for the welfare of the majority of followers of the *vinaya*, and he himself had the motivation to join Tsongkhapa. Indeed, when he demonstrated the means by which one is liberated, on one occasion Six-Armed Mahākāla appeared and said, "If you are no longer the caretaker of Tsongkhapa's teachings, who will be?" Mahākāla then became impatient.

Another time, [Damchen] Chögyal appeared along with his retinue and said, "We were ordered by Yamāntaka to look after Tsongkhapa's instructions. Tsongkhapa has sent us to escort you [to him]."

Yet another time Four-Faced Mahākāla appeared. "If you are no longer, then who will uphold the pure views of Tsongkhapa, which are Nāgārjuna's legacy? There are so many who scandalize them!" he said, turning his face skyward. He continued, "I am Nāgārjuna's Dharma protector; I favor the Madhyamaka view; I favor the Guhyasāmaja teachings; there is no difference between Tsongkhapa and Nāgārjuna. Views that misconstrue cause and effect and that do not encourage the upkeep of vows and sacred commitments are wrong views."

Then, in the evening of the twentieth day of the year, Khedrup Jé was accompanied by many *devaputras* carrying canopies and banners and so on. He appeared many different ways to his followers. According to one he was carried off to Tuṣita on an elephant. Others saw him go north to Shambhala. (25b) Some even saw him depart for Mount Wutai and so on. At that time an astounding rain of flowers fell, and the sky was suffused with the light of rainbows. Many such wondrous signs established all on the path of devotion. It is said that many miraculous signs occurred when Khedrup Jé was in the clear-light state too. After investigating how long he remained in this state and so forth, I hope to put it down in writing.

This has been a brief explanation of Khedrup Jé's demonstration of passing beyond misery and the wondrous omens that occurred at that time.

[Colophon]

Based on the resolve to preserve Chöden Rapjor's biography [of Khedrup], Jamyang Kunga Delek Rinchen Gyaltsen Palsangpo said that this wonderful story must be on everyone's lips. I, the logician Chökyi Gyaltsen, who has devotion to Khedrup Jé born from knowledge, heard it directly and resolved not to alter it.

Bibliography

Tibetan Sources

Akuching Sherap Gyatso (Shes rab rgya mtsho, A khu ching). *Collected Writings of A khu ching*. New Delhi: [n.p.], 1973.

Chahar Geshé Losang Tsultrim (Blo bzang tshul khrims, Cha har Dge bshes). *Collected Works*. 10 vols. New Delhi: Chatring Jansar Tenzin, 1971.

Chimé Rapgyé, Sangsang Neringpa, ('Chi med rab rgyas, Zang zang ne rings pa). *Golden Wick: A Biography of the Lord Tsongkhapa. Rje rin po che'i rnam thar gser gyi mchod sdong*. In *Snga 'gyur gsang chen rnying ma'i bstan 'dzin chen mo zang zang ne rings pa 'chi med rab rgyas kyi mdzad pa rje rin po che'i rnam thar nor bu'i bang mdzod dang bu chen sbyon tshul gser gyi mchod sdong zhes bya ba gnyis dang gzhan yang ne rings pa'i gsung thor bu nang rnyed phyogs gcig tu bsdus pa bzhugs so*, 14–33. Delhi: Rakra Tethong, circa 2001.

———. *Jewel Treasury: The Story of the Precious Lord's Endowment with the Qualities of Learning, Dignity, and Excellence. Rje rin po che la mkhas btsun bzang gsum gyi yon tan mnga' tshul rnam thar nor bu'i bang mdzod bzhugs*. In *Snga 'gyur gsang chen rnying ma'i bstan 'dzin chen mo zang zang ne rings pa 'chi med rab rgyas kyi mdzad pa rje rin po che'i rnam thar nor bu'i bang mdzod dang bu chen sbyon tshul gser gyi mchod sdong zhes bya ba gnyis dang gzhan yang ne rings pa'i gsung thor bu nang rnyed phyogs gcig tu bsdus pa bzhugs so*, 1–13. Delhi: Rakra Tethong, circa 2001.

Chöden Rapjor (Chos ldan rab 'byor). *Short Biography of the Omniscient Khedrup. Mkhas grub thams cad mkhyen pa'i rnam thar bsdus pa*. In Khedrup Jé, *Collected Writings of Khedrup Gelek Palsang*, vol. *ka*, 109–34.

———. *Short Biography of the Omniscient Khedrup. Mkhas grub thams cad mkhyen pa'i rnam thar bsdus pa*. In Khedrup Jé, *Mkhas grub dge legs dpal bzang gi gsung 'bum* (Sherig Parkhang edition), vol. *tha*, 604–21.

———. *Short Biography of the Omniscient Khedrup. Mkhas grub thams cad mkhyen pa'i rnam thar bsdus pa*. In Khedrup Jé, *Collected Works (gsuṅ 'bum) of mKhas grub dge legs dpal*, vol. 12, 470–93.

Desi Sangyé Gyatso (Sangs rgyas rgya mtsho, Sde srid). *Golden Vaiḍūrya: A History of Ganden. Dga' ldan chos 'byung bai ḍūrya ser po*. Gangs ljongs shes rig gi nying bcud. Zi ling: Krung go bod kyi shes rig dpe skrun khang, 1989.

Drakné Kunsang Chöphel (Kun bzang chos 'phel, Brag sne). *Ruby Necklace: The Story of the Lineage of the Completely Liberated Tsang Domar Tradition. Rnam grol rtsang rdo dmar ba'i gdung rabs lo rgyus deb ther padma ra ga'i do shal*. Dharamsala: Dakney Tsang Domar Namdolling, 1998.

Dungkar Losang Trinlé (Blo bzang 'phrin las, Dung dkar). *Dungkar Tibetological Great Dictionary. Mkhas dbang dung dkar Blo bzang phrin las mchog gis mdzad pai Bod rig pa'i tshig mdzod chen mo ses bya rab gsal zhes bya ba bzhugs so*. Beijing: China Tibetology Publishing House, 2002.

Gorampa Sönam Sengé (Bsod nams seng ge, Go ram pa). *Distinguishing the Views: Moonlight to Illuminate the Main Points of the Supreme Path. Lta ba'i shan byed theg mchog gnad kyi zla zer*. Ma su ri: [n.p.], 1966.

Gungthang Konchok Tenpai Drönmé (Dkon mchog bstan pa'i sgron me, Gung thang). *Entryway to an Array of Wonders: Commentary on the Perfect Glacier Peak Praising the Way the Lord Master Achieved True Enlightenment. Rje bla ma mngon par 'tshang rgya ba'i tshul dang rnam par bstod pa rnam dag gangs ri ma'i 'grel pa rmad byung bkod pa'i 'jug ngogs*. In *Collected Works of Guṅ thaṅ dkon mchog bstan pa'i sgron me Reproduced from Prints from the Lhasa Blocks*, vol. 4, 849–80. Gedan Sungrab Minyam Gyunphel Series, vol.36. New Delhi: Ngawang Gelek Demo, 1973.

Gyaltsap Jé Darma Rinchen (Dar ma rin chen, Rgyal tshab rje). *Explanation of the Stanzas of the Pramāṇavārtika that Unmistakingly Reveals the Path to Liberation. Tshad ma rnam 'grel gyi tshig le'ur rgyas pa'i rnam bshad thar lam phyin ci ma log par gsal bar byed pa*. In *Rgyal thsab rin po che'i gsung 'bum*, vol. *cha*, 1–836. Sku 'bum Monastery: Sku 'bum byams pa gling par khang, 199?.

Gyalwang Chöjé Losang Trinlé Namgyal (Blo bzang 'phrin las rnam rgyal, Rgyal dbang chos rje). *Wondrous Jewel Garland Beautifying the Buddha's Teachings: The Biography of the Dharmaraja the Great Tsongkhapa, who is Indistinct in Essence from the Refuge Lord, the Perfect Master Vajradhara. Khyab bdag rje btsun bla ma dam pa thub dbang rdo rje 'chang dbang dang ngo bo dbyer ma mchis pa 'jam mgon chos kyi rgyal po tsong kha pa chen po'i rnam par thar pa thub bstan mdzes pa'i rgyan gcig ngo mtshar nor bu'i phreng ba*. China: Tsho sngon mi rigs dpe skrun khang, 1981.

Jampal Gyatso, Tokden ('Jam dpal rgya mtsho, Rtog ldan). *The Marvelous Tale of Lord Tsongkhapa's Very Secret Biography. Rje'i rnam thar shin tug sang ba ngo mtshar rmad du byung ba'i gtam bzhugs so*. In *Collected Works (gsung 'bum) of Rje Tsong Kha Pa Blo bzang grags pa: Reproduced from an example of the old Bkra shis lhun po redaction from the library of Klu 'khyil Monastery of Ladakh*, vol. 1, 209–14. Edited by Ngawang Gelek Demo. New Delhi: Ngawang Gelek Demo, 1979.

———. *Rje'i rnam thar shin tug sang ba ngo mtshar rmad du byung ba'i gtam bzhugs so*. In Tsongkhapa, *Collected Works*, vol. 19, 1–7.

———. *Supplement to the Great Biography of the Lord Tsongkhapa, the Biography Entitled the Treasury of Eloquent Teachings. Rje btsun tsong kha pa'i rnam thar chen mo'i zur 'debs rnam thar legs bshad kun 'dus*. In *Collected Works (gsuṅ 'bum) of Rje Tsoṅ Kha Pa Blo bzaṅ grags pa: Reproduced from an Example of the Old Bkra śis lhun po Redaction from the Library of Klu 'khyil Monastery of Ladakh*, vol. 1, 144–66. New Delhi: Ngawang Gelek Demo, 1975. [Cited as *Supplement*.]

———. *Supplement to the Great Biography of the Lord Tsongkhapa, the Biography Entitled the Treasury of Eloquent Teachings. Rje btsun tsong kha pa'i rnam thar chen po'i zur 'debs rnam thar legs bshad kun 'dus*. In Tsongkhapa, *Collected Works*, vol. 1, 149–73.

Jamyang Chöjé Tashi Palden (Bkra shis dpal ldan, 'Jam dbyangs chos rje). *Supplication of the Secret Biography of the Lord Master Losang Drakpai Pal. Rje btsun bla ma blo bzang grags pa'i dpal gyi gsang ba'i rnam thar gsol 'debs*. In *Collected Works (gsuṅ 'bum) of Rje Tsoṅ Kha Pa Blo bzaṅ grags pa: Reproduced from an example of the old Bkra śis lhun po redaction from the library of Klu 'khyil Monastery of Ladakh*, edited by Ngawang Gelek Demo, vol. 1, 202–10. New Delhi: Ngawang Gelek Demo, 1979.

———. *Supplication of the Secret Biography of the Lord Master Losang Drakpai Pal. Rje btsun bla ma blo bzang grags pa'i dpal gyi gsang ba'i rnam thar gsol 'debs bzhugs so*. In Tsongkhapa, *Collected Works*, vol. 1, 211–21.

Jamyang Shepa I Ngawang Tsondrü (Ngag dbang brtson grus, 'Jam dbyangs bzhed pa I). *Cittamaṇi Garland. The 153rd Scroll-like Biography of the Great Master Tsongkhapa, the Great Enjoyment Sea of Prosperity that Causes the Growth of the Buddha's Teachings. Rje btsun tsong kha pa chen po'i rnam thar ras bris kyi tshul brgya nga gsum pa tsitta ma Ni'i phreng ba thub bstan rgyas byed phan bde'i rol mtsho chen po*. In *Collected Works of 'Jam dbyaṅs bzad pa'i rdo rje: Reproduced from prints from the Bkra śis 'khyil blocks by Ngawang Gelek Demo*, vol. 4, 285–336. New Delhi: Ngawang Gelek Demo, 1972–74.

Jamyang Shepa II Konchok Jikmé Wangpo (Kon mchog 'jigs med dbang po,

'Jam dbyangs bzhad pa II). *Biography of the Omniscient Khedrup Gelek Palsangpo. Mkhas grub thams cad mkhyen pa dge legs dpal bzang po'i rnam thar*. In *Collected Works of Dkon mchog 'jigs med dbaṅ po, the Second Jam dbyaṅs bzad pa of La braṅ Bkra śis 'khyil: Reproduced from prints from the Bkra shis 'khyil blocks by Ngawang Gelek Demo*, vol. 5, 699–723. New Delhi: Demo, 1971.

———. *Jewel Garland: A History of Ganden. Dga' ldan chos 'byung nor bu'i phreng ba*. In *Collected Works of Dkon mchog 'jigs med dbaṅ po, the Second 'Jam dbyaṅs bźad pa of La braṅ Bkra śis 'khyil: Reproduced from prints from the Bkra śis 'khyil blocks by Ngawang Gelek Demo*. vol. 5, 529–698. New Delhi: Demo, 1971.

Jetsunpa Chökyi Gyaltsen (Chos kyi rgyal mtshan, Rje btsun pa). *Eliminating Doubts Concerning the Difficult Points of the Illumination of Intent of the Pramāṇavārtikakārikā. Rnam 'grel dgongs pa rab gsal gyi dka' ba'i gnad la dwogs pa gcod pa*. Bylakuppe: Sera Je Computer Project, 1998.

———. *Garland of Fortune: A General Elucidation on the Difficult Points of the 'Illumination of the Thought' Explicating the 'Entry into the Middle Way' Treatise. Bstan bcos dbu ma la 'jug pa'i rnam bshad dgongs pa rab gsal gyi dka' gnad gsal bar byed pa'i spyi don legs bshad skal bzang mgul rgyan*. Mundgod, India: dGa' ldan byang rtse thos bsam nor gling grwa tshang, 2nd ed., 1996.

———. *Means for Eliminating Wrong Views of the Kālacakra Sādhana Entitled Oral Instructions of Puṇḍarīka. Dus 'khor gyi sgrub thabs pad ma dkar po'i zhal lung la log rtog sal tshul*. In *Collected Works (gsung 'bum) of Mkhas grub dge legs dpal*, vol. *cha*, 1a–75a. Delhi: Ngawang Gelek Demo, 1985.

———. *Secret Biography of the Omniscient Khedrup. Mkhas grub thams cad mkhyen pa'i gsang ba'i rnam thar.* In *Collected Works (gsung 'bum) of Mkhas grub dge legs dpal*, vol. 12, 421–70. New Delhi: Ngawang Gelek Demo, 1985.

———. *Secret Biography of the Omniscient Khedrup. Mkhas grub thams cad mkhyen pa'i gsang ba'i rnam thar.* In Khedrup, *Collected Writings*, vol. ka, 1–77.

———. *Secret Biography of the Omniscient Khedrup. Mkhas grub thams cad mkhyen pa'i gsang ba'i rnam thar.* [Manuscript in author's possession, n.p., n.d.]

Jikmé Drakpa Choklé Namgyal ('Jigs med grags pa phyogs las rnam rgyal). *Rain of Accomplishments, Harvest of Faith: The Biography of the Dharma Lord of Gyantsé. Rgyal rtse chos rgyal gyi rnam par thar pa dad pa'i lo thog dngos grub kyi char 'bebs*. Edited by Tshe ring don grub. Lhasa: Bod ljongs mi dmangs dpe skrun khang, 1987.

Kharnak Lotsāwa Paljor Gyatso (Dpal 'byor rgya mtsho, Mkhar nag Lo tsā ba). *History of Ganden: The Wish-Fulfilling Bough that Delights Scholars. Dga' ldan chos 'byung dpag bsam sdong po mkhas pa dgyes byed.* [Photocopy manuscript in author's possession, n.p., n.d.]

Khedrup Jé Gelek Palsang (Dge legs dpal bzang, Mkhas grub rje). *Collected Works (Gsuṅ 'Bum) of the Lord Mkhas Grub Rje Dge Legs Dpal Bzaṅ Po: Reproduced from the 1897 Lha sa Old Źol (Dga' Ldan Phun Tshog-Gliṅ) Blocks.* 11 vols. New Delhi: Mongolian Lama Gurudeva, 1982.

———. *Collected Works (gsung 'bum) of mKhas grub dge legs dpal.* 12 vols. Delhi: Ngawang Gelek Demo, 1983.

———. *Collected Writings of Khedrup Gelek Palsang. Mkhas grub dge legs dpal bzang gi gsung 'bum,* 16 vols. Sku 'bum Monastery: Sku 'bum byams pa gling par khang, 199?.

———. *Commentary on the Svārtha Chapter of the Ocean of Reasoning: An Extensive Explanation of the Extensive Commentary on Prime Cognition. Rgyas pa'i bstan bcos tshad ma rnam 'grel gyi rgya cher bshad pa rigs pa'i rgya mtsho las rang don le'u'i rnam bshad.* In Khedrup, *Collected Writings,* vol. *nga,* 1–410.

———. *Elucidation of Suchness: An Extensive Explanation of the Great Vimalaprabhā Commentary of the Illustrious Kālacakra. Dpal dus kyi 'khor lo'i 'grel chen dri ma med pa'i 'od kyi rgya cher bshad pa de kho na nyid snang bar byed pa.* In Khedrup, *Collected Writings,* vols. *ja* (1–805) and *nya* (1–251).

———. *Entryway of Faith: The Wondrous Biography of the Lord Teacher Tsongkhapa. Rje btsun bla ma tsong kha pa chen po'i ngo mtshar rmad du byung ba'i rnam par thar pa dad pa'i 'jug ngogs.* In Tsongkhapa, *Collected Works,* vol. 1, 1–147.

———. *Entryway of Faith: The Wondrous Biography of the Lord Teacher Tsongkhapa. Rje btsun bla ma tsong kha pa chen po'i ngo mtshar rmad du 'byung ba'i rnam par thar pa dad pa'i 'jug ngogs.* In *Collected Works (gsuṅ 'bum) of Rje Tsoṅ Kha Pa Blo bzaṅ grags pa: Reproduced from an Example of the old Bkra śis lhun po Redaction from the Library of Klu 'khyil Monastery of Ladakh,* vol. 1, 1–143. New Delhi: Ngawang Gelek Demo, 1975.

———. *Miscellaneous Writings of the Precious Khedrup. Mkhas grub rin po che'i gsung 'bum thor bu.* In Khedrup, *Collected Writings,* vol. *ba,* 345–752.

———. *Oral Instructions of Puṇḍarīka: Sādhana on How to Completely Achieve the Body, Speech, and Mind of the Illustrious Kālacakra. Dpal dus kyi 'khor lo'i sku gsung thugs yongs su rdzogs pa'i sgrub thabs pad ma dkar po'i zhal lung.* In Khedrup, *Collected Writings,* vol. na, 1–130.

———. *A Record of the Teachings Received by the Omniscient Khedrup Gelek*

Palsang. Mkhas grub thams cad mkhyen pa dge legs dpal bzang po'i gsan yig. In Khedrup, *Collected Writings, vol. ka*, 143–231.

———. *Secret Biography of Tsongkhapa: Grain Tips of the Precious Story Thoroughly Discussing Certain Parts of the Ocean-Like Secret Biography of the Precious Lord Master. Rje rin po che'i gsang ba'i rnam thar rgya mtsho lta bu las cha shas nyung ngu zhig yongs su brjod pa'i gtam rin po che'i snye ma.* In *Collected Works (gsuṅ 'bum) of Rje Tsoṅ Kha Pa Blo bzaṅ grags pa: Reproduced from an Example of the Old Bkra śis lhun po Redaction from the Library of Klu 'khyil Monastery of Ladakh*, vol. 1, 167–201. New Delhi: Ngawang Gelek Demo, 1975.

———. *Secret Biography of Tsongkhapa. Grain Tips of the Precious Story Thoroughly Discussing Certain Parts of the Ocean-Like Secret Biography of the Precious Lord Master. Rje rin po che'i gsang ba'i rnam thar rgya mtsho lta bu las cha shas nyung ngu zhig yongs su brjod pa'i gtam rin po che'i snye ma.* In Tsongkhapa, *Collected Works*, vol. 1, 175–210.

———. *The Story of My Own Realizations. Rang gi rtogs pa gtam du bsnyad pa.* In Khedrup, *Collected Writings*, vol. *ba*, 415–19.

——— et al. *Compendium of Polemical Literature. Dgag lan phyogs bsgrigs.* Chengdu: Si khron mi rigs dpe skrun khan, 1997.

Lechen Kunga Gyaltsen (Kun dga' rgyal mtshan, Las chen). *Lamp Illuminating the History of the Kadam Tradition. Bka' gdams chos 'byung gsal ba'i sgron me.* New Delhi: B. Jamyang Norbu, 1972.

Lodrö Rinchen Sengé, Müsepa (Blo gros rin chen seng ge, Mus srad pa). *Elucidation of Suchness [as presented in Tsongkhapa's] Commentary [Entitled] Illumination of the Thought. Rnam bshad dgongs pa rab gsal gyi de nyid gsal byed bzhugs so.* In *The Literary Works of the Omniscient Lodrö Rinchen Sengé. Kun mkhyen blo gros rin chen seng ge'i gsung rtsom bzhugs.* Lhasa: Dpal brtsegs bod yig dpe rnying zhib 'jug khang, 2007.

———. *Maṇḍala of Qualities: Prayer to Jamyang Chöjé. 'Jam dbyangs chos rje'i stod pa yon tan dkyil 'khor ma.* In *Dge lugs pa'i zhal 'don phyogs bsgrigs*, edited by Nor bzang O rgyan, 208–10. Lhasa: Bod ljongs mi rigs dpe skrun khang, 2000.

———. *Practice Manual of Padma Wangchen. Bcom ldan 'das padma dbang chen gyi 'phrin las.* [Photocopy manuscript in author's possession, n.p., n.d.]

Longdöl Lama Ngawang Losang (Ngag dbang blo bzang, Klong rdol bla ma). *A List of Writings by Kadampa and Gelukpa Masters. Bka' gdams pa dang dge lugs bla ma rag rim gyi gsung 'bum mtshan tho.* In Chandra 1973, 1285–1413.

Losang Könchok (Blo bzang dkon mchog, Byes bsam). *Moon-Jewel Mirror:*

A Short Presentation of the History of Sera Jé Khenyen College, Companion of the Gentle Lord Tsongkhapa's Teachings. Jam mgon bstan pa'i rtsa lag ser byes mkhas snyan grwa tshang gi gdan rabs mdo tsam brjod pa zla ba nor bu'i me long. Bylakuppe: Ser byes dpe mdzod khang, 2002.

Paljor Sönam Lhundrup (Dpal 'byor bsod nams lhun grub). *Meaningful to Behold: A Biographical Supplication to Sera Chökyi Gyaltsen. Se ra chos kyi rgyal mtshan gyi rnam thar gsol 'debs mthong ba don ldan.* Composed at Se ra monastery, printed at Se ra byes, 7 fols., [n.d.].

Paṇchen Delek Nyima (Bde legs nyi ma, Paṇ chen). *Delightful to the Scholar's Mind: The Biography of the Omniscient Khedrup. Mkhas grub thams cad mkhyen pa'i rnam thar mkhas pa'i yid 'phrog.* In *Collected Works (gsung 'bum) of mKhas grub dge legs dpal: Reproduced from a set of prints from the 1897 Lha sa Old Źol (Dga' ldan phun tshogs gling) blocks*, vol. 1, 5–31. New Delhi: Mongolian Lama Gurudava, 1982.

———. *Delightful to the Scholar's Mind: The Biography of the Omniscient Khedrup. Mkhas grub thams cad mkhyen pa'i rnam thar mkhas pa'i yid 'phrog.* In Khedrup, *Collected Writings*, vol. *ka*, 79–108.

———. *Rain of Accomplishments: The Liberation Story of the Glorious and Good Jetsun Chökyi Gyaltsen. Rje btsun chos kyi rgyal mtshan dpal bzang po'i rnam par thar pa dngos grub kyi char 'bebs.* Lhasa, Tibet: Ser byes mkhas snyen grwa tshang, 33 fols, [n.d.].

Paṇchen Sönam Drakpa (Bsod nams grags pa, Paṇ chen). *Mind's Ornament: The History of the Old and New Kadam Traditions. Bka' gdams gsar rnying gi chos 'byung yid kyi mdzes rgyan.* In *Two Histories of the bKa' gdams pa Tradition from the Library of Burmiok Athing*, 1–206. Gangtok: Gonpo Tseten, 1977.

Phurchok Ngawang Jampa (Ngag dbang byams pa, Phur bu lcog). *White Lotus Garland: The Formation of the Four Great Monastic Colleges and of Gyütö and Gyümey Colleges. Grwa sa chen po bzhi dang rgyud pa stod smad chags tshul pad dkar 'phreng ba.* In *Three dKar chag's*. Gedan Sungrab Minyam Gyunphel Series, vol. 13, 46–169. New Delhi: Ngawang Gelek Demo, 1970.

Rongpo Drupchen Kalden Gyatso (Skal ldan rgya mtsho, Rong po grub chen). *Versified Biography of Sera Jetsunpa. Se ra rje btsun pa'i rnam thar tshigs bcad ma.* In *Secret Biography of the Sixth Dalai Lama together with Rong po grub chen's Collection of Biographies of Eminent Gelukpa Masters*, 256–65. New Delhi: Ngawang Gelek Demo, 1970.

———. *Prose Biography of Sera Jetsunpa. Se ra rje btsun pa'i rnam thar tshigs lhug ma.* In *Secret Biography of the Sixth Dalai Lama together with Rong *po grub chen's Collection of Biographies of Eminent Gelukpa Masters*, 265–95. New Delhi: Ngawang Gelek Demo, 1970.

Serdog Paṇchen Shākya Chokden (Shākya mchog ldan, Gser mdog Paṇ chen). *Impartial Wisdom's Delight: Writing on How the Presentation of the Turning of the Wheel of the Dharma Is Established. Chos kyi 'khor lo bskor ba'i rnam gzhag ji ltar grub pa'i yi ge gzu bor gnas pa'i mdzangs pa dga' byed*. In *Complete Works (gsung 'bum) of gSer mdog paṇ chen Shākya mchog ldan*, vol. *ma*, 457–82. Thimpu: Kunsang Topgey, 1975.

Sermé Drakpa Khedrup (Grags pa mkhas grub, Se ra smad pa). *Jampal Nyingpo's Mind Ornament: The History of the Shartsé Norbuling College of Ganden, Residence of Ten Million Scholars. Mkhas grub bye ba'i brtsi gnas 'brog ri bo dge ldan rnam par rgyal ba'i gling gi ya gyal shar rtse nor bu gling gi chos 'byung lo rgyus 'jam dpal snying po'i dgongs rgyan*. New Delhi: Nawang Sopa, 1975.

Thuken Losang Chökyi Nyima (Blo bzang chos kyi nyi ma, Thu'u bkwan). *Commentary on Philosophical Systems. Thu'u bkwan grub mtha'*. Lanzhou: Kan su'u mi rigs dpe skrun khang, 1989. Translated in Thuken Losang Chökyi Nyima 2009.

Tsangtön Kunga Gyaltsen (Kun dga' rgyal mtshan, Gtsang ston). *Lamp Illuminating the Wondrous Story of the Full Enlightenment of the Omniscient Jamyang Chöjé Tashi Palden as Related by Himself. Thams cad mkhyen pa 'jam dbyangs chos rje bkra shis dpal ldan pa'i zhal snga nas kyi rnam par thar pa ngo mtshar rmad du byung ba'i gtam rab tu gsal ba'i sgron sme*. [Photocopy manuscript in author's possession, n.p., n.d.]

Tsechokling Yeshé Gyaltsen (Ye shes rgyal mtshan, Tshe mchog gling). *Biographies of the Eminent Gurus in the Transmission Lineages of the Teachings of the Graduated Path: Being the Text of Byang chub lam gyi rim pa'i bla ma brgyud pa'i rnam par thar pa rgyal bstan mdzes pa'i rgyan mchog phul byung nor bu'i phreng ba*. Gedan Sungrab Minyam Gyunphel Series 18–19. New Delhi: Ngawang Gelek Demo, 1970.

Tsongkhapa Losang Drakpa (Blo bzang grags pa, Tsong kha pa). *Collected Works (gsung 'bum) of the Incomparable Lord Tsongkhapa Losang Drakpa*. 19 vols. Sku 'bum Monastery: Sku 'bum byams pa gling par khang, 199?.

———. *Essence of Elegant Sayings: Treatise Differentiating the Interpretable and the Definitive Meaning. Drang ba dang nges pa'i don rnam par phye ba'i bstan bcos legs bshed snying po*. In Tsongkhapa, *Collected Works*, vol. *pha*, 442–687.

———. *Illumination of Thought: Commentary on the Great Madhyamakāvatara Treatise. Bstan bcos chen mo dbu ma la 'jug pa'i rnam bshed dgongs pa rab gsal*. In Tsongkhapa, *Collected Works*, vol. *ma*, 1–606.

———. *Meeting with Lhodrak Drupchen and The Gift of the Tooth to Khedrup Jé. Lho brag grub chen dang mjal tshul // Mkhas grub rje la tshems gnang skor.* In Tsongkhapa, *Collected Works*, vol. 1, 223–32.

———. *Miscellaneous Writings of the Great Omniscient Lord Tsongkhapa. Rje thams cad mkhyen pa Tsong kha pa chen po'i bka' 'bum thor bu.* In Tsongkhapa, *Collected Works*, vol. *kha*, 1a–316a.

———. *Realization Narrative. Rtogs brjod mdun legs ma.* In *'Og min byang chub chos gling grwa tshang gi zhal 'don thub bstan dga' tshal*, 145–55. Kathmandu: Kopan Monastery, 2000.

Non-Tibetan Sources

Aris, Michael. 1989. *Hidden Treasures and Secret Lives: A Study of Pemalingpa (1450–1521) and the Sixth Dalai Lama (1683–1706).* London: Keegan Paul International.

Backscheider, Paula R. 1999. *Reflections on Biography.* New York: Oxford University Press.

Berzin, Alexander. http://www.berzinarchives.com/web/en/archives/e-books/published_books/kalachakra_initiation/pt1/kalachakra_initiation_01.html. Accessed January 2014.

Beuscher, John B. 2005. *Echoes from an Empty Sky: The Origins of the Buddhist Doctrine of the Two Truths.* Ithaca: Snow Lion Publications.

Bhattacaryya, Benoytosh. 1993. *The Indian Buddhist Iconography Mainly Based on the Sādhanamālā and Other Cognate Tāntric Texts of Rituals.* New Delhi: Asian Educational Services.

Blackburn, Anne M. 2001. *Buddhist Learning and Textual Practice in Eighteenth-Century Lankan Monastic Culture.* Princeton, NJ: Princeton University Press.

Bourdieu, Pierre. 1991. *Language and Symbolic Power.* Edited and introduced by John B. Thompson. Cambridge, MA: Harvard University Press.

Bunce, Fredrick W. 1994. *An Encyclopaedia of Buddhist Deities, Demigods, Godlings, Saints, and Demons.* New Delhi: D. K. Printworld.

Cabezón, José Ignacio. 1988. "The Prāsaṅgika's View on Logic: Tibetan dGe lugs pa Exegesis on the Question of Svātantras." *Journal of Indian Philosophy* 16.3: 217–24.

———. 1992. *A Dose of Emptiness: An Annotated Translation of the Stong thun chen mo of mKhas grub dge legs dpal bzang.* Albany: State University of New York Press.

———. 2001. "Authorship and Literary Production in Classical Buddhist Tibet." In *Changing Minds: Contributions to the Study of Buddhism and Tibet in Honor of Jeffrey Hopkins*, edited by Guy Newland, 233–63. Ithaca, NY: Snow Lion.

———. 2007. *Freedom from Extremes: Gorampa's "Distinguishing the Views" and the Polemics of Emptiness*. Boston: Wisdom Publications.

Chandra, Lokesh, ed. 1963. *Materials for a History of Tibetan Literature*, vol. 3. New Delhi: International Academy of Indian Studies.

———.ed. 1973. *Collected Works of Longdol Lama*, parts 1 and 2. New Delhi: International Academy of Indian Culture.

———. 1999–2005. *Dictionary of Buddhist Iconography*. New Delhi: International Academy of Indian Culture and Aditya Prakashan.

Chosspel, Samten. 2011. "The First Jamyang Zhepa, Jamyang Zhepai Dorje." *Treasury of Lives* (http://www.treasuryoflives.org/biographies/view/Jamyang-Zhepai-Dorje/6646).

Cornu, Philippe. 2006. *Dictionnaire Encyclopédique du Bouddhisme*. Paris: Editions du Seuil.

Davidson, Ronald. 2005. *Tibetan Renaissance: Tantric Buddhism and the Rebirth of Tibetan Culture*. New York: Columbia University Press.

Desi Sangyé Gyatso. 2010. *Mirror of Beryl: A Historical Introduction to Tibetan Medicine*. Translated by Gavin Kilty. Boston: Wisdom Publications.

Dreyfus, Georges B. J. 1997. *Recognizing Reality: Dharmakīrti's Philosophy and Its Tibetan Interpretations*. Albany: State University of New York Press.

———. 1998. "The Shuk-den Affair: Origins of a Controversy." *Journal of the International Association of Buddhist Studies* 21.2: 227–70.

———. 2003. *The Sound of Two Hands Clapping: The Education of a Tibetan Buddhist Monk*. Berkeley: University of California Press.

———. 2005. "Where Do Commentarial Schools Come From? Reflections on the History of Tibetan Scholasticism." *Journal of the International Association for Buddhist Studies* 28.2: 273–97.

Ehrhard, Franz-Karl. 2000. *Early Blockprints from Mang-yul Gung-thang*. Lumbini: Lumbini International Research Institute.

Garfield, Jay L. 2002. *Empty Words: Buddhist Philosophy and Cross-Cultural Interpretation*. New York: Oxford University Press.

Gayley, Holly. 2007. "Patterns in the Ritual Dissemination of Padma gling pa's Treasures." In *Bhutan: Traditions and Change*, edited by John Ardussi and Françoise Pommaret, 97–119. Leiden: Brill.

Geertz, Armin W. 1992. *The Invention of Prophecy: Continuity and Meaning in Hopi Indian Religion*. Berkeley: University of California Press.

Gö Lotsāwa Shönu Pal. 1976. *The Blue Annals*. Translated by George N. Roerich. Delhi: Motilal Banarsidass.

Goldstein, Melvyn C. 1989. *A History of Modern Tibet, 1913–1951: The Demise of the Lamaist State*. Berkeley: University of California Press.

Gyatso, Janet. 1992. "Autobiography in Tibetan Religious Literature: Reflections on Its Modes of Self-Presentation." In *Tibetan Studies: Proceedings of the 5th International Association of Tibetan Studies Seminar*, edited by Shoren Ihara and Zuiho Yamaguchi, vol. 2, 465–78. Narita: Naritasan Institute for Buddhist Studies.

———. 1993. "The Logic of Legitimation in the Tibetan Treasure Tradition." *History of Religions* 33.2: 97–134.

———. 1998. *Apparitions of the Self: The Secret Autobiographies of a Tibetan Visionary: A Translation and Study of Jigme Lingpa's Dancing Moon in the Water and Dakki's Grand Secret-Talk*. Princeton, NJ: Princeton University Press.

Haarh, Erik. 1969. *The Yar-luo Dynasty: A Study with Particular Regard to the Contribution by Myths and Legends to the History of Ancient Tibet and the Origin and Nature of Its Kings*. Copenhagen: Gad's Forlag.

Heller, Amy. 2005. "The Second Dalai Lama Gendun Gyatso." In *The Dalai Lamas: A Visual History*, edited by Martin Brauen, 43–50. Chicago: Serindia Publications.

Hopkins, Jeffrey. 1987a. *Emptiness Yoga: The Middle Way Consequence School*. Ithaca, NY: Snow Lion.

———. 1987b. *Deity Yoga in Action and Performance Tantra*. Ithaca, NY: Snow Lion.

———, trans. 1989. *The Kālachakra Tantra: Rite of Initiation for the Stage of Generation*. 2nd rev. ed. Boston: Wisdom Publications.

———. 1999a. *Emptiness in the Mind-Only School of Buddhism: Dynamic Responses to Dzong-ka-ba's The Essence of Eloquence*. Berkeley: University of California Press.

———. 1999b. *The Tantric Distinction: A Buddhist's Reflections on Compassion and Emptiness*. Boston: Wisdom.

Ishihama, Yumiko. 2003. "On the Dissemination of the Belief in the Dalai Lama as a Manifestation of Avalokiteśvara." In *The History of Tibet*, edited by Alex McKay, vol. 2, 538–53. London: Routledge.

Jagou, Fabienne. 2005. "The Panchen Lamas and the Dalai Lamas." In *The Dalai Lamas: A Visual History*, edited by Martin Brauen, 202–11. Chicago: Serindia Publications.

Jinpa, Thupten. 2002. *Self, Reality and Reason in Tibetan Philosophy: Tsongkhapa's Quest for the Middle Way*. London and New York: RoutledgeCurzon.

Kapstein, Matthew. 2000a. "The Purificatory Gem and Its Cleansing: A

Late Tibetan Polemical Discussion of Apocryphal Texts." In *The Tibetan Assimilation of Buddhism*, 121–37. New York: Oxford University Press.

———. 2000b. *The Tibetan Assimilation of Buddhism*. New York: Oxford University Press.

———. 2003. "Remarks on the Mani-bKa'-'bum and the Cult of Avalokitesvara in Tibet." *The History of Tibet*, vol. 2, 523–37. London: Routledge.

Kaschewsky, Rudolf, trans. 1971. *Das Leben des Lamaistischen Heiligen Tsongkhapa Blo-Bzao-Grags-Pa (1357–1419), dargestellt und erläutert anhand seiner Vita: Quellort allen Glückes*. Wiesbaden: Otto Harrassowitz.

Komarovski, Yaroslav. 2011. *Visions of Unity: The Golden Paṇḍita Shakya Chokden's New Interpretation of Yogācāra and Madhyamaka*. Albany: State University of New York Press.

Lamotte, Etienne. 1960. "Mañjuśrī." *T'oung Pao* (Leiden) 48: 1–96.

Lopez, Donald S., Jr. 1987. *A Study of Svātantrika*. Ithaca, NY: Snow Lion.

———. 1996. "Polemical Literature (*dGag lan*). In *Tibetan Literature: Studies in Genre*, edited by José Ignacio Cabezón and Roger R. Jackson, 217–28. Ithaca, NY: Snow Lion.

———. 1998. *Prisoners of Shangri-La: Tibetan Buddhism and the West*. Chicago: University of Chicago Press.

———. 2006. *The Madman's Middle Way: Reflections on Reality of the Tibetan Monk Gendun Chopel*. Chicago: University of Chicago Press.

Maher, Derek. 2003. *Knowledge and Authority in Tibetan Middle Way Schools of Buddhism: A Study of the Gelukba (dge lugs pa) Epistemology of Jamyang Shayba ('jam dbyangs bzhad pa) in Its Historical Context*. Doctoral dissertation, University of Virginia.

Mullin, Glenn H., trans. 2005. *The Second Dalai Lama: His Life and Teachings*. Ithaca, NY: Snow Lion.

Nāgārjuna. 1995. *Mūlamadhyamakakārikā*. Translated by Jay L. Garfield in *The Fundamental Wisdom of the Middle Way: Nāgārjuna's Mūlamadhyamakakārikā*. New York: Oxford University Press.

Newland, Guy. 1996. "Debate Manuals in dGe lugs Monastic Colleges." In *Tibetan Literature: Studies in Genre*, edited by José Ignacio Cabezón and Roger R. Jackson, 202–16. Ithaca, NY: Snow Lion.

Ngawang Lobsang Gyatso, Dalai Lama V. 1995. *A History of Tibet*. Translated by Zahiruddin Ahmad. Bloomington: Indiana University Research Institute for Inner Asian Studies.

Nussbaum, Martha C. 1990. *Love's Knowledge: Essays on Philosophy and Literature*. New York: Oxford University Press.

Olivelle, Patrick, trans. 2008. *Life of the Buddha by Aśvaghoṣa*. New York: NYU Press.

Onoda, Shunzō. 1989. "The Chronology of the Abbatial Successions of the gSang phu Sne'u thog Monastery." *Wiener Zeitschrift für die Kunde Sudasiens und Archiv für Indische Philosophie* 33, 203–13. Vienna: Österreichische Akademie für Wissenschaften.

Phuntso, Karma. 2005. *Mipham's Dialectics and the Debates on Emptiness: To Be, Not to Be or Neither*. London and New York: RoutledgeCurzon.

Ricoeur, Paul. 1970. *Freud and Philosophy: An Essay on Interpretation*. New Haven: Yale University Press.

Robinson, James B. 1996. "The Lives of Indian Buddhist Saints: Biography, Hagiography and Myth." In *Tibetan Literature: Studies in Genre*, edited by José Ignacio Cabezón and Roger R. Jackson, 57–69. Ithaca, NY: Snow Lion.

Ruegg, David Seyfort. 1981. *The Literature of the Madhyamaka School of Philosophy in India*. Wiesbaden: Otto Harrassowitz.

Sakyapa Sönam Gyaltsen. 1996. *The Clear Mirror: A Traditional Account of Tibet's Golden Age*. Translated by McComas Taylor and Lama Choedak Yuthok. Ithaca, NY: Snow Lion.

Samuel, Geoffrey. 1993. *Civilized Shamans: Buddhism in Tibetan Societies*. Washington and London: Smithsonian Institution Press.

Schaeffer, Kurtis. 1999. "Printing the Words of the Master. Tibetan Editorial Practice in the Collected Works of 'Jam dbyangs bzhad pa'i rdo rje I (1648–1721)." *Acta Orientalia* 60: 159–77.

———. 2004. *Himalayan Hermitess: The Life of a Tibetan Buddhist Nun*. New York: Oxford University Press.

———. 2005. "The Autobiography of a Medieval Hermitess: Orgyan Chokyi (1675–1729)." In *Women in Tibet*, edited by Janet Gyatso and Hanna Havcnik, 83–109. New York: Columbia University Press.

Shakabpa, W. D. 1967. *Tibet: A Political History*. New Haven: Yale University Press.

Smith, E. Gene. 2001. *Among Tibetan Texts: History and Literature of the Himalayan Plateau*. Boston: Wisdom Publications.

Snellgrove, David. 1957. *Buddhist Himālaya: Travels and Studies in Quest of the Origins and Nature of Tibetan Religion*. Oxford: Cassirer.

Sørensen, Per. 1994. *The Mirror Illuminating the Royal Genealogies: An Annotated Translation of the XIVth Century Tibetan Chronicle: rGyal rabs gsal ba'i me long*. Wiesbaden: Harrassowitz Verlag.

Stearns, Cyrus. 2010. *The Buddha from Dölpo: A Study of the Life and Thought of the Tibetan Master Dölpopa Sherab Gyaltsen*. Ithaca, NY: Snow Lion.

Stevenson, Daniel. 1996. "Visions of Mañjuśrī on Mount Wutai." In *Religions of China in Practice*, edited by Donald S. Lopez, Jr., 203–22. Princeton, NJ: Princeton University Press.

Stock, Brian. 1983. *The Implications of Literacy: Written Models of Interpretation in the Eleventh and Twelfth Centuries*. Princeton, New Jersey: Princeton University Press.

Stoddard, Heather. 1985. *Le Mendiant de l'Amdo*. Paris: Société d'Ethnographie.

Thuken Losang Chökyi Nyima. 2009. *The Crystal Mirror of Philosophical Systems*. Translated by Geshé Lhundub Sopa et al., edited by Roger Jackson. Boston: Wisdom Publications.

Thurman, Robert A. F. 1978. "Buddhist Hermeneutics." *Journal of the American Academy of Religion* 46.1: 19–39.

———, ed. 1982. *The Life and Teachings of Tsong Khapa*. Dharamsala, India: Library of Tibetan Works and Archives.

———. 1984. *Tsong Khapa's Speech of Gold in the Essence of True Eloquence: Reason and Enlightenment in the Central Philosophy of Tibet*. Princeton, NJ: Princeton University Press.

Tsongkhapa. 1999. *The Fulfillment of All Hopes: Guru Devotion in Tibetan Buddhism*. Translated by Gareth Sparham. Boston: Wisdom Publications.

———. 2000. *The Great Treatise on the Stages of the Path to Enlightenment (Lam rim chen mo)*, vol. 1. Translated by the Lamrim Translation Committee. Ithaca, NY: Snow Lion.

———. 2006. *Ocean of Reasoning: A Great Commentary on Nāgārjuna's Mūlamadhyamakakārikā*. Translated by Jay L. Garfield and Ngawang Samten. New York: Oxford University Press.

Tucci, Giuseppe. 1949. *Tibetan Painted Scrolls*. Rome: Libreria dello Stato.

———. 1980. *The Religions of Tibet*. Berkeley: University of California Press.

Tun Aung Chain. 2000. "Prophecy and Planets: Forms of Legitimation of the Royal City in Myanmar." In *Proceedings of the Myanmar Two Millennia Conference 15–17 December 1999*, vol. 3, 133–55. Yangon: Universities Historical Research Centre.

van der Kuijp, Leonard W. J. 1985. "Studies in Mkhas-Grub-Rje I: Mkhas-Grub-Rje's Epistemological Oeuvre and his Philological Remarks on Dignaga's *Pramāṇasamuccaya*." *Berliner Indologische Studien* 1: 75–106.

———. 2001. "On the Fifteenth Century Lho rong chos 'byung by Rta tshag Tshe dbang rgyal and Its Importance for Tibetan Political and Religious History." *Lungta* 14: 57–76.

———. 2005. "The Dalai Lamas and the Origins of Incarnate Lamas." In *The Dalai Lamas: A Visual History*, edited by Martin Brauen, 15–31. Chicago: Serindia Publications.

Vose, Kevin A. 2009. *Resurrecting Candrakīrti: Disputes in the Tibetan Creation of Prāsaṅgika*. Boston: Wisdom Publications.

Vostrikov, A. I. 1994. *Tibetan Historical Literature*. Richmond, Surrey: Curzon Press.

Wang, Françoise. 2000. *Dje Tsongkhapa: Rencontre avec un Maître Remarquable*. France: Détchène Eusèl Ling.

Wayman, Alex, trans. 1997. *Calming the Mind and Discerning the Real: Buddhist Meditation and the Middle View, from the Lam rim chen mo of Tsong kha pa*. Delhi: Motilal Banarsidass.

———. trans. 1999. *Chanting the Names of Mañjuśrī*. Delhi: Motilal Banarsidass.

Willis, Janice Dean. 1985. "On the Nature of Rnam-Thar: Early Dge-Lugs-Pa *Siddha* Biographies." In *Soundings in Tibetan Civilization*, edited by Barbara Nimri Aziz and Matthew Kapstein, 304–19. New Delhi: Manohar Publications.

———. 1995. *Enlightened Beings: Life Stories from the Ganden Oral Tradition*. Boston: Wisdom Publications.

Woolf, Virginia. 1986. *The Common Reader: Second Series*, edited by Andrew McNeillie. London: Hogarth Press.

Wylie, Turell V. 2003. "Monastic Patronage in 15th Century Tibet." In *The History of Tibet*, vol. 2, 483–91. London: Routledge.

Zongtse Champa Thupten. *History of the Sera Monastery of Tibet, 1418–1959*. New Delhi: International Academy of Indian Culture and Aditya Prakashan, 1995.

Index

- *Page numbers followed by "(2)" indicate two discussions.*
- *Page numbers followed by "n"/"nn" plus a number/numbers indicate footnotes.*
- *Page numbers followed by "+n"/"+nn" plus a number/numbers indicate discussions plus footnotes.*

About the Author

Elijah Sacvan Ary was born in Vancouver, Canada. In 1979, at age seven, he was recognized as the reincarnation, or *tulku,* of a Tibetan scholar and spent his teenage years as a monk at Sera Monastery in South India. He went on to study at the University of Quebec in Montreal and the National Institute for Eastern Languages and Civilizations (Inalco) in Paris, and he earned his PhD in the study of religion from Harvard University. His writings have appeared in the books *Little Buddhas: Children and Childhoods in Buddhist Texts and Traditions*, *Oxford Bibliographies Online: Buddhism*, *Contemporary Visions in Tibetan Studies*, and *Blue Jean Buddha: Voices of Young Buddhists*. He lives in Paris with his wife and teaches Buddhism and Tibetan religious history at several institutions.

Wisdom Publications

Wisdom Publications is the leading publisher of classic and contemporary Buddhist books and practical works on mindfulness. Publishing books from all major Buddhist traditions, Wisdom is a nonprofit charitable organization dedicated to cultivating Buddhist voices the world over, advancing critical scholarship, and preserving and sharing Buddhist literary culture.

To learn more about us or to explore our other books, please visit our website at www.wisdompubs.org. You can subscribe to our eNewsletter, request a print catalog, and find out how you can help support Wisdom's mission either online or by writing to:

Wisdom Publications
199 Elm Street
Somerville, Massachusetts 02144 USA

You can also contact us at 617-776-7416 or info@wisdompubs.org.

Wisdom is a 501(c)(3) organization, and donations in support of our mission are tax deductible.

Wisdom Publications is affiliated with the Foundation for the Preservation of the Mahayana Tradition (FPMT).

Studies in Indian and Tibetan Buddhism
Titles Previously Published

Among Tibetan Texts
History and Literature of the Himalayan Plateau
E. Gene Smith

Approaching the Great Perfection
Simultaneous and Gradual Methods of Dzogchen Practice in the Longchen Nyingtig
Sam van Schaik

Buddhism Between Tibet and China
Edited by Matthew T. Kapstein

The Buddhist Philosophy of the Middle
Essays on Indian and Tibetan Madhyamaka
David Seyfort Ruegg

Buddhist Teaching in India
Johannes Bronkhorst

A Direct Path to the Buddha Within
Gö Lotsāwa's Mahāmudrā Interpretation of the Ratnagotravibhāga
Klaus-Dieter Mathes

Foundations of Dharmakīrti's Philosophy
John D. Dunne

Freedom from Extremes
Gorampa's "Distinguishing the Views" and the Polemics of Emptiness
José Ignacio Cabezón and Geshe Lobsang Dargyay

Himalayan Passages
Tibetan and Newar Studies in Honor of Hubert Decleer
Edited by Benjamin Bogin and Andrew Quintman

Luminous Lives
The Story of the Early Masters of the Lam 'bras Tradition in Tibet
Cyrus Stearns

Mipham's Beacon of Certainty
Illuminating the View of Dzogchen, the Great Perfection
John Whitney Pettit

Omniscience and the Rhetoric of Reason
Śāntarakṣita and Kamalaśīla on Rationality, Argumentation, and Religious Authority
Sara L. McClintock

Reason's Traces
Identity and Interpretation in Indian and Tibetan Buddhist Thought
Matthew T. Kapstein

Resurrecting Candrakīrti
Disputes in the Tibetan Creation of Prāsaṅgika
Kevin A. Vose

Scripture, Logic, Language
Essays on Dharmakīrti and His Tibetan Successors
Tom J. F. Tillemans

The Svātantrika-Prāsaṅgika Distinction
What Difference Does a Difference Make?
Edited by Georges Dreyfus and Sara McClintock

Vajrayoginī
Her Visualizations, Rituals, and Forms
Elizabeth English